Co2o

SPITFIRE DIARY

SPITFIRE DIARY

The Boys of One-Two-Seven

E.A.W. SMITH

WILIAM KIMBER · LONDON

First published in 1988 by
WILLIAM KIMBER & CO. LIMITED
100 Jermyn Street, London, SW1Y 6EE

ISBN 0-7183-0692-9

Typeset by Ann Buchan (Typesetters), Middlesex
and printed in Great Britain by
Redwood Burn Limited, Trowbridge, Wiltshire

Contents

List of Illustrations

Illustrations in the Text

Foreword
by
Walter Cronkite

This is a most unusual and very special book. Almost half a century after World War II, here comes a volume of personal reminiscence, a collection of diary and letters, that takes you right into the Spitfire cockpit, the briefing room, the ward room, the barracks in a manner that few novels and no histories ever have done.

Ex-Spitfire Pilot Smith, with his utter disdain for literary pretence, has given us an unusually candid, colourful and, yes, affectionate picture of the brave and brazen men of the RAF.

I found the book a real delight.

Preface

'Spitfire Diary' is a combination of two sources. In effect, it is two books in one. The base is the official Operations Record Book, the daily diary of 127 Squadron, from a few days before I joined, up to the last mission before the squadron was disbanded on 30th April 1945. The nature of the operations record was necessarily comprised of third person fact. Occasionally, the adjutant or his assistant injected a personal, if understated note. The entire record may well be viewed as understatement, yet, somehow; perhaps by sheer number of missions, the interminable, unrelenting story of war, shines through.

Set in counterpoint to the operations record and interfaced, is my personal story, in diary form, of what it was like for those of us who made the history of No 127 Squadron, RAF.

'Well, of course, whatever other things that you could say of the Spitfire, I would say that she was a lady. She was a lady in every definition of the word. And of all the World War Two aeroplanes – she remains the only *lady. Every line of her – the beautiful ellipse of the wings, the unmatched grace of her tail unit . . . the unmistakable* sit *– as she banked in a steep turn – displaying that feline waist.* She was a lady. *Comparably, the Hurricane was a prize fighter. You could fly* it *as tough as old Harry. You could bash it, and even try to smash it. It would go through shrubs, and trees, and even Cornish stone walls, and people did, and walked away from it. But the Spitfire was a lady. She was sensitive to the touch, and if you treated her right, she would take care of you. And if you didn't treat her right – she gave it back to you in* full *measure. She let you* know *that she was a lady, and she would not forgive you easily, if you gave her brutish treatment. That was what she was* about, *I think . . .'*

Freddie Lister, DSO, DFC, speaking on Transatlantic telephone, Lincolnshire to Texas, June 1985.

Introduction

The purposes of this book are twofold. First, to put into perspective the enormous accomplishments of the Tactical Air Forces between D-Day 1944 to the end of the Second World War, as documented through just one Royal Air Force Squadron. Second, to present a very personal history to those members of 127 Squadron who served in that period, in whatever capacity. . .

With all of the books that have been written of the campaign in France, Belgium, Holland, and Germany, the workings of the Tactical Air Forces seem to have been glossed over, or missed completely.

With this book, I hope to set the record straight, with extracts from the detailed operations record of One-Two-Seven Squadron, Royal Air Force, compiled daily by the squadron adjutant and his assistant, from reports notated by the squadron intelligence officer, set side by side with my own recollections of them.

It was the practice of the RAF to gather the pilots together after each operation, within minutes after their return to base. The purpose was to procure detail from the mission of every pilot's observation, while it was still fresh in everybody's mind. This de-briefing was probing in every aspect, with each question answered, to be followed by another question, to determine accuracy and substance.

I am specially indebted to Peter Coxell, one of 127's pilots, with whom I flew many missions.

I became re-acquainted with Peter Coxell in 1984 after an absence of 39 years. In June 1985 I made another trip to England, to pick up on more reminiscences. He told me that he recently learned, that after all of forty years, our squadron records were finally de-classified from secret – and available at Public Records Office at Kew.

I went to Kew the very next day. I spent some hours with the record book, and decided to have all the records copied, from just prior to my joining the squadron, through to 127's last operation, on which I flew.

The day before I went to the Public Record Office at Kew, I asked Peter of the circumstances that brought us together under arms. His simple story has a pertinence that will ring through this story, on many levels. Peter Coxell, born and raised in Peterborough, England was, like me, a product of Grammar School. (In those days, all English schoolboys were given an elementary school education until eleven years. In our eleventh year, we sat through two or three days of examination which would determine our future. These exams were, in fact, known slangily as 'Elevenses'. Those who passed, went on to Grammar School. Those who did not, ended their schooling with an elementary education). At eighteen, Peter Coxell joined the RAF, applying for air crew training. He was trained in South Africa, and then was sent to the Middle East. After ten weeks or so, he joined a fighter-bomber squadron equipped with Kittyhawks. His squadron served in the Western Desert, until the Italian offensive began. He was on an armed reconnaissance mission, strafing enemy transports, when he was shot down. The mission was over Sicily. He was hit by small arms fire – possibly a rifle, and he made it over the water before crashing on Italian soil. He was clad only in flying boots, socks, undershorts and a light flying suit, as well as flying gauntlets and helmet. He did not even have a shirt, or undershirt. Though he was seen to crash by the Germans, close to a village, he was able to elude his would-be captors. The villagers hid him in an attic for days, sneaking bread and water to him. He was outfitted with peasant rags and indescribable footwear, and went on the run. After many weeks, living off the fields with Italian peasants, he got through to our lines. Shortly thereafter, he got to London, and was interrogated for three days by RAF Intelligence Officers. He was sent on a week's leave, and on returning to RAF Headquarters at Kingsway, was asked his preference for assignment. One of his options was to be grounded, to sit-out the war, in *safety*. With this option, he told his RAF mentor: 'I have never flown a Spitfire, so I'd like to try that. . . .'

As this is written, the boys of 127 Squadron are scattered. Peter is retired, from thirty years' duty in the Thames Police Force.

Squadron Leader Freddie Lister, DSO, DFC, is retired in Lincolnshire.

Reginald Eckert retired from the Adelaide Telephone Communication Corporation; he lived in Felixstowe, an Adelaide suburb, for all of his remaining years. He died, suddenly, in 1986.

Flight Lieutenant Harry Lea, DFC, retired from British Airways, lives in Portugal.

Sergeant 'Jock' Wallace, retired from a career in plumbing, lives in Edinburgh, Scotland.

Squadron Leader Frank Bradley served a full career in the RAF. He retired as Group Captain. He lives in a suburb of Johannesburg, South Africa.

The hours I spent in June 1985 in the PRO at Kew, London, were an eye-opening revelation. Reading these combat reports took me back again, as if it were yesterday. It was, at once, a heart-warming, heart-breaking experience. I was very moved. I wanted to open up my many experiences. To my family, my friends, and, mostly, to all those who shared with us – those momentous months from August 1944 to May 1945.

The originals of these reports were typed on very questionable machines, often with worn ribbons. In places, they were very difficult to read. Place names, in particular, in Holland, were typed with a certain spelling licence, albeit a creative licence! Many words were coded – for brevity, and I had to use my own creative powers to spell out the meanings of such as – AFV's, SE, E/A's, MY, HDV's, and the like. (Armoured Fighting Vehicle, single-engined enemy aircraft, Marshalling Yards, Horse-Drawn Vehicles.) Beyond these minor edits, no changes have been made. Every phrase, every word, every nuance is original, as typed by an unknown adjutant or squadron clerk.

In re-living this history, I was struck by a number of incongruities, beginning with the realisation that I was reviewing, and involved with, a microcosm of history – the history of one squadron, in relationship to the enormous force of the 2nd Tactical Air Force, being two groups of relatively equal weight. (83 Group and 84 Group.) I was somewhat overwhelmed by the great number of dangerous missions which we flew; literally, relentless opportunities for many more of us to fall from flak, than actually *did*.

It was incongruous to me, to note the constant emphasis on weather conditions – though, in perspective, weather *was* of prime importance. I found it ironic, that there is constant documentation of conditions in the air, and literally none of ground conditions, living conditions, or human conditions . . . how we felt, or how we accepted the odds that we had to accept. In putting this history together. I have tried to supply the missing elements.

In this area, I was aided greatly by this combination of factors. First, the reports gave an instant memory jog as I lived it again. Second, my pilot's flying log book, in which I documented not only my own impressions, but also a factual report, here and there, which I 'liberated' from the adjutant's daily input. The two final elements were notes that I had written at the time, or within a year of the events, plus about 150 pages written six years later, as 'work in progress' for a novel. As I lived it all again, I found mental notes hidden, such as the curious irony concerning my leave to the UK February 1945. Four of us were detailed to catch a 'compassionate special' DC3 transport, or Dakota. Our transport was delayed by fog. An Anson landed and we learned that it was returning immediately to the UK. We took up the pilot's offer to fly us to London. It was a trip fraught with danger. In the heavy fog over the Channel, we came close to crashing into one of the Seven Sisters – the seven distinctive cliffs of Dover. We were lost in fog over England. We were saved by the keen eyes of Larry Hyland, who spotted the FIDO flames at Manston – the Fog Intense Dispersal Operation – where they burned the fog away by lighting kerosene in a pipe alongside the runway of this major emergency crash base. The navigator was angry at Larry, because he gave his findings directly to the pilot. ('It's Manston. *Get down*, for Christ's sake!') We made our way to London by hitchhiking an RAF lorry. One week later, we found out that our intended transport from Holland crashed, en route to England. There were no survivors . . .

I have done my best to give the human element. Unfortunately, nowhere can I give adequate recognition or thanks to those who most deserve it. These were our ground crews; the armourers, fitters, mechanics, and clerks, who performed magnificently in conditions which were always sub-standard, often, appalling. I am sure that every one of the boys of 127 will remember our squadron corporal, who woke us up, every day, seemingly, before first light. Probably *none* of us will recall his name . . . only that he shook us by the shoulder, saying, sotto voce 'Show on, Mr Smith, there's a *show on*.' 'Show on, Mr Crozier. *Show on*' . . . It was RAF understatement . . . there is a show on, this morning, and *you are in it!*

In the main, this is a history. If readers find a certain beauty in these combat reports, it is in the terseness of reporting. Those who flew with us, the pilots, will get, I suspect, a lump in the throat, as they read the last entry, which comes without warning. I believe, in today's parlance, this is known as – a 'grabber'.

E.A.W. Smith
One of the 'Boys of One-Two-Seven'

I

July

D-Day Plus Four, Tactical Exercise Unit, Tealing, Scotland
When I got back here from sick leave today, minus tonsils,and one stone in weight, realized what a silly decision I had been talked into. One simple decision put to me by Squadron Leader McCardy, the senior medical officer. 'Your name has come up on the waiting list for a bed. Decision by tomorrow, when you'll have to be there, Smith. Yes, or no?'

How could I refuse? I had had more than my share of sore throats from infected tonsils, and as of the last two months I have not been able to go to the ablutions after breakfast. The stink from the urinals and the stalls would make me vomit. Of course, I had no idea the invasion would start without me.

The operation was a success. A huge, bloody success. For nearly eleven days I was in agony, craving only one thing. Aspirins to gargle with to allay pain for the time being. The surgeon who operated visited me after the operation, but I did not remember. I was told he wore rubber Wellingtons on his feet, and that his smock was splattered on over with other people's blood. I was also told that he operates exclusively with looped piano wire. I would not be surprised.

I ate nothing for eight days, because I could not open my mouth wide enough to pass a lead pencil between my teeth. I was one of twenty tonsillectomies done in one day. A wardful. Two airmen in the ward chattered incessantly from the day following our operations. They smoked a packet of Woodbines every day. Finally, after eleven days, I was discharged with a seven day sick leave pass. My mother's cooking put four pounds back on this gaunt frame.

Boy! Was I looking forward to getting back here today. Surprise! Everyone has been posted. Now, I sit here, more alone than I have ever been since the day I joined up. With all the postings I have had, 23, not counting six weeks on the SS *Mooltan* to Africa, and four weeks on the SS *Liverpool* back to Blighty, I have always had at least one or two pals who were posted with me. Now there's just me. Ken Hopley (Hoppy), Bill Williams, Dicky Peters, Woody, Church, Don Hind, Jackie Frost, all posted.

I asked them to look after my case while I was away, and somebody did. It was still under my bed. The contents have been stolen. 'Lifted' or 'liberated' is the popular term. I am so miserable, I could cry. The camera I bought in Bulawayo is gone, as is my Wilkinson auto strop razor. Someone probably took the razor with spiteful glee. Most of the pilots in this hut hated the razor, because it made a racket with the stropping. 'Clack – clack – clack – clack – clack!' Even Hoppy threw a pencil box at me one morning. What hurts me most is the thieving or vandalism of my papers. These were my diary notes, one big clump of notes weighing probably two pounds in which I recorded everything that happened to me since the day I joined up at Blackpool in January 1941. Nobody could mistake my bundle of memories for anything but what they are – or were. They were held together by two elastic bands, and one of them is still in the case.

No more today.

D-Day plus Nineteen, Tealing, Scotland

I still haven't received one word from my 'oppos' – Hoppy, Bill and the two Kens, and all. Welcome, flight sar'nt E.A.W. SMITH, 1333127, to the world of reality. I was thinking today of old Sergeant Hawkins, my first drill instructor of Blackpool. The day we broke up from our Initial Training, or 'square bashing' as we called it. Our squad all went down to the Crown, the pub on Coventry Street. He got a bit tearful after about six pints of wallop, as I'm told is his sentimental practice. What he told me was, 'Hang onto yer gear. Never lend it to *nobody*. Borrow money if you 'ave to – but don't lend any to *any* bugger. Never trust anyone but *yourself* – and you won't go wrong. Don't have any belief in service pals, unless you knew 'em in civvy street.' Well, I hope he was wrong. Hoppy and the others are probably at Group Support Unit, unless they've joined squadrons.

A rumour came through that they've all been posted onto Rocket Firing Typhoons, but its only a rumour. I wish they'd write. Even a postcard.

The weather has been generally good. I've got about thirteen hours' flying time since D-Day. The weather over the Second Front is supposedly vile, from all reports. It seems that those of us here are off Hurricanes, because we are all flying Mark V Spits. They are a delight to fly. I've been getting used to the new gyroscopic gunsight. It takes up most of the forward vision, but it's a wizard improvement over the fixed reflector sight. For aerial use you set the graticule in front of your face to the aircraft you are attacking, such as Me109, FW190, Ju87, and then you rotate the twist grip on the throttle to expand or contract the diamond shaped lights in the reflector to fit the wingspan. Then you press the gun buttons and the target plane blows up. That's the theory, anyway.

I have been flying with some of the Polish airmen stationed here, and they are excellent at dogfighting, aerobatics, and bouncing out of the sun. Their flight commander is ex-303, one of the two Polish Battle of Britain squadrons. He lectured me like hell, yesterday, and said if I didn't keep my head 'out of the office' I would be dead in the first action. I can learn a lot from Captain Karnowski.

Outside flying, this place is enough to make me perpetually browned off.

Will I miss the war entirely? Here in Scotland it seems a world away.

July 16th, 1944, Tealing, Scotland

I've given up all that D-Day plus, nonsense. I lost count on the days following June 6th, and having to remember 'Thirty Days hath September, April, June and November.' In June I flew sixteen hours and fifteen minutes. I now have 1242 hours as pilot, and I still haven't fired guns in anger.

One of our former instructors at OTU flew in yesterday from Ford, in Sussex. That's where they have the crash landing runway which is so long and so wide that anyone, any*thing* can land on it. Flight Lieutenant 'Dutch' Kliemeier, NZ. Dutch said he was sure Hoppy, Bill, Dicky Peters and the two Kens are all on Typhoons – but mostly split up. No letters or cards.

This is what I have done, flying, this month so far. Squadron Balbo – that means we took up every aeroplane which was serviceable on this 'drome, and put them all in formation. Balbo was named after the Italian General in Mussolini's air force. In Africa, before the war, Balbo used to get every aircraft they had in the air to intimidate the Abyssinians. I suppose it worked. I have flown in two Balbos, four fours formations, one practice scramble and one interception. Also, one shot at air gunnery firing at a canvas drogue. I did very well on that, using the old reflector sight. All for now.

July 19th, 1944

I flew twice today. I led a section in practice interceptions, in which we got the cooperation of a US Army Air Corps B.24. We intercepted over the Highlands, and bounced it well, never giving the crew a chance to turn in against our attack. Then control broke in, telling us that the B.24 had a bad port outer engine, and had to return to base at Turnberry. I took the section down into the valleys at deck level, and reminded myself of the last time I had done that, in late March, with Hoppy leading. There was just Hoppy, Bill Williams and me on that trip. That was the most split-arsed, frightening trip I remember. Hoppy said he knew every inch of those valleys, having been at glider-instruction school up on the east coast. Hoppy said he'd take us on a deck level tour of stately Scottish mansions. This was strictly against rules, since we were to be nowhere near our low level flying area. We agreed to radio silence, took off separately, and formed up at angels five, north of Tealing. Hoppy led us up the coast, then turned west, and took us down to the deck through the valleys. It was not long after first light, and we hadn't calculated on morning mist. Pretty soon we were flying tight on wingtip under a ceiling of mist which was between 50 and 100 feet. It was like threading a path in a dark grey tunnel at 200 mph. Without warning, we would be confronting a wall of mountain, and Hoppy would steep turn, port or starboard, with Bill or me on the low side, frantically steep turning, with a wingtip dangerously close to the ground. There was no way to turn back, and it was too dangerous to chance flying up through the layer of mist. It went on and on, and all I saw of stately homes were two grey castle-like houses, miles apart, where I felt one of us would knock off a turret, or plough through a roof. The mist finally broke, and as we came into the clear, I looked down and saw perhaps 50 panic-stricken sheep run into a stream that was laden with rocks, and blocks of ice. I looked at the clock and saw that we had been valley sweeping for almost twenty minutes. As we climbed to a safe height of 3,000 feet, I felt that my feet were as numb and dumb as those ice blocks in the stream. At the same moment, rivulets of sweat were running down my face and my spine. We flew home in silence, and when we landed, Bill and I cursed Hoppy in no uncertain terms.

He laughed and laughed. He said, 'Now, you know what thrills are. Did you see the stately homes?' Bill answered with a deliberate, 'Fuck you, Hoppy.' That night, in the bar at the sergeants' mess, we were laughing about it. Bill referred to Hoppy as 'Thomas Cook of the Scottish Highlands.'

My other trip today was air to ground gunnery, at the coastal range. I took a lesson from the Polish ace. Fire only when the target fills the reflector gun sight, and only fire a short burst on each pass. ('You don't get medal for flying through ground target.') When the range commander telephoned, he recorded a good score for me. Two hundred and seventy-five hits out of 600 rounds fired.

Letter from home. Mickey Cross confirmed as a POW. His Stirling bomber was posted missing months ago. His parents got a postcard, finally. The letter contained a picture of Mum and Wendy with Sally, our Alsatian. It also contained a ten shilling note.

II

August

August 1st, No 84 Group Support Unit, 2nd Tactical Air Force, RAF Thruxton

FINALLY. Finally my posting came through. It came through, *actually* (as they say!) July 25th. I got a travel warrant to London, a four-day leave pass, and a travel warrant to here. It was a *name* posting, so my name and number was on it. I almost forgot to collect my log book, which was in Wing Commander Gordon Haywood's office. His sergeant caught me at the gate. On the camp bus to Dundee I opened the log. Inside was a new 'Summary of Flying and Assessment' label, glued to a new page.

It reads as follows:

As a F (Fighter) Pilot:	Average
In Ground Strafing:	Average
In Bombing:	Average
In Gyro Gunsight:	Average
Then it reads:	Gyro Trained Pilot
Signed:	Gordon Haywood, W/Cdr.

I flew my first Spitfire IXB today. It is everything I hoped it would be. It has *power*. It is a kick up the arse, compared to any Mark V. One can take off easily at 7+ boost; it cruises beautifully at twelve plus, and above all it has automatic pitch control. This means as soon as you get airborne, wheels and flaps *up*, you can pull the airscrew lever into automatic. From there the throttle controls the pitch. In combat, one can boost up to eighteen pounds. It is a wonderful aerobatic machine. It will perform a full loop at 300 mph, and a half roll off the top at 340 mph. From the ground, the high whine of the supercharger is surely louder than any Spitfire ever built.

August 2nd: I felt very good, yesterday, until I went to the sergeants' mess for a pint. George Dickson dropped in with an RP Typhoon. George was with us all at OTU. He never joined us at Tealing. George got a little drunk. Then he told me that Hoppy got the chop two days ago, in Normandy. He was attacking panzers. I felt sick when I heard. I feel empty now. Bill Williams is on 247 (Typhoon) Squadron.

August 7th, 1944, 84 GSU Thruxton

It has been a very busy day today. I was called to the adjutant's office at nine o'clock this morning. He was a bit agitated, because his orderly sergeant had forgotten to tell me on arrival that I could not go to a squadron without a khaki (Army type) battledress. This involved getting another set of stripes, two crowns (for flight sgt) one new brevet (wings) and (curses of curses) bribing, for a few shillings, one of the overworked camp tailors to machine sew the above by close of work.

From here on in I am to wear khaki because, I was told, 'That's what every 2nd TAF pilot wears.' The idea is that if one is shot down, one will be a less obvious target to German ground crews, than if clad in blue. I was also given a slip by the adjutant which authorized me, by name, rank and number, to draw from stores my first issue of the new 'Escape' flying boots. These are sheepskin-lined boots of a special design. They are basically black walking shoes, plain leather, sturdy in build, with black mohair laces. The shoes are affixed to black sheepskin leggings, which have a zip fastener on the side of the calf. Inside the top of the legging is a concealed small pocket, and in the pocket is a blued steel, single bladed, razor sharp penknife.

The penknife is wrapped in a white piece of paper on which is printed 'Do not remove, except for purpose intended.' The 'purpose intended' is the cunning part. Should he be shot down alive, and be lucky enough to be picked up by the Maquis, or underground, said pilot would need walking shoes, not flying boots. The penknife would be used to cut the leggings away from the shoes, which would probably fool any Hun who had not seen shoes cut away from a pair of 'Boots, Flying, Escape type'. Anyway, they are comfortable and warm. I also drew my escape kit today, which included three silk maps. Two of these are kerchief sized, one with map of Northern France, one of Belgium and part of Germany. One scarf-sized silk map is a map of most of Western Europe. Also in the kit are two packets of two steel fly buttons. These, the tailor sewed onto my battle dress khaki trousers. Any matching two buttons together make a crude compass. Finally, the kit contains 200 French francs in new notes. I signed, in triplicate, for the francs.

There was a note for me to call the adjutant's office on the notice board of the sergeants' mess, when I walked in for tea, at tea-time. He wanted to see me right away. He was very brief. 'Flight sar'nt Smith, this is Flight sar'nt Attwooll.' He pointed to a tall, lean, pale-complexioned individual, who rose from a chair by the wall, extending his right hand. 'You are posted together to 127 Squadron, effective immediately. 127 Squadron is one of four squadrons flying under the command of 132 (Norwegian) Wing. As of now, they are at Funtington. You will be flown over there tomorrow. Be ready to go by eight-thirty tomorrow. Report to parachute section by eight o'clock. You will need to draw parachutes, dinghies, and Mae Wests. Good luck.'

That was all. Attwooll is very talkative. He tells me his name is Peter. He introduces his surname very colourfully – as if it is accompanied by a drum roll. 'Ay – double tee – double you – double oh – double ell. Attwooll!' Very clever.

August 8th, Funtington

Pete and I were delivered – by Anson. Dumped, would be more like it. The pilot did not even shut off the engines, as his navigator pushed us out onto the steel 'Somerfeld' matting. I have never seen this makeshift runway surface before, and am curious to see that it is nothing more than the steel matting that is usually an integral part of concrete re-enforcement. It comes in huge rolls, and it is simply unrolled, flattened to the ground, and tied down with twelve-inch steel pegs, driven into the ground. A brilliant idea for supporting aeroplanes, at least until heavy rains fall, and loosens the pegs. . . .

Our exchange with the navigator was brief – or, pointedly – curt. 'Get your kit out.' So saying, he threw a kit bag out of the door. Then another. Then a third. Pete said, 'Will somebody come and meet us?'

'Get your parachute.'

I said, 'Will somebody meet us?'

'And I said, "Catch!" ' He threw the parachute. Pete dropped it.

The Anson took off, and left us standing there. It seemed a long time that we were waiting, and we simply made a pile of the kitbags and 'chutes. Then we sat down. Pete was first to notice that all the

Spitfires have had the wingtips cropped. The beautiful ellipse is gone. As I told Pete, there must be a reason.

Finally, a 30 hundredweight vehicle pulled up, with squealing brakes. The driver was our CO, of all people, Squadron Leader Bradley. He is tall, and broad, and quite impressive. I noticed that he has big features, and a black heavy moustache. What does not seem to fit the face are his small ears. They are no bigger than two-shilling pieces. Florins. He introduced us to his companion. Flying Officer Gollins, New Zealand.

Squadron Leader Bradley drove us all around the perimeter of the strip to the squadron tent, where he dropped us, and asked Flying Officer Gollins to find us a tent. On the way, he asked question after question. Where were you born, when did you join up, where did you train, how many flying hours, how much night flying, how many hours on spits, how much air gunnery, how much air to ground firing, how much bombing. I thought the questions would never end. Since Pete put a Sir on the end of every answer to Bradley's question, it sounded like an endless Sir, Sir, Sir, Sir, Sir. I don't think the CO noticed. All the time, Gollins was staring at us, his head turned to face us, moving rapidly from Pete to me and back again, like a man at the net, watching a tennis match. He seemed to be appraising us as two strange creatures. I felt very uncomfortable; and wearing a new khaki battledress with unblemished new brevet, stripes, ditto, and new flying boots, did not put me at ease.

Gollins showed us to an unoccupied tent, helping us to carry our gear. Gollins is a *talker*. He talked all the time. He is known, apparently, as 'Golly', and he refers to himself in the third person. It was for example, 'What do *I* think about it? What does *Golly* think about it? What Golly thinks is. . . .'

Gollins introduced us to all the pilots, one by one, not always telling us their rank. Some of them were wearing Irvin jackets, with no insignia. All that was accomplished was accomplished from their point of view. 'Today, two sprog flight sergeants have been posted to 127 Squadron. They will either make it, or they won't. See them in their new khaki battledresses and new boots.'

I am only certain that the pilots of 127 are not impressed with us. For my part, I stand in awe of every one of them. They are *operational*, and they stand on the balcony, while I shuffle my feet, in my non-operational boots, on the threshold. One day soon, if I last, I will, too, be *operational*.

August 9th, 1944

Some of the things I have found out in one day. Our wing is comprised of four squadrons. These are 331 and 332 (Norwegian). 66 and 127, both RAF. The wing commander is Rolf Berg. 66 is quite a famous squadron. 127 is *not*. 127 was first formed in the First World War.

It was formed at Catterick, January 1st 1918. It saw no war action. It was disbanded July 4th 1918. It was re-formed in the Middle East at a place called Haditha in June 1941. 127 has made its way all across the Middle East over about twenty different aerodromes, getting back to the UK April this year. The whole wing only got here at Funtington two days before Pete and I were posted. No wonder the squadron tent is such a shambles. Mae Wests, gauntlets, parachutes and helmets strewn all over the place. All the cooks are Norwegian. The food is dreadful. *Dreadful.*

The officers seem very conscious of being officers. Some of them sound like outright snobs. From their talk, they are very browned off at not still being in some place called Nicosia. They must be, they keep nattering on about it, and Beirut. The speech of all the Middle Easters is larded with words like *char* for tea or *shai*. ('Time for *char*?' 'I could drink a cup of *shai* right now'). *Baksheesh* is another. It means money. *Gharry* means lorry. Pete mentioned *lorry*, yesterday, was looked at *pityingly*, and corrected. *'Gharry'*.

The NCO pilots are friendly enough. There are two who are presently grounded. 'Chalky' White is skinny, with dishwater-blond hair, and a ring of pustules around his mouth. Each pustule has a dab of some white ointment on it. Chalky was detailed by Peter Hillwood to brief Pete and me today. The subjects were long range drop tanks and bomb switches. The briefing was to make clear (drop tanks) that you always take off on main tanks, switch off main tanks *before* engaging drop tank, to obviate a possible air lock, and follow the same procedure back to mains before jettisoning drop tank. Bomb switches. Chalky showed us, out of ten switches, which will arm bombs, and which you use for eleven-second delay fuses.

We didn't have to ask Chalky about his ring of pustules; he was all too eager to talk. He is more of a talker than Pete, even. Chalky claims to be the first pilot to ditch a Mark IX successfully. That is, to belly land in the sea and not go down with the plane. In most cases when you ditch, your scoops under the wings ram into the water and the plane upends and dives nose first into the deep, and you can't get out of the cockpit. In Chalky's case he was shot up over Dieppe, and the engine, which was on fire, blew oil all over the cockpit cowl. He says he slid the hood back as the oil was thrown, and black oil covered his goggles and oxygen mask. From 20,000 plus feet, he glided to sea, hoping to bale out. He was about to half roll *out* – when, wiping his goggles back, he saw that he was only a few feet above the water. 'Too late! I said a quick prayer, pulled the stick back, and *stalled*! The tail wheel hit first, and I mushed onto the water. I had stretched the glide to get as far away from Dieppe as I could, and being stupid and blind, saved my life!' Chalky said that when he got in the dinghy he wanted to paddle it as far away from Dieppe as he could – and hoped the Germans hadn't seen him ditch. When over two hours passed, and no Air/Sea Rescue launch or seaplane showed up, and dusk had arrived, Chalky began hoping that, (by God!) the Germans *had* seen him ditch! He was picked up at last light, seasick, retching sea water, and bone-shaking cold. I learned all this in walking from dispersal back to our tent lines. (Chalky White, *Talky* White). I also learned about his pustules. The ring is exactly where his oxygen mask fits. Ever since his ditching, Chalky's face breaks out within two days of his first flight. At first, our squadron 'Doc' thought it might be caused by some chemical in the mask. They know now that the pimples are *not* caused by the mask. They are probably caused through fear, or more probably *shock*. And why not?

I also learned today that every Spitfire on this wing has had the wings clipped permanently. They call this model Mark IXB (LF) That means low flying. The other NCO pilot grounded as of now, is Sergeant Barker. He shares tent space with Chalky. Chalky told me a preposterous story about Barker. I'll have to get this verified before I believe it.

I have a funny feeling about this squadron. I don't feel welcome. The fellows don't laugh much. I feel very awkward in this khaki battledress. It makes me look exactly what I am, a sprog. I am keeping my mouth shut. I am not so much scared about going into action as I am in *not belonging* – not making the team. When I got back to the tent after tea, there was Pete, with his big doe's eyes, organizing things. He has made it look quite homey. He even got out my best blues and hung them out to air. He is neat in what he does. I will have to strive to be neat, also, so we won't have arguments. You can't have arguments in close quarters like this. There's no future in it, as they say.

August 10th, Funtington

This is the story that Chalky White told about Barker, his tent sharing oppo. Barker joined 127 in Cyprus, not too long before the squadron was posted back to North Weald, UK. Chalky explained the crapper system which is common from El Alamein to Cyprus and Cairo and everywhere. The latrines are built by sinking oil drums into the ground. The lowest oil drum has the top cut out. Another drum is sunk, resting on top of the first. This drum has the bottom cut out, with a generous hole cut into the top, to represent a toilet seat. When the crappers are reasonably filled, the lowest paid natives on the camp come round and pump them out. Then they supposedly sanitize the drums with carbolic, which is later pumped out. According to Chalky they either ran out of carbolic or someone didn't understand. It is believed that kerosene might have been in by accident. Barker, who had not been with 127 for more than a week, apparently went to the crapper with cigarettes in hand. Chalky says that Barker seated himself, lighted a cigarette, and dropped the lighted match between his legs. There was a loud explosion, and all within earshot came running. They found Barker face down in the sand, showing a bare arse and exposed genitals, with a fourteen inch circular burn all around his buttocks. Chalky couldn't wait to tell Pete and me.

Here on this strip we have only tents, and chemical crappers, with a canvas screen five feet high to keep us from prying eyes. Chalky claims that Barker will go nowhere near the camp bogs. He says Barker shits in the woods.

I did two ops today. Both were convoy patrols, and we went off in pairs. It was very overcast over all of the Channel. We never got above angels five. We did as we were told. That is, not to go too near any ship without waggling wings to show the broad black and white stripes underneath. These are 'invasion' markings and all aircraft of 2nd TAF have them. Convoy ships are very trigger happy, and no wonder. People on ships have nowhere to hide, and no speed to either run or evade. The sea was choppy, and spume was cascading the bows of every ship. What was not white on the water was green, light green to darkest green and hostile looking. We are all flying with seat dinghies attached to the parachute. This is a big change from the sponge cushion I've been used to sitting on. Sitting on packed rubber is not comfortable. After thirty minutes, one shifts buttocks almost every minute. Packed inside the rubber dinghy is a seven inch steel

CO_2 bottle. Unerringly, one buttock finds it, and after ninety minutes that buttock becomes first numbed and then painful. We came back to cheese and potato pie. The potatoes are lumpy, only half cooked. The tea is loaded with saltpetre. The only way to drink it is to gulp it, while pinching nose with fingers. The smell of saltpetre is sickening.

Pete says Chalky is right about one thing. He says he saw Barker going into the woods carrying a copy of the *Sunday Express*.

Pete went to town this evening with Ron Reeves, among others, plus a new bod among the officers, Flight Lieutenant Covington. This gave me the tent to myself, so I wrote three letters. I wrote home, to thank them for the money, and to tell them where I am. I wonder whether they will see anything significant in the fact that 127 coincides with the last three digits in my serial number, 1333127? I thought that was a hell of an omen when the adjutant at Thruxton gave me this posting. I could feel my face glow. I am not superstitious. I *do* carry the silver horseshoe with me every day, and I re-checked that I had it with me today when I climbed into the cockpit. One-Two-Seven, for One-Three-Three-Three-One-Two-Seven. That's a good omen. I won't mention it to *anyone*.

August 12th, Ford, Sussex

We moved here today. What a change from Funtington! There, I felt as if I were living in a field, which I was. The reason we are here, is so that we can get all the gear we need for the four squadrons, to equip us for Normandy. Ford is one of the biggest aerodromes in the South, the other being Manston.

The main runway is so long and so wide that it is hard to believe. You could just about take off with the entire squadron in echelon, wingtip to wingtip. Ford and Manston are both known as crash bases. All the crippled bombers coming back controlled by May Day are directed to one place, or the other. I suppose that many prayers have been answered here, not only on the runways, but on the grass as well. There are huge dispersal bays here, with the carcasses of every kind of operational aircraft you can think of. We are back inside, sleeping in huts, and all of us have abandoned our brown battledresses for RAF blues, accompanied by shoes, as opposed to flying boots. They have a number of messes here, two of which are kept for permanent staff. One huge mess is called 'Aircrew Mess', and it is open 24 hours a day, for officers and NCO's together.

Anyone aircrew can walk in and get a meal at any time. They even have fried eggs and bacon, periodically.

The gigantic crash runway has a foot high steel pipe running along the ground on each side of the tarmac. These steel pipes would be hazardous if the runway were not as wide as it is. The pipes have holes bored in them, which are actually flame jets. They call this operation FIDO which translates as 'Fog-intense-dispersal-operation'. When heavy fog blankets the southern coast and counties, FIDO is lighted. Kerosene or coal oil is the fuel. The flames, they say, go up five feet or so, and the heat burns the fog away up to five hundred feet or more. Fog or no fog, FIDO makes Ford visible for miles.

Pete spent a lot of time with Flight Lieutenant Covington the night before last at the pub. He calls Covington 'Covie', so some camaraderie is developing. Covington is an unusual fellow. He is tall, and slim to the point of being gaunt. Moustached, with blinking blue eyes. They blink, and his head shakes in cadence with each sentence he speaks. His hair is long, which I am sure is typical affectation common to a number of Battle of Britain types. The blinking and head shaking are due to the fact that he suffers from the malady they call 'Operational Twitch'. It is rather unsettling to anyone confronting a sufferer for the first time. It certainly was with Pete, until I pointed out that there are many sufferers today – particularly in Bomber Command. Apparently this nervous disorder does not affect a person's ability to function completely, as long as he is game to continue. It tells me, in Covington's case, that he has gone through hell. Is he game? As game as a fighting cock. Just to volunteer for another tour, after being grounded for three years, interned in Southern Ireland, on top of a hairy, deadly Battle of Britain tour. . . .

He crash landed in Southern Ireland when he was flying an Airspeed Oxford to Belfast. He got off course in intense fog, ran out of petrol, and had to pancake.

His main problem, as he tells it, was that he was too distinctive as a type, physically, facially; that he would be *missed* – by those conducting the International inspections on monthly tours of the Internment camp. Thus, he was used as 'window dressing' to make up for others, less distinctive, who were allowed to be 'slipped away' to freedom. He became a renegade. He could have given his parole, and led a fairly cushy life. He refused so he was confined to prison camp, until he got someone on the outside to help him escape.

Anguishing at his imprisonment, with a wife and child in England, he sweated, while other officers were freed. The guards were hostile to any officer who refused to give parole. On one appalling occasion, Covington was awakened by a guard who gleefully announced, 'We've sunk the *Hood*!'

No wonder that Covington is bitter. His dislike of Frenchmen, as opposed to his dislike of Irishmen, is almost comic relief. He calls Frenchmen 'B-bloody – p-pouffs!'

Covington, Pete, and I, all got our pictures taken today. These are our 'escape' pictures, small photos taken while each of us takes turn in wearing a civilian suit. The main purpose of the photos is, in case we get shot down and are lucky enough to be picked up by Free French Underground, that we will have passport photos ready for use. That's three things that the underground cannot provide. Escape pictures, shoes, and cash. How far will two hundred francs go – in France – let alone in Holland or Belgium?

There's another reason for the photos, and Covie says it's the main reason. Every squadron has a board with two-inch slots in it that shows every pilot's picture. Thus, when someone gets shot down, there's a picture of the unfortunate one that the CO can look at to refresh his memory on what the fellow looked like. Covie says it helps the CO in writing his 'next of kin' letter. Covie is probably right. I have only been a member of 127 for four days, so I'm still not comfortable.

Pete has apparently 'put up a black' in something he said to one of the officers. He was answering some questions, and according to *him*, he just told the truth, that, yes, 'We did it at OTU.' Of course, because I came with Pete, we are linked together as if we are co-conspirators. 'The *new* boys'. This won't go away easy.

August 13th, Ford, Sussex

We are enjoying life here. Thank God that the Norwegian cooks are not in charge of this aircrew mess. I'm convinced that they could ruin eggs and bacon, and that is what we load up on here, when we time it right. Timing it *right* certainly includes after midnight, when we get back from sampling the beer, when available, at the pubs. Eggs and bacon are on the menu from midnight to six o'clock, so that returning night fighter and bombing crews can get their reward – right after de-briefing. So we get a midnight breakfast, before turning in. We have bicycles here, so we have more freedom to go where we want to go, when we want to go. Good laundry service here.

127 has NCO pilots, as well as Pete Attwooll and me. Pete has a fine sense of humour and he knows a lot of jokes. He is also a very sensitive person. He has not had an easy life, poor chap, having been brought up in South London with an aunt and uncle as guardians. He has a sister who is eighteen, and I gather he is very Big Brother to her. They were both orphaned at an early age, and it seems he has never been away on holiday, either with his guardians, or even on a school journey. He is a good pilot, particularly since he has only flown 300 odd hours. He has been very fortunate not to have been encumbered by staff piloting of any sort, as have most of us. He is outwardly very keen, to the point that I wonder if he knows that people get shot down and killed with the increased emphasis on bombing and strafing.

The other NCO pilots. Warrant Officer 'Dinger' Bell, Australian: tall and rangy with a seamed face and leathery tan. The outdoor man to the life 'Dinger' has been on 127 for a long time. He must be near tour-expired, I would think. He is a leader on 'A' Flight on every sortie he flies. He is very calm. They say you can't shake Dinger Bell.

Warrant Officer Reginald Eckert: Some call him 'Reg' – but nearly everyone settles for Eckert. Australian. He joined 127 at Lympne, so his tour has a long way to go. He is over six feet in height, is 21, and balding prematurely. He is the second son of a dairy farmer. Eckert is quiet, in the way that Dinger Bell is quiet. He has an enormous capacity for beer, for someone his age. He is very strong, with hands that could cover most of a newly cut cabbage, and mash it.

Flight Sergeant Griffin: He was at Tealing when I was there, but he never ran with my crowd, or I, with his. He is neat, to the point of perfection. He parts his black hair in the middle, and not a hair out of place. His shirt is always starched, and clean. His battle dress is wrinkle free. He has a Clark Gable moustache, which could be glued on his upper lip, it is so razor neat. His chin has the bluish shadow of the just shaved, and he uses toilet water. He is very self-confident, and speaks in short sentences that leave no doubt as to meaning. He is a loner by choice. When he has eaten his last bite, drunk his last drop of tea – he leaves the table, abruptly.

Flight Sergeant Barker: I have put him down before, so all I see in Barker is 'odd man out'. I caught a glimpse of Barker in the showers today. He didn't see me but he heard me humming the tune 'Idaho', which was on my mind. He turned away and shut the shower door. He was too late. He has a coffee-coloured scar which covers most of his arse.

Flight Sergeant Reeves: Ron is one of what Pete calls the Middle Easters. Reeves has nearly two hundred ops flying hours, so, he will soon be, tour-expired. He talks his fair share of *gharry*, *shai*, and *dhobi wallah*, although I think that *dhobi* and *wallah* come from India. *Dhobi* is laundry and *wallah* is fellow. Reeves has a very animated face. He can purse his mouth and give an illusion of having almost no chin. Ron Reeves has a memory catalogue of David Langdon cartoons, and nearly all the men in them are chinless wonders. Reeves can describe the cartoons, one after another, and with his facial animation can bring them to life. He keeps us all amused, between *this*, and squadron stories from the Western Desert.

Sergeant Macey: He is about five feet nine, no more. I would say he is middleweight – not that he looks like a boxer. He has sandy hair, and looks very young. He is not assertive. He is serious about some dark-haired, dark-eyed girl. I know this because he keeps her photo in a reversible leather frame. On one side is her picture, and on the other side is a shaving mirror. At Funtington it was hung on a nail on his tent pole. The photograph was showing mostly because Macey only shaves every so often. This is why he looks so young. *Schoolboy*.

Paddy Crozier: Paddy's Pig. Paddy is Irish as *that*. Boy! can Paddy Crozier talk! Paddy could probably out talk a Member of Parliament, and talk one out of his seat. He has a really engaging singsong to his voice, and his way of speaking ranges from understatement all the way to unbelievable exaggeration. He says things like 'listen to this because it's the basic, unvarnished *truth*. I know ye'll find it hard to believe – so trust me.' Yesterday, Paddy was shooting a line about meeting his old schoolmate, by chance, in London. After describing every nuance of his oppo's dress, in the Fleet Air Arm, (and all the reasons *why*) he said, '*Swordfish*. He's flyin' bloody Swordfish. That bloody old stringbat, tied together with balin' wire and not much else – a bloody biplane that only goes about a hundred knots (they call it *knots* in the FAA don't ya know) with a *fish* (they call the torpedo a fish) between the wheels of the undercart. They fly at zero feet over the drink and they hold course, mind you, flyin' straight at a ship's guns. Then they drop the fish if they're *not dead*, and they pray for *Jesus Christ Almighty*! *My considered opinion* is that every one of those boys should get the Victoria Cross! *Every man, Jack*. Nothing less would do!' Paddy has an aversion to khaki battledress. He says he'll never wear it. He says, 'I left the mountains o' Mourne to join the Royal Air Force to be an *airman*, not a bloody *brown job*. If I meet the Hun in the sun or my *maker*, tis all the same to *me*. I'll meet him as an airman, and not garbed in brindleshit brown.'

I am writing this bit before I turn in. We have spent the evening at the Lamb and Flag. Some of the officers, too. We ran into Covington who said he only went out to buy a toothbrush. They must have been serving ale in the chemist's shop, because he was quite pissed. When Covie drinks he acquires a stammer, which adds to his bizarre twitch. Every other word is 'Fu-fu-fucking'. The toothbrush story (he pronounces it '*toth*brush') revolved around his rooming with a Free French Airforce captain for three days before his posting to Funtington. On the second morning, it seems Covie slept late, and when he went to use his toothbrush, he found it was *wet*. Furthermore, his toothpaste tube had a new pinch in it. Covie searched and found the Frenchman's toiletry case, ransacked it, and found neither brush or paste. As he told us the story, high hilarity took over, dictated by emotions ranging between affront, disdain, contempt, despair, anger, hatred, and revenge. As the third day dawned in Covie's shared quarters, he lay awake awaiting the French captain's ablutions. He peeked from under his blanket as the Frenchman showered, shaved, and helped himself to Covie's toothpaste and toothbrush. No sooner had the object of Covie's emotions rinsed his mouth, Covie leaped out of bed, grabbed the wet toothbrush, swept his pyjama pants down, dropped into a squat like a Russian dancer, and began scrubbing his anus. The captain apparently stared in horror. Covie broke the silence with, 'Don't worry about *me*, old boy, I always start the day by doing *this*!'

The saloon bar of the Lamb and Flag rocked with laughter – not the least of which being that of the landlord's wife, who reacted like a jarred plate of jelly. Covie took great joy out of acting the story out in the bar, including the new toothbrush. He did, for the sake of decorum, keep his trousers on.

August 14th, Ford

We are doing stepped up escorts. B25's (Mitchells) B26's (Marauders) which are nearly all silver – no camouflage, with some gaudy pictures painted below the cockpit. It seems that all the Marauders are also USAAF. The Mitchells are either painted in grey or matte black, and many of these are 2nd TAF. Whether RAF or Yanks, these crews have a lot of guts. They usually dog leg past the target, then make a sudden turn back across it. This is supposed to fool the flak crews on the ground, but it seldom does, with possible exception of the first few 'boxes' of six. After that, they don't fool anybody. They fly the last two minutes or less straight through the flak, mostly 37 mm. When the Hun 88 mm guns fire, it is in fours, and you see four big mushroom shaped black puffs. One barrage of four 88s could blow a big goodbye to a box of six bombers. Sudden events have turned Lancasters and Halifaxes into daylight bombers. They are bombing the hell out of an area surrounding a town called Falaise. They say the Lancs and Halis are raining thousands of bombs in an enormous acreage where they have Hun Panzer divisions trapped. It seems like a terrific wastage of high explosives to bomb open fields. They say there's hardly a live cow or horse left alive, God knows how the German army must feel.

Sergeant Macey got shot down today. He got hit by flak, and was seen to bale out – but nobody seems clear on detail. Almost everyone ran out of petrol and had to pancake on airstrips in Normandy. At least Macey is probably still alive.

August 18th, Ford

We are making the most of our stay, here, with what the adjutant calls 'the amenities'. He is a pretty stodgy old codger is Watkins, with a heavy black moustache not unlike a brush. Very public school – and very thoughtful and scholarly. The amenities which we are enjoying are: the aircrew mess, with hot meals and fresh vegetables, toast, marmalade, and tons of margarine. Even hot fried potato chips, as good as any from the fish and chip shop. We also enjoy: the movies, the laundry, the showers, and nearby pubs. Mostly, though the aircrew mess.

Saw flak fired in anger yesterday. It was fired at the squadron of

Mitchells (B25) that we escorted to targets east of Caen. The bunch which we escorted were about sixth in the mission, and by the time my box got there you could almost walk on the black layer of smoke from the 37 mm flak. It took so much time getting them in and away from target that we ran short of fuel. We landed at B2, refuelled, and flew back here.

No word, so far, on Sergeant Macey – whether he is POW or not. He hasn't walked back, to anyone's knowledge. Paddy Crozier packed his gear, the private stuff – razor, wallet and such, to be sent to his home. (It must be a very upsetting parcel, when it arrives.)

We heard a funny one, today. 66 Squadron was being led by Flight Lieutenant Walton. When they were taking off, they were surprised to hear the voice of a WAAF airwoman in control, because until now we thought that all controllers were men. 66 was taking off in two echelons of six. Since there is a pretty big rise near Ford's very big runway, there are a number of seconds during take-off when the tower people cannot see the aircraft taking off. Johnny Turk, an Australian W/O, says it went like *this*.

Walton: (Very public school voice) 'Control. This is Roundtop Red Leader. In position to take off. Roundtop Squadron, Red Leader, over.'

Female voice: 'Roundtop Red Leader, you may take off. Off you go. Over.' 66 opened the taps, and were rolling *well along* when the WAAF broke in again.

'Roundtop Red Leader – are you there?' Walton and 66 were too busy to answer. By now, they were moving fast, and were out of sight behind the big knoll.

'Roundtop Squadron, this is Control. Are you airborne yet?' By now, all twelve tails were rising. *Much* too critical for Walton to reply. 'Roundtop Squadron. This is *Control*. Are you airborne yet? Say again. *Are you airborne – Over.*' At this precise moment, in the last fifty yards, when the wheels are bouncing and begging to leave the ground, Walton flipped the RT switch, and in his most affected, impatient manner, said, 'Ac-chu-ally – Na-a-ooo!' Johnny Turk said everyone got his own individual chuckle. At about 200 feet Walton flipped the switch again.

'Hello, Control. This is Roundtop Red Leader. Let me speak with *Chief Controller* – I say *Chief* Controller. Are you there? Over.'

Male voice: 'Roundtop Red Leader, Chief Controller here. Can I help you? Over.'

Walton: 'Yes, you *can*! Would you please get that silly fucking woman off the air?'

Controller: (Very matter of fact) 'I haven't the faintest whom you mean, Roundtop Red Leader, but – Wilco – *out*. . . .'

Walton: 'Roundtop Squadron, setting course. Over to B – Baker. Out.'

Reading this over, it was funny, the way Johnny Turk told it in the bar. He's quite a card. Hard as nails.

Four new bods have been posted to us. Two flight lieutenants. Truscott, Shillitoe, a flying officer, Bill Malone, and a flight sergeant from New Zealand, Alan (he says call me *Sandy*) Powell. Sandy Powell is smaller than most of us. Wavy-haired, neat, good for a laugh or two. He will fit in with us NCO's very well, I think.

August 20th, Ford

Chalky White says we will be moving over the drink to Normandy before the week is out. He says he overheard the Group Captain talking to Winco Rolf Berg and Bradley. Chalky says we ought to have been over there weeks ago but there is a shortage of Somerfeld steel matting for the strip. The way the bomb line moves, we could be in Normandy and be out of range, without resorting to drop tanks.

We had a devil of an experience today, just after lunch. Four of us were riding our bikes to squadron dispersal, Paddy Crozier, Pete, Sandy Powell, and me. We were way out on the perimeter track, as far from Ford HQ as you can get. We were all alone, except for one big vehicle which was parked, or seemingly abandoned, twenty yards off the Tarmac track. We heard the familiar 'plack – plack – plack – plack' of a V1 buzz bomb coming from the south. In a flash it was in sight, then above us at about 1200 feet, and just as suddenly the engine stuttered, and cut out. Somebody screamed, 'It's diving! *Take cover*, for Christ's sake!'

Four bikes were thrown down, almost simultaneously, as we ran in panic and dived under the vehicle. We were in such fear that none of us even considered the muddy puddle *under*, and surrounding the vehicle. We threw our bodies into the puddle. The buzz bomb exploded about three miles away, and the blast was so frightening and so powerful that it seemed to lift our cover, wheels and all, a foot high. Perhaps that was only our imagination, but we all swore to it as we discussed it with the other pilots, later. After the blast, we picked ourselves up, soggy and muddy as street urchins. We were still shaking from fear when Sandy said, 'For God's sake, you twerps! Look at your bloody cover!' He was pointing to the huge cylinder which ran from the driver's cabin to the four rear wheels. Stupidly, unthinkingly, we had taken refuge under a petrol bowser. We didn't stay to find out whether it was *full*, or empty. We ran for our bikes, and pedalled away as fast as we could. Nobody complained about being muddy or wet.

I am still keeping my mouth shut as far as the officers are concerned. There is no future in talking unnecessarily and having anyone think of me as a know it all, as they do of Pete. I have not changed my mind as far as the Middle Easters are concerned. They seem to be very clique-ish, and very superior. As Pete says, it's not *our* bloody fault that we're not older, more experienced than we are, or not having had the luck to be in the desert or Nicosia, or Beirut. The new officers, like Covie and Malone, are okay. Truscott, and Dave Shillitoe, too. Of the Middle Easters, the NCO's *all* like I.I.R. (Bill) Campbell.

I spotted Campbell as soon as Pete and I arrived at Funtington. Why wouldn't I? On the back of his yellow Mae West, between his shoulder blades, there is a cartoon of Mister Chad, done in India ink. Mister Chad's long nose is drooped over the familiar brick wall. Below, is the question mark, with 'Oo's watchin' yer?' Chalky White says Campbell got the idea from a neighbour visiting his family on his last leave before going overseas. The neighbour had brought her youngest child with her, who was five. The child was apparently prone to butting in grown ups' conversation. Each time the kid butted in, his mother fixed him with a withering, pugnacious stare. 'Oo's watchin' yer, Timothy?' she demanded. 'Oo's watchin' yer?' She repeated this, until the poor kid whimpered, '*Gawd*'s watchin' me, mum!' To which the neighbour added, 'I should bloody well 'ope so!'

Today, all of us new arrivals since Funtington met with Wingco Berg. He is a very intense man, 25 or 26. He is Norwegian, clean-shaven, blue eyed, and exactly what I would think of as a true Viking, but without a ginger coloured beard or a helmet with horns on the sides. His speech is clipped, almost staccato. As Pete said, later, you wouldn't think of interrupting Wingco Rolf Berg. He refers to Germans as *only – The Hun*. 'You are here to *kill the Hun*.' Our meeting was, I suppose, what the Yanks refer to as a 'Pep Talk.' Rolf Berg is said to be superb fighter pilot, and a superior shot. He speaks perfect English, even though it is a sentence-by-sentence English, without, seemingly, direct continuity. Rolf Berg's only affectation seems to be his wearing of pigskin gloves. Here, in August, he wears *gloves*. He tugs at the uppers, left, right, as though he is pulling them on and on, constantly. He punches one hand into the other, left, right, to emphasize a point. Chalky White says Wingco Berg is so keen to get at the enemy that he spends part of his leave with Bomber Command, flying two or even three sorties in seven days as a crew member. Chalky says Berg can fly Halifaxes, Lancasters, and is equally at home in a gun turret. I wonder whether he flies with gauntlets, or just those pigskin gloves? His hands must get bloody cold on escort missions in the Spitfire's unheated cockpit.

August 22nd, Villon les Buissons, B.16, Normandy

Eighteen Spitfires, 127 Squadron, led by Squadron Leader Bradley, flew here around lunch time today. 66, 331 and 332 Squadrons arrived first. The rest of 127, pilots, doc, adjutant, Flying Officer Johnson, Intelligence and Pete and I, all came in one Dakota. *We* arrived at tea time, only there wasn't any tea. This is a Somerfeld – steel matting airstrip. It is in between two orchards, which was probably one big orchard until the Yankee bulldozers ripped hundreds of apple trees out to make the landing strip. One reason B.16 was behind schedule, among many, was the lean-up from fierce fighting, which left many dead bodies on both sides which, like cows and horses, had to be buried.

We had two briefings before we said goodbye to Ford, goodbye to good food, to laundry, to barber shop, and clean beds. Wingco Rolf Berg briefed the wing, and told us what to expect, and what *not* to expect. Don't expect white bread, until further notice. Do *not* trust anyone, no matter what uniform he is wearing. (There are, literally, thousands of displaced people all over Normandy, not the least of which are Wehrmacht deserters). Do *not* expect them to be in German uniforms. They may well be in civilian clothing, and may well pose as members of the Maquis. Wear your sidearm (Enfield or Smith & Wesson – 38 – at all times. Do not drink any water that has not been boiled. Stick strictly to tea – because you *know* that tea has been boiled. Do not eat any orchard apples. (We wouldn't, anyway – they are cider apples, or more properly, apples to distil Calvados). There is a sweet sickening stench all over B.16, which they believe is a combination of smells from rotting apples, dead carcasses of cows, horses, and men. Wingco Berg made a call for superior airmanship, piloting, and aircraft handling. Watch out for the steel matting, particularly try to avoid puddles underneath it. The wet ground will not always hold the steel retainer pegs, so the matting can bounce up without warning. No stupid, avoidable accidents, such as taxying accidents, ground looping. Above all – everyone be on guard at all times. If we see anyone strange around the aircraft challenge once – then shoot – but not where we might hit an aircraft.

We had another briefing from Squadron Leader Bradley. This one was more controlled anger than anything else. It was *This is War*, by God – and we had better be prepared to answer the call. To the older hands, be prepared to do the job even if you are close to tour-expired. 'There will not be any let up as long as I'm running One-Two-Seven . . . and as long as God made little Green Apples. . . .' (How prophetic!) Then he told us that he had just sacked a pilot for LMF (Lack of Moral Fibre) who didn't want to fly any more operations. He did not name the pilot, so we all looked at each other.

Flight Lieutenant McNally (Australian) was appointed 'A' Flight Commander today. Pete, Eckert and I are all in 'B' Flight under Peter Hillwood, ex-Battle of Britain. I wonder how we will all sleep tonight?

August 23rd, B.16, Normandy

It was war today, and the trip ended with an angry confrontation. We were sitting around, sorting out gear, shooting lines about all sorts of things, and four people were playing draughts. Chalky White found the checkerboards, the draughts, the cards and cribbage board, and the dartboard and darts.

We were on thirty minutes standby, and suddenly the red telephone flashed and rang. 'Scramble'. We were airborne in two minutes or less. We went up to Angels fifteen, vectored to supposedly twenty plus Bandits. There were twenty all right, but they were Mustangs. Twenty silver bright Mustangs. We switched to armed recce. Not ten miles east of the bomb line, flying at Angels eight, someone said, 'Monty Red Leader – large MET's twelve to one o'clock below, moving into woods.' Bradley: 'Monty Squadron. In we go.' I was flying Red Four, and followed Red Three down to the target, four big MET's. Even as I fired my cannons and point fives, I could see that it was all over. Three of the four vehicles were smoking, and number two was rent apart, flaming. Enemy troops were running in all directions for their lives. All four vehicles had white canvas tops with big Red Crosses painted on them. As we pulled up from our first strafing pass, I could see Blue section coming in from starboard, cannons tearing into the other trucks. 'Monty Yellow. This is Monty Red Leader. Proceed to attack, over.'

'Monty Red Leader. I don't think so, actually. This is Monty Yellow. Over.'

Bradley: 'Monty Squadron, re-form Angels eight. Return to base.'

After we landed, Bradley called us together. He was in an angry mood, red-faced and agitated. he could hardly wait for Flying Officer Johnson, our 'Spy' or Intelligence Officer to debrief us, taking notes. Johnson was dismissed – rather – rather curtly, I felt. Then followed a showdown of two officers, the like of which I have never heard.

Bradley began. 'Why did you not attack, Peter?'

Hillwood scratched his chin. 'Actually, sir, when I saw that Red Section had a flamer I didn't think it needed us. Besides . . .'

'Besides, *what*?'

'They all had big red crosses on them – *all four*. . .'

'What difference does *that* make?'

Peter Hillwood (almost diffidently):. 'Well, sir, I'm sort of *squeamish* about attacking Red Cross ambulances, as I wouldn't attack a Red Cross ship . . .'

Frank Bradley (very angry in tone): 'A Red Cross gharry is *not* a Red Cross *ship*.'

Peter Hillwood: 'Pertains to the same thing, *sir*.'

Bradley: 'No, it bloody well does *not*! A ship is a *ship* – and I'll accept that. If you studied the directives, *here* – you'd know that we are directed to attack any and all *enemy transport* bearing Red Crosses or not – if they are moving *south* or east. These were moving *south*-east – *away from the front*. Transport moving away from the front can be *presumed to be carrying troops on retreat*! And if you'd seen the action, as *we* saw it, down on the deck – you'd agree that those bastards who baled and ran were hardly wounded soldiers! *All* of you – dismiss!'

We walked away. I was too stunned to speak, let alone discuss the rights or wrongs of the matter with anyone. We walked back to the tent lines in silence. *Somebody* – think it was Griffin, said, 'Lunch time.' We walked to our tents, to pick up our eating irons, and our canteens. Nobody cracked a joke, all day long.

August 25th, B.16

Yesterday, the squadron got an early release. The officers went on a trip to the Falaise Gap. We, the NCO's, were left here, to 'mind the fort'. Bradley, Fyfe, Shillitoe, Truscott, Asboe, and McNally, all left with the 30 hundredweight. Oh, and Peter Hillwood caught it – on the 'fly' as they were gunning the motor. He took a flying leap, and many hands pulled him up over the dropped tailgate. 331 and 332 pilots preceded them by half an hour. Somebody came up with a rumour, and a wild idea. The rumour turned out to be true.

The Falaise Gap is reputed to be the aftermath of immense carnage. The German army, trapped in the closing of the Gap, were slaughtered by the thousands. They say that those who got out alive were totally mindless, having been bombarded for weeks. They had faced bombing on an unprecedented scale. After many days of unending tactical strikes – Rocket Typhoons, strafing Spitfires, Mitchells, Bostons, Marauders, the Lancs and Halifaxes went over with the heavy stuff. There were 700 heavies on some raids.

The stench of rotting corpses of men, cows, horses, they say is unforgettable. The rumour that the Polish army is in charge of the cleanup, is a *fact*. In practicality, they have turned a portion of the area into a used vehicle lot. Hundreds of vehicles, all incapacitated in one way or another, are passed in bargaining, for from 100 to 1,000 francs.

Bradley and company came back with a dispatch rider's BMW motorcycle, which only needed new plugs, and some work.

Dave Fyfe's sharp eye caught on an SS Mercedes Benz, looking, on the cursory inspection, to be undamaged. He paid a Polish staff sergeant 500 crisp new francs, from his own, and Asboe's escape pack. He was handed the keys, and got in the driver's seat. The others watched, as he leapt out immediately – threw himself on the ground – then choked, and vomited. He got up and staggered away, retching. The headless cadaver of an SS major was on the rear seat. The head was on the floor.

331 Squadron fared better. They came back with two DUKW amphibeans, used for fording rivers. They drove them to a creek on the north end of the strip. We all watched as they drove over the bank, into the water, the amphibious propellers churning perfectly. There were five pilots in one, four in the other. They bounced into the water, and sank within ten feet of entry.

Mechanically, the DUKW's were in fine condition. Nobody

bothered to check that the understructures were riddled with grenade and rocket shrapnel. . . .

Our BMW motorcycle is shaft driven, apparently far more practical than chain drive. It has skid-proof platforms for the feet. It is very big, compared with a BSA – or a Norton. Paddy *loves* it, and so does Griffin. Pete has been thrown off it, hitting a ditch at forty, he said, *kilometres*. The speedometer reads in kilometres – not miles – per hour. Pete was white-faced when he rode it back. I want no part of it. I will not be killed on a liberated German army motor bike. Spitfires are safe, and reliable. No gears to shift, for one thing. . . .

Today has been one hell of a day. Busy, and quite unsettling. Flying Officer Bill Malone got shot down. He pancaked okay, in a field, but he was apparently on the wrong side of the bomb line. It is thought that he will be all right – but, at best a POW. Officially, he is posted 'Missing'. Bill Campbell force-landed, we don't know whether due to mechanical or flak. At squadron release, he was still not back. Bradley shot an Me109 down. I was not on the trip. They said it was great shooting, from 800 yards! The Me109 blew up.

Chalky White packed his gear up today. Posted sick, by the doc. The sores around his mouth did not clear up. Better, I suppose, that we get a replacement who can fly every day. We will miss Chalky, if only for his ghoulish humour. He spends time among the patches of yellowed, dead grass, claiming he can identify the places where dead Germans lay for many days. He's a good scout, though.

August 27th, B.16

I could easily have got a bullet last night, and all for a souvenir for Griffin's young brother. One German helmet was what he asked for.

The Norwegians, 331 and 332, got here before we did, so they got their hands on the war loot left behind in the German army flight. These are assorted belts, boots, broken rifles, one machine pistol, and steel helmets. They have 'liberated' about a dozen helmets, which they have posted on the tops of their tent poles.

Griffin came into the tent we are sharing, at ten o'clock. Apparently he had been wandering in between the Norwegian tent lines, looking for the best souvenir, which happened to be on the furthest tent pole from us. He had a flashlight masked with black sticky electrical tape so that the lighted aperture showed only as a square, the size of a sixpence.

He spoke in hushed tones, and made the appeal emotionally. His little brother, Ronnie, is only twelve, and he idolizes Griffin, and he has begged for a German helmet, or a dagger, bayonet, or even a belt buckle. And why did Griffin need *me*? 'You're taller than I am, and you can give me a boost. I'm going on leave tomorrow, Smitty, so this will be my last chance. All you've got to do is crouch, let me get on your back, and stand up so that I can lift the helmet. It won't take but a minute. It's raining again. Let's do it before we get soaked!'

Griffin led the way, carefully picking out guy ropes and tent pegs, crisscrossing between the tents for no reason that I could fathom. It seemed ages before he stopped, spotlighted the desired helmet and switched the flashlight off. He shoved the torch into his tunic, and put his hands on my shoulders in a note of caution.

Someone in the tent was talking in his sleep, not only garbled, but in Norwegian. The rain was heavier, and the wind was rising. Griffin put a hand on my head, and pressed down. I turned toward the tent pole, crouched, then raised as he got up on my shoulders. As he lifted the helmet he started to lose his balance, and the tent pole jerked violently. Shouts came from the tent, and Griffin jumped down, and ran right. I followed him, my heart pounding like a hammer. Griffin tripped over a guy rope, and I caught the one behind him, sprawling head first into a grass clump, sodden with rain. Yells rent the night air, and we ran, and tripped, and ran and tripped. Between the Norwegian lines and our lines, there is a merciful space of fifty or sixty yards, with dozens of crab apple trees, the ground being covered with rotted apples. We covered the distance to our tent in about ten seconds, slipping and tripping, and expecting the discharge of revolvers at any second. Back at the tent, I fell on my cot, face down, wet with rain, and the sweat of stark fear. I could still hear angry yells and shouts from the Norwegian lines. It must have been five minutes at least, before we caught our breath enough to speak. Griffin stood up, shining his torch on the helmet. 'Ah, Ronnie is going to *love* this one, when I get it home. There's hardly a scratch on it. Take a look.'

I looked. Inside the helmet was a name and a number, painted in white dope. 'Schultze – 565.' Schultze must have been quite a draughtsman. The legend was expertly painted, in *Gothic*. In a rush, forgetting my fear, my anger at Griffin, and my breathless frustration, I said, 'My God! They are just like us! Just like *us*!'

'What are you talking about?'

'Don't you see? Schultze – 565. *Five-six-five* – they use their last *three* – Just like us!'

'What about it?' Griffin asked. I did not reply. I have been brought up so much on our propaganda of *The Hun* – in two world wars, bayonetting babies in Belgian streets, killing civilians violently in dozens of films, the supermen from another world. The myths were shattered by one glance into a steel helmet: Schultze – 565.

Griffin packed last night, while I tried to get warm under my blankets. He was gone when I woke this morning, leaving an odour of scented soap and after shave. He emptied his canvas wash basin outside the tent. His parachute is on his cot, with this helmet, oxygen mask and gauntlets. His blankets are neatly folded. The steel helmet is gone. He has left his shoes, so that means he is wearing his flying boots to England. It is one thing to be stranded at an aerodrome without issue footgear, but why wear flying gear on leave? Surely it's enough just to wear one's tunic on leave, with the top button undone. That's what we all do. People *know* that it means: fighter pilot.

August 28th, B.16

We NCO's have our private, small, special squadron. We talk, endlessly, and between ops, and trips to the crappers. (Everybody has some form of dysentery, which only Doc calls dysentery, because we all call it the *shits*. More about this, later. All the officers have the shits too, so human equality prevails!) These are the subjects which revolve endlessly in discussion. The officers. The *food*. (Not only the fact that it is lousy, and always cold, but we vie with each other to discuss memorable meals of the past. Only the man describing the M.M. is *really* interested.)

The *weather*. In England, the weather would be warm and wonderful. Normandy is cold and wet, and prone to 'cow pissing' rainstorms. *Living conditions*. Any illusions that tent living was to be adventurous was dispelled with the first rainstorm. Every one of us, it seems, forgot what Squadron Leader Bradley proposed, when he issued Foxhole shovel-diggers. (US Army issue). This was an order that each of us dig a personal foxhole, in case Jerry planes come over, strafing. He also *recommended* that we dig a small trench all around the tent walls, so that in case of rain, the water would run *out* – not in. Of course we didn't, and when it rained, the water ran in, and around our entire tent interior is a quagmire. Nobody told us that you should *never* scrape tent canvas inside, when it is pouring rain *outside*. It causes leaks, so when it pours, everything gets wet. *Personal Hygiene.* We long for a bath. All that we have is a canvas affair three feet square that hooks onto a wooden frame. It has to be filled from Jerrycans, or canvas buckets. It is no more than nine inches deep. Taking a bath (stand up) means building a fire to heat water. It is a bloody mess. What we *don't* talk about is that most of us go for days without changing underwear, because we sleep in our battledress, because of the cold. Some of us don't take our socks off! *Flying.* We talk about *tactics*, *formation flying*, *bombing*, whether dive bombing or low level, *strafing*. Of all topics, flying is most constant. We talk about women, but not much. We haven't seen one since arriving here.

We don't talk about fear, but I am sure it is a sometime experience with everybody. At briefing, you can *smell* it.

Back to the shits. We all have 'em, and the pills don't seem to work. Fear, in the air, puts a severe strain on the sphincter. (Wow. I learned that word at Cranwell, from Gerry Lilly, whose brother is a Wingco Doc, in the Middle East). Pete says the shits are with us because of the flies. He says flies breed by the millions because the banquet meals they get from the rotted corpses of cows, horses, and men. He says flies regurgitate before they eat. According to this logic, flies eat rotted flesh, then regurgitate it on our food. We eat the food, and we get the shits. Some of us defecate five times a day. Paddy Crozier calls us 'Sore-arse-one-two-seven'. He got very angry with Pete, at telling us what Doc told *him* – since we were eating whatever passes for supper.

We have been issued new cots with quarter inch steel frames. These replace, immediately, our wood and canvas cots. The canvas used on the new cots is coloured orange, a violent orange, to boot. Because they have steel frame, they have much more bounce than a wooden cot. Still, you wouldn't try to use them as a circus trampoline, that clowns bounce on. Amazingly, one can assemble or disassemble the cot in three minutes, and one can roll up the entire canvas and stretchers into a three-inch core, with a length of sixteen inches. Here is the *disadvantage*. When the cot is assembled, it stands only seven inches above the ground. Sergeant Powell brought the first one to us and assembled it. Eckert pointed a finger at it, and we all began laughing, and holding our sides.

August 29th, B.16
Food is abysmal, since our standby, white bread, is not available. We are told we may not see white bread before we advance to a city, where we can buy from, or 'liberate', a bakery.

Pete has turned into a craftsman. His large, doe eyes have a rested, if hollow look, and he is in good spirits. He has the hands of an artisan, large boned, and strong. Using not much more than metal scissors and pliers, he has fashioned water basins and feet-washing basins out of five gallon petrol tins. He has learned how to bend tin, in corrugation, making a workable scrubbing board. This is practical, since we have to do our own laundry. Pete's work even impressed Peter Hillwood, our flight commander, who has asked Pete to make one for the officers.

Norman peasants showed up for the first time, today. We were on thirty minutes readiness, as usual. Our readiness team was down at flight, and it was early afternoon. We had had morning showers, and now, clearing skies. There was a breeze, with a chill to it. Pete was hanging laundry on a line between two apple trees. Griffin, Dinger, and Eckert had built a blazing bonfire, which, after the flames depleted, was warming petrol tins for water for laundry, and bathing. Eckert was standing in four inches of water in a green canvas field bath, soaping his huge hirsute (Pete calls it 'hair suit') body, when the villagers appeared, through a small copse of saplings. The women and children were 'Sunday church' dressed, in starched white bonnets, white blouses and floor length homespun skirts. Eckert went white, bringing up one foot and then the other, trying to hide his genitals, hopelessly, behind a bent knee. He looked like a man standing on hot coals, as he hissed at Dinger to throw him a towel. This, Dinger did, as the party advanced. It was Pete's moment of delight, stepping forward to greet them in schoolboy French with his astounding cockney accent. He diverted the villagers' attention, as Eckert gathered towel around his privates, his face blushing red in bashfulness. He stood, smiling awkwardly, as the villagers came up to him. They were studying him, in the way that people might study a man from Mars. In rapid country French they were obviously describing parts of Eckert's anatomy, marvelling, it seemed, at his hair-covered torso. Finally a matronly woman could stand curiosity no longer. She lifted the flap of his wrap-around towel as he leaped out the field bath, and ran for his tent, pursued by laughter and catcalls. Not the least, were unkind guffaws of Pete, Dinger and me.

Eckert came back after a while, dressed, and bearing gifts. These were four bars of Cadbury chocolate with cream filling. The villagers were all brightened, visibly, by the chocolate. I noticed that the bars all had the last row of squares missing. I asked Eckert about this. His answer: 'Well, I couldn't give 'em the end pieces, sport, because that was the end the wasps got in, through the back o' my night stand. Those little buggers fair cleaned out the cream from the end rows – like a bloody honeycomb. The least I could do was give the Frogs what was left.'

August 30th, B.16

Today – this afternoon – Bradley gave the NCO's a 'Sunday break' or, afternoon off. This was his joke, really, as Sunday is no different from any other day, as far as ops are concerned. When 'the show's *on* – the show's *on*' as they say. Doc Blanchard drove us to Bayeux, dropping us off at a church annex, to see the Bayeux Tapestry, which he recommended. He went on to a HQ Hospital Supply detachment. We are out of many drugs and pills – bandages – and, notably *morphine*. He told us to meet him at the Town Major's HQ at 1700 hours, which we did.

There were Eckert, Paddy Crozier, Dinger, Bell, Pete and me – and our newest 'bod', Sandy Powell. The building housing the Bayeux Tapestry is a centuries-old building. Hardly a museum – it is more like a stone barn. Most of the wooden floor is rotted, exposing the dirt foundation. The first thing we learned, was that the tapestry on exhibition is a canvas replica. The real Bayeux Tapestry is a priceless work of art, recording the history of centuries. It is still in hiding, somewhere. *This* tapestry is a facsimile, hung all the way around the wall of the building, and overlapping itself by thirty feet. All the historical figures, and data, are recorded in India ink. The lady who told the story was patient, but since she spoke only French, it was an incomprehensible bore to everyone but Pete and me. Less, in fact to Pete, because he has an excellent knowledge of French, though his accent is London Cockney *atrocious*. We left after half an hour, without more than a modicum of newly-gained knowledge of Norman knighthood.

The damage done to Bayeux is shocking. It is a desolate, mute testimony to man's disregard for the value of property, labour, history, or *life*. An old, old country town, with every other building defaced, de-walled, de-windowed, de-roofed. The civilians' faces are masks of absentmindedness. Most of them seem to be, mentally – *somewhere*. The town is overloaded with soldiers and airmen of many nations, all with – no purpose. There is nothing to buy, in Bayeux. Whatever is left in the shops, seemingly, nobody wishes to purchase. Troops of all nationalities pick their way through rubble on the streets, avoiding holes in the cobblestones that would wreck anything but a tank. A number are drunk, and for every drunk there are two sober militiamen with dry throats, wondering where the drunk got his supplies. They sit on broken pavement and they lean on walls. Any young woman, walking from one end of Bayeux to the other, runs a gauntlet of leers, jeers, catcalls, whistles, and groping hands. . . .

We met Doc Blanchard at the Town Major's. It was marked with flags, the SHAEF shield, and military banners. We walked in silence, and *then*, in Doc's wagon, rode *back* in silence. We were private heroes, reduced to private shame, and inner humiliation.

There was a row when we got back. It was touched off by a thoughtless observation – 'I wonder where the prossies went to?'

'Who?'

'The prossies. Prostitutes.'

Pete blew up. He gave a verbal tirade, accompanied by angry tears, welling in red-rimmed eyes. Those who did not feel the shame before had a chance to feel it now. 'Corpse explorers,' he called us, and included himself. With a final ejaculation of 'Jesus Christ!' accompanied by a sweeping look of impatient disdain, he strode back to the tent lines. The rest of us had tea. Few words were exchanged, between the six of us.

August 31st, B.16

I was so pleased, today, to get a letter from Bill Williams. He is the only one of the Tealing crowd to put pen to paper – but that is his bent. He is a very funny fellow in that he can mirror the life of a London cockney, and take flights of fancy, wherein he will play all the parts. I would be with him today, assuming that I would be among the living. I think about the happy months we were all together at Tealing, flying tactical exercises daily, simply waiting for D-Day, and being absorbed in a squadron – as we would replace other bodies. When the Tealing Doc referred me to the surgeon at

Dundee General Hospital, who performed my tonsillectomy, neither of us had the slightest idea that the Second Front would start – as I lay on a recovery cot. I had eight days in hospital, and was given seven days' leave, on my discharge. When I got back to Tealing, my hut was deserted, and most of the pilots were gone.

Bill, Ken Hopley, Ken Morse, Dicky Peters, Brownie, and Lowe. Higgins, Harris, Beamish, and Ternhill: all gone to war. Everyone to rocket-firing Typhoons. This is the most dangerous game in TAF. Each 'Tiffie' is armed with eight rockets, four under each wing. You dive on the target, like a dive-bombing Spit, but at a lesser angle. You aim the plane at that gun battery, that locomotive, and you stay in the dive until you discharge those rockets. By now you are flying at 400 plus, and you are flying down their 20 millimetre gun barrels. You know that one of those shells will blow your wing off, and your chances of baling out are literally – zero. Bad tonsils took me away from Bill and Hoppy, and put me into Spitfire Mark IXs.

Bill Williams – Stanley Lionel, to be correct. He will never be anything but Bill to us. Cockney, born and bred, Kilburn. Bill Williams, (how he hates *Stanley*! and Lionel, perhaps even more!) is, like me, a product of the London Metropolitan School System. Like me, he did not get too serious about Elementary School until he was but one year away from the 'Elevenses' – that series of exams in which in one stroke, the fates of all eleven-year olds in every school are decided. There are a limited number of scholarships, between ten and fifteen percent. This small percentage allows an escape to higher learning, through Grammar School. All the rest, those who don't win a scholarship, are destined to end their formal education at age fourteen. Some of these go into 'Trade Schools'.

Bill is a cockney sparrow, even though he can speak King's English with the best, and mimic the Public School accent to a point of high hilarity. There is nothing he loves more than to go through an improvised charade of cockney fantasy, in a pub – in the hearing of those officers born in the upper class. I have played the 'straight' man to his cockney 'only *just* this side of the law' – more times than I can count. I only have to hear such words as 'Wotcher, Cock! an' 'ow's yer belly orf fer spots?' to know that Bill Williams is present, in the bar. I will retort 'None o' yer business, you motherless *git* . . .' almost as a reflex action. Bill writes, always, to me in the cockney idiom . . . even in notes, at flight.

Bill's favourite story, probably, is a true one. ''Ere I am mate, 'ome on leave from Canada. Got me new sergeant's stripes, and me silver wings. So I gotta go over ter Islington ter see me mother's sister, auntie Lil – right? Gotta show auntie Lil me new stripes and Brevet. No bullshit, nar. I git orf the bus at the Angel, which ain't open at the time, so I take a ball o' chalk over to me auntie Lil's house, not arf a mile from the Angel. All these bleedin' rows of houses and the streets full o' kids. 'Ere is this little snot nosed bastard with his snot faced little brother, who is screamin' his bleedin' head orf. Mother, who's bullshittin' with 'er old china across the street, 'ears, snotfaces' screams.

'"Oi!" she shouts. "Timmy! What's wrong wiv Raymond?'

'"'E"s crying', mum!"

'"Don't tell me he's cryin'! I can 'ear he's cryin! What's 'e cryin' for?"

'"Raymond, 'e's, er – 'e's shit 'imself."

'"Why didn't you say so! 'as 'e done it much?"

'"Now – 's Gawd is my judge. . ." Timmy reaches round the arse of Raymond. 'e feels for the package. "Well?" the old lady shouts. "Not much, mum" says Timmy. "Oh." And she turns right back to 'er ol' china and starts bullshittin' again! "'as 'e done it much!"' His shoulders shake, in his laughter. . . .

As I read the letter in the food line, I wondered what a field censor would think. He would be sure that Bill William is fugitive from a loony asylum, and be very sceptical of *me*. Bill always addresses me 'Spiv' as though it is my given name which, in a sense it is. Cockneys call other cockneys 'Spiv', in affection. The word is supposed to originate from London Metropolitan Police Stations, a corruption from 'Suspicious Persons, Itinerant Vagrants.'

567 W/O. Williams, S.L.
SERGEANTS' MESS
ROYAL AIR FORCE,
124 Wing
247 Squadron
B.W.E.F.

Dear Spiv, or what have you,

and how's me ol' cock sparrer gittin on, still strugglin I hope.

I don't know if Hoppy has written to you lately, no doubt he has in which case you will know that he and I are at different air fields; I was hoping to get over to see him today but was unable to get my washing finished in time; terrible weather for drying these days don't you think?

As regards news of myself: it's not too bad here been on worse places (but can't remember where) and the food is improving a great deal as we are beginning to get more fresh eatables now, and only just in time as very shortly I shall be wearing a 'MEAT & VEG' wrapper around me if things continue as they are.

As regards working hours it's not going too bad, we are very seldom troubled with Jerry fighters whilst 'hitting the Hun where it hurts most,' to coin-a-phrase, but he has certainly got a few clues when it comes to flak and it is very, very accurate but, of course, despite this remarkable Keenness to knock us down we go on, on, and – well, we go!

Ol' —— is on this squadron and has managed to put up quite a number of blacks since he has been here, (not regards flying) his latest effort was getting well jugged up, on whisky of which there is ample supply at 5 fr. a tot (6d) but no, repeat NO, beer; and then, together with another chap he did attempt, whilst on active service, to commit rape on a French citizen which is just not done by a liberating army, (so they say). He was lucky enough to get away with being prevented from partaking in liquor, alcohol, and all villages were put out of bounds to him.

Speaking of blacks, I'm sorry to hear that you have fallen in the eyes of the guardians of this fine Air Force of ours and I sincerely hope that you will do your utmost to reinstate yourself.

The question of leave has been quite a topic the last few days here, unusual I know, and it seems likely that we may be permitted to have the above time off in which case, at a later date, I hope to be able to see you.

Ralph Reader put on his *Gang Show* for us the other day and he appeared in person as well and it was a pretty good effort and the picture at our 'Odeon!' this week is very good also. I have forgotten to mention the fact that I am a teetotaler now. Ahem!!

Dicky Peters lobbed in here a week ago with a pretty badly shot up Kite and he tells me that he has been recommended for a DFM. Good show what? (I got my DSO back-dated, by the way).

The ol' man wrote to me the other day and tol' me he's goin' on them laves soon and they're goin' to give 'im one of them NAAFI gongs and some stripes, upside darn, on his arm. Says he told the Warden 'is son was a W/O and they considered 'im for premotion as well, yus and 'im wiv 10 kids to feed reclining in the Scrubbs, t'aint right I says to 'im. Now they've taken the mangle back Gaw'd know's what muvver's doin' about taking in washing. I saw ol' Alf Overt 'ere, 'es in the Pioneers, yer know, and he said its like bein' back on the demo again, all shovel and lean. My brovver Tom did 'iself a bit of good down the dawgs, did a tanner treble if cash all on maidens virgin and it come off lucky b' – 'aint he? Me young brovver says there's a load of Kifer gits in the Caf these days I wish we 'ad some of it art 'ere.

So from the ridiculous to somewhere or the other I must close and finish by saying that I sincerely hope to see you again soon Spiv. Please let us know how you are going along,

Cheerio for now

Your oppo
Bill

Bill Williams' reference to my own troubles is a reference to a totally avoidable and senseless lapse of mine, a taxying accident (June 15th). I have deliberately pushed this outside my mind. My log book endorsement 'Gross Carelessness' is *enough*.

This letter has been around a long time, chasing me from Scotland to Thruxton to Funtington to here. Bill must know by now that Hoppy is gone. I wonder if Bill, or any of the gang have been shot down in this short space of time? Whether they *will* get the 'chop' is another matter, as it is with us, *here*. The difference is that rocket Tiffies are very dangerous ops. They don't get *any* escort trips, guarding bombers. It is all assault work, unrelieved.

All for today. We still have the runs.

Extracts from the
Operations Record Book 127 Squadron, RAF 132 (Norwegian) Wing

Funtington, 8th August 1944: Ramrod 1177 – Twelve aircraft took off from base at 2020 hours as top cover to heavy bombers. Two aircraft returned early owing to one mechanical plus one, technical trouble, remainder completing the mission. Bombing appeared very accurate. Intense heavy flak in target area at bombers. 2/10ths at 22,000′ slight haze at 10,000′. Visibility good above that height. Ten aircraft landed base 2215 hours.

Funtington, 9th August: Eleven aircraft took off from base at 0925 landing Manston 1010. Took off from Manston at 1210 as Close Escort to Lancasters. Two aircraft landed Manston technical trouble, remainder completing mission. Uneventful. Visibility good. Nine aircraft landed base 1420.

Twelve aircraft took off from base 1920 – Fighter Sweep over Touquet/Cambrai/Hardelot area. Three aircraft returned early owing to one technical one mechanical and one as escort to damaged bomber, remainder completing the mission landed at base at 2125. Ten miles west of Arras meagre inaccurate heavy flak Le Touquet moderate light and heavy. Slight accurate heavy flak Caeux. Moderate inaccurate light flak at Tournai. Clear, slight haze up to 9,000′ bulk of cumulus up to 10,000′

covering St Margaret's Bay North Foreland. Mission uneventful. F/Lt Covington – F/Sgt E.A. Smith – F/Sgt Attwooll arrived on posting from No 84 GSU.

Funtington, 10th August: Twelve aircraft took off in sections of four – On convoy patrol south of Selsey Bill. First section taking off at 0725 hours and last section landing at 1215 hours. Nothing exciting was seen. Mission uneventful. Visibility good.

Six aircraft took off from Base on Fighter Sweep between Cherbourg and Le Havre – at 2115 hours landing base 2240 hours. This trip also proved uneventful.

Funtington, 12th August: Eleven aircraft took off from Funtington at 1235 hours – Ramrod 1190, as target and withdrawal cover to Lancasters and Halifaxes bombing marshalling yards, Etours. One aircraft landed at B.10 at 1515 hours. Five aircraft landed B.3 – at 1515 hours. Five aircraft landed at B.9 at 1515 hours, due to fuel shortage. Aircraft took off from respective landing strips at 1630 hours landing Ford 1700 hours. Escort uneventful.

Bombing concentrated. Meagre inaccurate heavy flak. Moderate accurate heavy flak Falaise area. Visibility good. Squadron moved from Funtington to Ford. F/Lt J.E. Schofield 'A' Flight commander posted to 84 GSU pending repatriation to Australia having served for thirteen months in that capacity.

Ford, 13th August: Eleven aircraft took off from base at 0905 hours – Patrol over Le Mans area. One aircraft failed to take off owing to technical trouble. Two aircraft escorted damaged bomber back to base, landing at 1105 hours. Due to shortage of fuel one aircraft landed at B.10 at 1050 hours, one aircraft landed B.2 at 1055 hours. One aircraft landed at B.5 at 1045 hours. Mission uneventful. Visibility good.

Twelve aircraft took off from base at 1845 hours – Ramrod 1196 Escort Marauders bombing targets in Péronne area. One aircraft landed at Exeter owing to R/T failure, remainder landed at base at 2110 hours. Red section attacked enemy aircraft taking off from A/D SE Amiens. No claims but fire seen later near aircraft. No cloud – Hazy. Visibility fair.

Ford, 14th August:
Twelve aircraft took off from base at 0845 hours – Ramrod 1200 – Close escort to B.26s bombing 25/B/25. Escort uneventful – No enemy aircraft seen. Bombing appeared concentrated. Two aircraft of Red Section escorted damaged bomber back to base landing at 1040 hours. Remainder completing mission landed base 1110 hours. No cloud – slight haze up to 6,000′.

Twelve aircraft airborne at 1535 hours – Patrol Vire–Argentan area also support to 670 Lancasters and Halifaxes bombing target at 48.58 N. 0015 W, in waves of no small number. One aircraft was hit by flak at Falaise – Pilot (serial number) 1801876 Sgt Macey, Middle East Forces seen to bale out. Two aircraft landed B.3 at 1530 hours. Four aircraft landed B.2 at 1535 hours, returning to base at 1710 hours and 1715 hours, respectively. Bombing concentrated. Vehicles attacked, strikes observed. Troops seen to enter wood north of Thiéville – Wood strafed – intense accurate light flak woods Mezidon. Visibility good.

Twelve aircraft took off from Base at 1925 hours – Ramrod 1202 – Target and withdrawal cover to 140 Lancasters bombing Brest Harbour. Escort uneventful. Bombing appeared good. Intense inaccurate heavy and light flak. Visibility good. One aircraft landed at B.13 owing to engine trouble. Remainder landed base 2145 hours.

Ford, 18th August: Shipping Patrol convoy 'Central' 20/30 SSW Selsey Bill going south. Fourteen aircraft (seven scrambles two aircraft) from 0840 hours to 1625 hours. F/O W.L. Malone arrived on posting from 83 GSU.

Ford, 20th August: Squadron moved from RAF Station, Ford to B.16 (Villons les Buissons). Eighteen aircraft took off from Ford at 1300 hours landing B.16 1335 hours.

B.16, 22nd August: DD.127 – twelve aircraft took off from B.16 at 1415 hours as top cover to No 66 Squadron on Armed Recco, mission uneventful. Visibility good. 5/10ths at 6,000′.

DD.184 – six aircraft took off from B.16 at 1730 hours on shipping recco, for shipping lost by the Navy, but without result. Two aircraft returned early owing to technical trouble, remainder landing base 1839 hours. Weather slight haze, cloud 4/10th at 11,000′. Visibility 25 miles.

F/Lt D.J. McNally was posted from 127 Squadron (supy) to No. 127 Squadron as Flight Commander replacing F/Lt Schofield.

B.16, 23rd August: Two aircraft took off from base at 0910 on weather recco. Argentan, Laigle, Lisieux and Base. Weather 9/10ths Base 18,000′. Top 25,000′. Visibility below and above cloud 60 miles, on ground fairly good. Uneventful. Aircraft landed base 0950 hours.

Twelve aircraft scrambled at 0945 hours for enemy aircraft reported to be in the Le Havre area. These proved to be friendly so the squadron was vectored to Port Audener area where one M.T. vehicle moving East to L.9211 was completely destroyed. Meagre medium accurate flak M.1812. Inaccurate heavy flak Le Havre area. Squadron sighted a number of small ships moving in Le Havre outer harbour, while medium shipping tied to the quay of the inner South harbour was also observed. Visibility good. Twelve aircraft landed base 1110 hours.

Two aircraft together with two aircraft of 331 Squadron took off from base at 1855 hours on Air Sea Rescue mission, an empty dark brown dinghy was sighted approx. ten miles west of Le Havre 2035 hours. One aircraft with a column of smoke coming from it was seen to dive into the sea three miles west of Le Havre. Weather 10/10ths at 3,000′. Visibility good. Uneventful. Aircraft landed base 2050 hours.

Two aircraft took off from base at 1745 hours on weather recco. River Loire area – Weather cumulus cloud Rennes area 6/10ths at 10,000′. River Loire 6/10ths 16,000′. 10/10ths at 25,000′. Cloud increasing towards S.E. Uneventful. Landing base at 1910 hours.

B.16, 24th August: Squadron released.

B.16, 25th August: 127 Squadron started wing ops. – F.216 – Armed Recco North Seine. Twelve aircraft took off from base at 0645 hours landed base 0830 hours. The squadron sighted two armoured fighting vehicles and ten METs, they were stationary and facing east towards Puthy M.4029 – an attack was made – three destroyed and two damaged were claimed. Strikes were also seen on two armoured support units. Unfortunately one Spitfire IX LF piloted by 51113 F/O W.J. Malone was hit by flak and force landed at M.3307. The fate of this pilot is yet unknown. Weather, thick haze in valleys, otherwise clear. Visibility excellent.

Twelve aircraft took off from base at 1420 hours to patrol Yvetot and Rouen area. Landing base 1600 hours. One heavy lorry was sighted and destroyed M.1034. One Spitfire piloted by F/O Campbell force landed approx two miles south of Carpiquet – Pilot uninjured – Weather hazy. Visibility good.

Eleven aircraft took off from base at 1650 hours as top cover to Typhoons on armed recco north Seine – No enemy aircraft were sighted – The squadron was then vectored by control to another area without result. An armed recco could not be carried out owing to the shortage of fuel. Weather 5/10ths cumulus 3,000′ to 6,000′. Visibility good. Landed base at 1810 hours.

Eleven aircraft of No 127 Squadron together with No 66 Squadron took off from base at 1930 hours on patrol Rouen area F.229. Three FW190's were sighted by Red Section led by Squadron Leader C.F. Bradley – M.1000 – Flying west at 19,000′. Singling out No 1 enemy aircraft, S/Ldr Bradley put his aircraft into a dive, closing in and giving it a few bursts at approx. 800 yards, causing smoke to pour from its rear. Coming in to closer range he gave it a few more bursts resulting in the FW190 blowing up in mid-air M.2803.

Weather cumulus 3/10ths 10,000′. Visibility good. Aircraft landed 2030 hours.

B.16, 27th August: Four aircraft took off on weather recco Rouen–Fécamp area at 1010 hours, landing 1110 hours. A few vehicles were sighted, one AFV seen damaged during the mission which was otherwise uneventful. Visibility fair.

Eight aircraft took off at 1105 hours on an uneventful armed recco DD.278 landing at 1225 hours. Ground haze to 10,000′ prevented a full scale operation from being carried out. Visibility poor.

Six aircraft took off at 1715 hours on convoy patrol SW Fécamp landing 1835 hours. Mission proved to be uneventful. Visibility good.

Six aircraft took off at 1800 hours on Convoy SW Fécamp DD.294 landing at 1900 hours. This mission also proved to be uneventful. Visibility good.

B.16, 28th August: Eleven aircraft took off from base at 0725 hours on an armed recco F.302 – Rouen–St Valéry area, coming back with a bag of six MT destroyed and one tank damaged landing at Base at 0920 hours. One aircraft returned early owing to mechanical trouble. Visibility good.

Three sections of four aircraft took off from base in relays from 1930 hours, 1950 hours, and 2000 hours. All aircraft down at 2120 hours. Operation armed recco DD.323. Targets were scarce though sections searched diligently. Flak still powerful and in appearance moving north of the Seine. The results were three MT smokers destroyed – two MT damaged. One of the sections found a curious vehicle – like a camouflaged haystack. After an attack it looked as though some Hun soldiers had started a smoke screen around it. Visibility good.

B.16, 29th August: Bad weather prevented flying. F/O I.I.R. Campbell posted to No 84 Group Commander Squadron.

B.16, 30th August: Another day of exceedingly poor flying weather. Squadron had been detailed for beach-head patrols the first section taking off at 0650 hours, the mission was cancelled after three sections had been on patrol, the last section landing at B.17 at 1005 hours due to the weather.

B.16, 31st August: The start of the day found the squadron once again on beach head patrol, four sections of two aircraft taking part in the mission, all of which proved uneventful. The first section took off at 0645 hours the last landing at 1035 hours. Visibility good.

DD.341 – The next operation was in the Big Ben area in which twelve aircraft took off at 1530 hours – each returning to base at 1735 hours and (Blue Section) four aircraft landing at Lympne. At L.9238 and M.5685 the squadron sighted a number of sunken buildings into which lead a number of communicating trenches. These, it is believed, are Buzz Bomb sites of one kind or another. The eight aircraft which landed at base claim for this trip two trucks (explosives) destroyed, and one flak post attacked of which no result was observed. Blue Section claimed one MET probably destroyed and three MT damaged.

A section of five aircraft taking off at 2005 hours including G/C Morris, and W/C Berg closed the day's work on an armed recco south of Dieppe. They sighted considerable movement of Hun vehicles moving in an N.E. direction, landing back to base with a bag of MET destroyed and two damaged.[1]

Signed: C.F. Bradley
Squadron Leader, Commanding
No 127 Squadron, R.A.F.

[1] This and all following extracts from No 127 Operations Record Book can be found in the Public Record Office, Kew, reference AIR 27/929. Crown copyright material in the Public Record Office is reproduced by permission of the Controller of Her Majesty's Stationery Office.

III

September

September 1st, B.16

As of today, we seem to be better off, concerning dysentery. Doc's new pills seem to be working much better. We are still cold, nearly all the time. When we are airborne, the cold is *much worse*, particularly at 12,000 or 15,000 feet, and particularly on escort missions. Perhaps the only drawback to the Spitfire is the cockpit. It is bone chilling cold. Since you have no room to begin with, you can't even shift your buttocks. Your left hand, the throttle hand, is just cold enough to be *almost* painful. Your right hand, like both your knees, goes *numb*. You beat it against your knees, left right, left right, and when the blood comes back, it is so painful, you could cry. We are supposed to be getting electrical heated kimonos soon, which plug into the gloves. It sounds like a dream, but there's a *catch*. The catch is that you have a plug on the kimono, and that plugs into a socket. It represents one more disconnect if you have to do a panic bailout. We are getting to know the officers better. Squadron Leader Bradley has, I think, a cross to bear. Frank Bradley (nobody calls him *Frank*) is a countryman from Wiltshire, and he speaks with that very comfortable 'moonraker' (rounding of r's) accent. Bradley is ticked off with the lackadaisical attitude of some of the Middle Easters. You only have to look at Frank Bradley to know that he can't stand *any* attitude that isn't *positive*, or 'take charge'. Some of the older pilots have been much more comfortable with the easier – 'desert life'.

Not Bill Campbell, mind. Bill (''oo's watchin' yer' on his Mae West) crash landed a few days ago, was into it until he was tour-exed, yesterday or the day before. 'Big Mac' McNally has a cruel streak in him. He pulls snide practical jokes on Bradley, behind his back. It has to do with Bradley's one deaf ear. McNally says that Bradley lost the hearing chasing an Me109 right to the deck in a vertical dive, pulling out by a miracle. After he landed, McNally says Bradley had a trickle of blood coming out his ear. Bradley must have shot down half a dozen 109's, at least. He is not only a superb pilot, but he has more guts than anyone I know. When he leads us on a mission, he loves to steep turn right after take off, swinging straight back over the strip at about thirty feet, at full bore. For us in Blue section it is a fright. He flies straight at us, pulling up over us at the last split second. Blue leader always has to dip – flashing over trees with only a few feet to spare. But it's not only that. Bradley charges. He strafes below tree tops, flashing over targets (like the Red Cross trucks!) with inches to spare. McNally is loud of voice, disdainful, and sarcastic. Mac's 'Oppo,' or mate is 'Bex' Asboe. Bex, whose nickname comes from a Middle East hangover cure, ('Take Bex! It will make *today* – as bright as yesterday!') is the most non-committal man I have ever met – at least, for a pilot. Bex is McNally's *foil*. 'Hey Bex! Remember the time we went in 'at fuckin' after hours club in Cairo? Those belly dancers with the fuckin' turbans on with the blinkin' bulbs? Remember that, Bex?'

'Yeah. I remember, Mac.'

'Bex got fuckin' plastered, see. Remember 'at, Bex?'

'Yeah, Mac. I remember.'

'Well then, Bex passed out, in the Jacks, with his strides down around his ankles. Remember that, Bex?'

'Mac?'

'Yeah, Bex, what is it?'

'Shut the fuck-*up*, Mac. Wontcha?'

'Bex is *too tight*. Bex needs another shot o' mother's ruin to loosen up. 'ow about another Gilbeys, Bex, I've still got 'alf a bottle 'ere.'

'Mac?'

'Yeah, Bex?'

'Shut yer fuckin' mouth, and *pour*. . . .'

Asboe has earned the right to two special privileges which go back to the desert. He is the only one who has a picture painted on his nose cowling. It depicts a foaming pitcher of beer, and there are painted flecks of foam alongside the cockpit. This is one privilege. The other is that nobody else has the right to fly his 'B' Beer. Actually, I don't think anyone else would particularly *want* to fly it. For one thing, to we of the 'post desert' joiners, we are *told* which aircraft we will fly – without preference. For the older hands, there is almost certainly a superstitious prejudice against flying 'B' Beer. Why we are so prone to superstition, nobody knows – but we would agree that superstition goes along with the job. I am getting away from my 'rundown' on the officers. More about this, later.

It is dark. I am hungry. The mess tent is long since closed, and the food packed away. We have a new sergeant pilot, Sergeant Housden, who came the day before yesterday. Paddy says he doesn't have a 'fat' log book. That means he probably doesn't have any more hours than Pete. About 400 hours, total. I only met him today, after briefing. He was dressed in his brass-buttoned tunic, with a white aircrew sweater underneath. According to Sandy Powell, his battledress did not arrive. He is six feet tall, and has blond straight hair. Not more than 22 years. He took off with the squadron on his first op, just around tea time. The squadron has not returned. They must have landed somewhere else.

September 2nd, B.16

It is always a thrill when the squadrons come back, whether it is just *us* – or *US* – and sixty six, or the whole wing, four squadrons, or even the Norwegians, 331 and 332 Squadrons. When the squadrons are up, the orchards and the strip are fairly quiet. Occasionally the silence is broken by an engine, started, run up to max, down to idle, switched off. Now and then, Typhoons go over, always at angels five or less. Sometimes, boxes of Mitchells go over, and almost daily one can look up, high, and see the long train of Yankee Fortresses, very high, stretching for miles, in very loose formation. They are usually up at angels 25 or more, and many are not even camouflaged. They shine like silver fish in the sun, when there is no cloud cover. The noise from them is mostly a continuous drone.

When the squadrons return, it is like *this*. The quiet is broken by a heavy throb from seeming far away. Almost with no pause, the throb becomes a crescendo, and you know that they are Spitfires even before they break cloud, because the high, piercing whistle of the superchargers become more dominant than the combined roar of the stacked exhausts. Then, there they are, at perhaps 800 feet, in tight formation, flying perfectly pretty, until Red Leader pulls up high, followed by Red Section, peeling off in a steep turn to port, the port section sliding underneath to starboard, as starboard section follows Red, steep turning, cutting the exact swath through the sky. By this time, Red Leader is on the approach, in that rate two turn to port, all the way down to the deck, that makes Spitfire pilots seem crazy, to the uninitiated. These are people who do not know that you cannot make a straight approach to land with a Spitfire. The cockpit is too far back to give forward vision, so you have to get your line of sight to the landing strip around the port side, between the propellers and the leading edge of the wing.

I will never get tired of sitting or standing on an airstrip and seeing the boys return. It is a thrill that has no end.

Pete and I and Dinger Bell got a ride on the gharry this morning, down to flight. Even before we saw our 'spy' Flying Officer Johnson, I sensed that something was *wrong*. I didn't know what. I felt an empty stomach feeling as the squadron flew above us, with two planes missing from Red Section. Then they landed, and we got the sickening news, from Paddy, Eckert, Sandy, and Gollins. But this was after Squadron Leader Bradley briefed us. We were all called together, and Bradley began speaking even before Johnson got his notebook out.

'Last night, we had an unnecessary crash at Lympne. Typically, it was not caused by enemy action. It was caused by pilot error. We were diverted to Lympne, because we were short of petrol. The crash was caused because one pilot failed to obey the rule to continue taxying down to the end of the runway. He attempted to turn off at the first intersection, and was rammed by the following aircraft. Sergeant Housden is dead, and Flight Lieutenant McNally is in the hospital with burns. In future remember the unbreakable rule. Never turn off the runway until you have to – at the *end*. That is all.'

As usual, Paddy had the most to say. 'It was too bloody awful. A fireworks display it was – and two full months before Guy Fawkes Day. That poor bloody kid. Gets killed on his first show. Mac had no chance to avoid the prang. He landed as normal, and was still runnin' at about 35 to 40 when he runs right up the kid's chuff. Mac ripped off his harness and his mask, jumped out of his cockpit, and ran and jumped on Housden's port wing. He saw a great flash of fire, as he grabbed the kid's head, and shouted, "Out! Out! Get out!" Well, the kid's head lolled forward, and Mac could tell he was dead of a broken neck. At that moment Housden's tank exploded, and Mac was blown back about fifteen feet. Then the ammunition started exploding, cannon shells and machine gun bullets flying everywhere. Everybody went down on the deck. Wasn't that the most awful, bloody helpless feelin' you ever had? Knowing that Housden was still in the cockpit, burning – and *not* knowing the kid was already dead. We must be on the shit end of *luck* – is all I can say.' Everyone agreed on *that*.

'What about Mac?'

A handful of 127 'Types'. These pictures were all taken on each man's arrival at 127 Squadron, partly as our 'escape' photographs and partly so that the Wingco and 'the Brass' could relate to a man when he did not return from an operational sortie. *(Top left)* Peter Hillwood, my flight commander. Battle of Britain pilot. He finished his second tour with 127 and was awarded the DFC. *(Top right)* Len Feltham, a 'good type', who survived. *(Bottom left)* My best friend, Peter Attwooll, who joined 127 and was shot down and killed. He apparently forgot to cut the switches when he crashed and burned to death. I buried him in a blanket sewn with string at Breda, Holland, on 1st January 1945. The incident marked my life. *(Bottom Right)* Gilbert (Zhilbare) Morisson, Free French. An incredible man who survived four years of prison in N. Africa. Shot down twice with 127. He was awarded the Medaille de Résistance and survived the war.

No 127 Squadron at B60, Grimbergen, near Brussels. *Front Row:* Chaplain, Doctor, Len Feltham, Gordon Richardson (killed at Alblassa dam, Holland), David Fyfe, S/L Sampson, Harry Lea, Adjutant, 'Spy' Johnson, (Squadron I0), Sammy Roth, Covington, *Second row:* Sgt Baecke (later shot down, killed), George Boudreau, unknown, Reg Eckert, Peter Attwooll (killed crash-landing), W/O Malandaine, F/Sgt Simpson, Peter Coxell, three Canadians, Sandy Powell. The author was on leave as were Paddy Crozier and some others.

'Mac'll be back. About three weeks. Thank God he still had his gloves on, and his helmet. Otherwise he'd have had a cooked head. On the *bad* side, he had his goggles up – and his oxygen mask off. Sandy saw him during the night. The flash fire in his face made Mac's head look like a gigantic, ripe *tomato*. Right, Sandy?'

'But how's Mac now?'

'Brad says he's chipper – when he can speak. He's in the famous 'burns' hospital. He spent all night with them dunkin' his poor tomato head in a special toilet bowl full o' sea water. In, out, in, out, all night long. They say you can't find a better prescription for burns than good old sea water. They bring it in bowsers every day, direct from the south coast. Imagine Mac, havin' his head dunked in water all night long – and not being able to speak a word, for fear of gettin' a mouth full o' saline!'

Golly Gollins added a hundred dimensions to the above. I have just recorded the important details.

September 5th, B.16

The prang at Lympne did more damage than you could expect. It brought the fright of fire back to everyone. We miss Mac, even with his big sarcastic, outspoken mouth. As for the NCO's, we have speculated over and over, what prompted Housden to turn off – because 'inexperience' does not answer the question 'Why?' Oddly, only a few people know much about him. We don't even know if he had his 'chop' – or 'escape' photos taken. It is Bradley's unhappy duty to write the sad letter to Housden's parents.

One thing we know. It might not have happened – probably would *not* have, if we had been able to advance our base. Almost since we landed here, we have been handicapped by our distance from the front – the bombline. If we had been further up there, the squadron would not have had to divert to Lympne. There has been talk for days, about when we will move up – to Lille, when they can repair the runways, of an established aerodrome named Lille-Nord.

The Group Captain briefed us at tea time today. Tomorrow, we move. To a new strip? No! To a farmer's wheatfield! We were told that the wheat was cut, less than a week ago. The sheaves were only stacked and moved to the granary or silo a couple of days ago. We were briefed in the ops tent, and it was cold. The tea was cold. The Group Captain was in a good mood, but he was very direct in his orders. It is a long field, and ten three-ton trucks ran up and down it all last night, to compress the soil and the wheat stubble. The field runs up a hill, from one end to the other. We were told to disregard the windsock, and simply land uphill, south to north. We were told *not* to taxy off the area which had been rolled over. We were also told that we had better land three point, because of the danger of nosing over. We will be staying here overnight – just the pilots and minimum crews. Nearly all the ground crews leave tonight by gharries, so they will be ready for when we arrive. It sounds like a real mess – but we have no choice. They have given the strip a number designation – B.33. It is called Camp Neuseville.

September 6th, B.33, Camp Neuseville

We are here, and it is miserable. Cold, blustery winds, sudden showers. All of our gear is wet. The entire wing landed safely, all but for two 331 Squadron pilots, who landed on soft earth, two point, and nosed over. One of them nosed over right at the end of the field, and sat there as a mute warning to the rest of us who landed later. As each of us landed at the top of the hill, we were met by our airmen, who braced themselves under our wings, so that we could taxy to a tarpaulin. It was slow, maddening slow work – and arduous for our hard-backed airmen. Food for lunch – M and V (meat and veg in cans) cold. The fires won't keep lighted, in the wind and rain. The hard tack biscuits are all wet. Thank God for the new orange canvas beds with the steel struts! We carried them in the gun ports, separate to our two rolled blankets.

We ate the M and V, and immediately turned to the task of setting up the cots, and opening our kit bags, and shaving kits. It seemed only an hour before we were called to briefing. It was an immediate show, and a dangerous one. We were to strafe a radar station in the precincts of Boulogne, a major city. Two squadrons called for – 331 and 127. At the briefing they showed us two or three aerial recce photographs, showing us clearly what we had to strafe – to put out of action. The photos were taken from angels eight. Good pictures.

Following the briefing, Bradley briefed us separately, standing in the open field with rain falling steadily. Here is what he said. 'When we roll over, it will be out of cloud, and directly over target. We will dive as close to vertical as we can make it. You will push your throttle through the gate, if you can. We will be going as balls out as balls out can go. Pull out when you see me pull out – not a foot higher or a foot lower. Expect flak like you've never seen before. This is Boulogne, and I can promise you that they've got the flak, and the bastards will be ready for us. Throttle through the gate, so we can all have tea together! Good luck!'

We took the same arduous procedure to get into the air. Two airmen shoulder each wing. At the given call 'Two-six!' they brace their bodies and lift. Pilot guns the throttle, and the Spitfire trundles three or four yards. Brace again – 'Two six' – gun the throttle – and move forward three or four more yards. Finally, we are on the compressed soil, the take-off strip which the trucks have pounded, before we arrived. We do not turn 'in herringbone', noses in to each other, because there is no room to take off in pairs. We must remember to hold the control column back, so that we don't hit a soft area with the tail up. Take-off is fraught with danger, and each aircraft staggers off the ground. Mercifully we are not carrying bombs, or 60-gallon belly tanks, as we would not get off the ground.

Once airborne, we had to circle base once, as the teams of three fours were slow getting off the ground. The target area was about six-tenths cloud covered, so we at least had some element of surprise. We flew in and out of cloud, with violent bouncing, and then Bradley spoke. 'Monty squadron sections – close up. Monty Red Section – in we go.' I was flying right behind Bradley, and I rolled over on my back, following him exactly. As he went into a vertical dive, he flipped to r.t. switch again. 'Balls out! Here it comes!' I shoved the stick and throttle hard forward, and saw the flak tracers coming up, slow at first, then increasing to incredible speed. I made sure that Bradley was not in my gunsight, and depressed the centre of the gun button. I picked the centre building on the ground, depressing the stick even more. I saw the airspeed indicator winding up, as the altimeter was winding down – very fast.

Suddenly, in a split second, I felt my heart stop as the target was obliterated by the black explosion of an 88-millimetre flak burst! In that same instant, my eyes picked out the other three bursts, as eighty-eights are always in bursts of four. My propeller chewed straight through the black puff, as I fully expected to be ripped apart by shrapnel. Apparently I was half a second too late – the shrapnel was already outside my span. I continued firing cannons and point fives, and suddenly, Bradley pulled out, and as I followed him, I was almost too late. I could clearly see the black ring around his duck-egg blue propeller, then he was way above me, and I surely felt the main span creak under 'G' forces that I had never deliberately caused before. Ahead and still above, Bradley dove for the deck once more, 20-millimetre tracers following him, like rain.

Clear of the target and the flak, Bradley spoke: 'Monty squadron, re-form angels eight, over river bend.'

My throat was very dry. My shoulders, my back, my buttocks, all were wet as though I had been soaked in a pool. My first thought was, 'Is it blood?' I slipped my left hand around my back. It was simply the sweat of fear. As we flew back to the wheatfield, my battle dress, tunic and trousers, became miserably – *cold*. We broke cloud, over the field, at under 1,000 feet. It was raining. The airmen were so soaked – you could have put them through a mangle. Their greasy blues could not have held any more rain. What men they are! *Two six! Two-six!*

It is raining into the night. Will this continue? Will we be able to fly out of here?

September 7th, B.33, The Wheat Field

It rained all night, and it has rained most of the day. Now, everyone is wondering if we will be able to fly out of here, as the strip, running uphill, is the only area that is not a morass. With Big Mac McNally not being here, there is no spark, no loud talk, not many shared jokes. Sandy Powell said today, 'I miss the big old shit. Without Mac everything's dead around here.' There are no ops today.

One of the new officers is Geoff Davies. He is young, blond, good looking, and obviously public school. He has good humour, and is a very fearless pilot. He is very good at aerobatics and can fly upside down at low level. (I don't think Bradley or Hillwood or anyone approves of that.) He is easy to talk to. Gollins, 'Gollie,' is forever Gollie. He always talks of himself in the third person. Only a few more weeks, lads, and Gollie is *gawn*. Gollie on the boat there – Gollie eatin' deelectable food. White fuckin' bread, fried egg, real, New – up yer chuff – Zealand butter! *Nurses on board*. Gollie will be cock o' the roost! Gollie, back 'ome in New – fuckin' – Zealand for Christmas! Christmas dinner wiv me *grand*mother! Roast lamb, green peas, new potatoes! Die of jealousy, you bastards!'

Covington seems to be doing okay. Considering that he has only had a few weeks of orientation into Spitfire mines, after three years as an internee in Ireland, I suppose he does very well. There's no question that he should have had a complete course at OTU as a refresher. It was bypassed because 'I couldn't *wait* to have another *go*, dontcha know. 'Magine me s-sitting the b-bloody war out in Ireland! What – what would I tell my kids – eh? eh? eh?' He accentuates the *last*, by three shakes of the head.

We have lost Covie a couple of times in cloud, recently, but his formation 'feel' will come with more practice. His mood can change in a flash – from the very intense – to the totally humorous, including the knowing wink, that signals the coming bawdy story.

We have a new non-com pilot who is French. His name *reads* English – Gilbert Morisson. It is pronounced – *very* French. Zhilbare Mor-*e*-sson. Nobody could *look* more French than Zhilbare. He stands about five feet eight, has black, straight hair swept back from a swarthy face that is blue shaded, not longer than one hour after shaving. He has such broad jaw bones that, head on, his head is pear-shaped. He said it himself. 'You see this face, Schmidt.' (He calls me 'Schmidt') 'I am told it is shaped like a pee-air. Even people have called me *tête-à-poire*!' He has an infectious chuckle, which is outstanding by strange sounds evoked from rolling his tongue between clenched teeth. A weird hissing is produced. Anything really amusing to Zhilbare is enough to make him hold his sides. *Well* may he laugh. His life has been one saga of danger, even condemnant to *death* – in a North African prison. He has one medal, for absolute bravery, which is the Medaille de Résistance. He was awarded this by General de Gaulle, and presented by him. Zhilbare is ranked as a warrant officer – non-commissioned – which in the Free French Forces is called *ajutant*. As he says: 'In Free French *ajutant* is a *rank* not a function.' He is broad-shouldered, narrow-waisted, cat-like in movement. A natural middleweight fighter, for want of better description. The irony of his medal, is that the same medal, at the same investiture, was presented to the ex-Governor of the prison in which Zhilbare was under sentence of death, and in solitary confinement for two years! Zhilbare bears scars all over his superbly muscled body, from whips, lashes, bayonet stabs, and what must have been ghastly boils. He also bears mental scars from unprecedented miscarriages of justice and incarceration. He is with *us* – because his disgust of French politics made him rebel at joining a Free French Squadron. Zhilbare is twenty-nine years of age, older than all of us, and he had over 2,000 hours in a long since lost log book, prior to the Vichy French Government of General Pétain.

Recce parties are out, looking for a new airfield. Rumour still says 'Lille'. To see a big city again!

September 9th, B.33, The Wheat Field

Squadron Leader Bradley told us that we received 'High Commendation' from the Army for our attack on the Boulogne radar station. Will I ever forget flying through that flak burst?

We have not operated for three days, and today is another 'scrub', due to this marsh land we are pleased to call an airstrip. It is rain, clearing, then more rain. Any idea that 'boy-scouting' was fun, or adventurous, has long since departed. Nobody is in much good humour. Even the jokes told, have a dampness about them. Mostly, the wind has held down, so at least the cooks can light the fires, and we can get hot meals. M and V, Spam, bully beef, canned bacon, and canned sausage. The canned sausage is largely composed of soya beans. The cooks cut the sausage in wedges. It looks so odd.

We are getting along quite well with the boys on 66 Squadron. Like us, they have a mix of different types, RAF English, Canadians, Aussies, New Zealanders, and two Dutchmen. When we first met them, they seemed to be quite supercilious, as though they were somehow superior to *us*. Sixty-six has a long battle record, so I suppose they looked upon us as 'Desert Sprogs', not worthy of much accord. Among their NCO's: 'Woody' Woodhouse, Mike Larson (a terrible North Country accent!), Mac 'Big Mac' McLeod, a New Zealander, and big and well-larded Johnny Turk, an outrageous Australian who has an eye, as they say, for 'any pair of legs wearing skirts'.

All for today. The paper is wet. Everything is wet.

September 11th, B.33, The Wheat Field

We got airborne today, and it was for us, a disaster. Neither Peter nor I was on the show. It was led by Ted Doyle, 'A' Flight Commander. Ted is a Canuck, and is a very steady leader. Among the NCO's were Sandy Powell, Zhilbare, Eckert, Ron Reeves, and – Dinger Bell. Longbow Control vectored them to Flushing, where they attacked two ships.

Pete and I were coming back from lunch, when they came back. Pete looked up. 'One missing' was all he said. We ran all the way to our dispersal.

It was Dinger Bell. Dinger, tour-expired. Pete and I stood by for the de-briefing. The facts were that they made three passes, in spite of intense flak. Eckert and Sandy agreed that the target vessels were 'Bloody near big as destroyers – and stubborn bastards, to boot.' Everyone, officers included, is very down in spirits. Dinger, tall,calm, leather lined face, reminded me so much of a Gary Cooper type who would always come through. We know he was tour-expired, but he was the kind you felt that one more trip wouldn't make any difference. It *did*. Three strafing passes made the difference. The irony was that usually *two* strafing passes, say, on an airfield, will usually expend all the ammunition. These were short strafes, because a ship is a small target. It wasn't Ted Doyle's fault, though. He just carried out the orders. Apparently nobody saw Dinger going into the drink. He was certainly going at 400 mph plus. Sandy was certain that he saw the water disruption, about five hundred yards further from the lead vessel.

Before the de-briefing ended. Ted Doyle asked or detailed Eckert and Sandy to handle Dinger's gear. Normally this is the adjutant's job, or Corporal Turner's. Doyle felt that since Dinger and Eckert were close (they usually tent, together) that it would be better for him to handle. Sandy, Pete and I tagged along. Nobody was in good humour, and we got into an argument right away. Our nerves were raw. Sandy picked up Dinger's camera, and Eckert slapped his wrist agitatedly. Sandy reacted with '*Three* fuckin' passes. If we hadn't made three passes. . . .'

'Well, we *did*. You think you're the only upset bastard? *You* don't know what *I* know. Dinger went *in* with his leave pass in his pocket. I saw the adj *give* it to him. Let's get this job done. We haven't got all day.'

Then Sandy asked, 'What about the camera?' Eckert picked it up and said, 'Goes *home*. All that goes home, put in this foot locker.'

Dinger's metal foot locker is a scratched, matt black marvel of hotel stickers, rail and bus stickers, from Australia all through the Middle East. The shaving gear, brush and razor, and zipper case, went in, minus blades and toothpaste. Two sets of never worn aircrew underwear were passed to Pete. Sandy got three pairs of civilian black socks. We found a shoe box, crammed with letters and photographs. Eckert examined each snapshot, each card, each letter carefully. 'No sense in bringing any unnecessary *pain*. . . .' he said. The shoe box was put into the locker. Eckert tried Dinger's best uniform on, and though it was tight under the arms and across the chest, decided to take it, anyway. It being Australian navy blue, it was no good for Sandy, me, or Pete. Eckert also had first call on Dinger's sheepskin-lined Irvin jacket, (you have to *steal* them) so inherit them these days, because the stores no longer issue them) so he lifted it from the cot, and put it on. We found a bottle of Gilbey's gin, unopened. Eckert poured a cupful, and sipped and passed it around. It was horrible to taste, but we drank it, anyway. He poured another cup, and we were all giggling, and on the edge of silliness, when Eckert saw the Vee mail letter on the little wooden chest of drawers, which had been begging to be seen. We read the letter, Eckert, me, Sandy and Pete.

> My dearest Mum and Dad,
> Sorry again, about not writing you before. Mum, I *did* get the cake, but it was bashed about a bit, because we've been on the move a lot. Thank you for that, and also, the gloves, and the tie. I'll be wearing the tie soon, with the civvies I've got waiting for me in London. They are in storage in a place in the Strand. Now, I must ask you both, please, not to worry. For your information, I've only got a few more to do, and I really *mean* it. They call it 'tour expired' and I can tell you, I'm on that list. The stuff we are doing is *not dangerous*, so please, don't bite your nails to the quick, either of you. By now you must have heard from Milly, and it's quite true. We're engaged by mail, and I have sent the ring. I only hope I picked the right size. I know you've always liked Milly, Mum, and I hope it's not *just* that she always volunteers to help you do the dishes. Milly is going to try to get the church for Christmas or New Year. We want it to be small, so please don't invite *everyone*. I know you *won't* – ha, ha.
> Much love, and expect a cable from me, from Aus House. Don't worry,
> Your loving son, Love to Timmy.

Pete was teary-eyed, perhaps from the gin. He wanted to destroy it. He got quite angry, and told us we were 'Bloody Ghoulish' if we were to send such a letter which would arrive *days* after the telegram. Eckert took charge, and made the decision to send it.

It is late afternoon. We were rounded up by Corporal Turner, who said, 'Briefing. Right now.' We are going to Lille Nord, right after tea. No more, now. Thank God for the orange canvas cots! We may have to sleep under a wing, tonight.

September 12th, B.57, Lille Nord

Last night was a hell of a party; which we needed after bad weather, bad food, bad morale, and bad, sad news about Dinger Bell, and which we *didn't* need after the Gilbey's gin consumption from the cup. Paddy Crozier, who was miffed because he didn't get Dinger's Irvin jacket, referred to the kit dispersal as 'Dinger Bell's *wake*.' He, being Irish, it is not surprising.

At the briefing we were told that Lille has been liberated only a few days. The British and Canadian armies moved through like a dose of salts, and only a Town Major, with a small staff, was left. 'Do *not* be surprised if half the Frenchmen you see are Germans in disguise. Be suspicious of everyone – particularly if he is *young*, and ostensibly *fit*. Nearly all the young men in France are crippled in some way. The able-bodied are working in Germany, in slave factories. German army bods, even in civilian clothes, will not hesitate to throw a grenade at *you* – *or* your Spitfire. Our advance parties may or may not get to the airfield tonight. If they *don't*, you will not leave your aeroplane for any purpose. Not even to *eat*, urinate, or defecate!'

Immediately after briefing, we stuffed our roll up canvas cots into the gun ports, as we did with our blankets. There was no room for a pillow, but we anticipated *that*, by wearing our Irvin jackets, which can be rolled up as a head rest. At the last minute prior to take-off Paddy Crozier made a small plea to God; that we get out of, 'This damnable morass of a French *bog*,' an observation that, 'If we run into the Hun, he'll be surprised to see us shooting brown blankets and orange canvas,' and a request to our maintenance flight sergeant that he loan us a screwdriver, 'So that we can get our bloody bedding out – assuming that we get down in one piece!'

We landed all eighteen aircraft at Lille, with two hours of daylight to spare. We were surprised to find our ground crews waiting for us. When we got to our dispersal, we found that the entire field is bounded by wire fencing. For a while, there was not a person in sight. Then, one by one, they came out of their houses, clapping hands, grinning and cheering, in some cases. They crowded the fence, beaming, and shouting greetings which only one person could properly assimilate. The one person was: Zhilbare Mor-i-sson!

Zhilbare was in his *element*! He was laughing, chattering, even crying tears of total *joy*! For the rest of the evening, and most of the night, he was our mentor, our guardian, our *translator* – and our *star*. After much excitement, most of the people left, presumably to go back to their homes, with many '*Oui! Le demain!*' assurances. It seems as though we were told the truth – that Lille was still awaiting official liberation! Zhilbare, waiting for the many to leave, was in earnest conversation with a small group of men and women. As dusk came upon us, one of the men produced a pair of wire cutters, which made short work of the fence. Zhilbare motioned to six or seven of us – me, Pete, Paddy, Griffin, Eckert and Sandy at least, and we slipped through the rent in the fence. . . .

We walked through two or three streets, not more than five hundred yards in a rather poor built-up neighbourhood. We walked in single file through an open door, seven or eight of us, perhaps even ten. We were inside an *estaminet*, which had a limited sized bar. It was obviously a working man's French version of a local pub. From the size of our heads this morning, we had imbibed not well at all. I remember that Pete struck a bargain with the owner, whom I suppose is *that* – as well as bartender. Pete produced two cartons of dreadful Yankee cigarettes, which are called 'Twenty Grand'. Pete says the Yank soldier who swapped the cigs for six Guinness, told him that 'Twenty Grand' was a racehorse which won the Kentucky Derby. You couldn't prove it by Pete. Pete swapped the 400 cigs for one drink for each of us, from every one of the cordial bottles on the bar. These were such exotics as banana cordial, raspberry, strawberry, kirsch, brandy, and even advocaat, which is full of beaten egg yolks.

The French people, when their tongues were loosened, gabbed all night. As they told their stories, Zhilbare rocked with laughter, chuckling his repulsive chuckle with his rolled tongue clenched between his teeth, with its attendant hissing noise and visible spume-laden lips. Then, he would interpret the joke. 'Three weeks ago – *three weeks ago* – this lady was down to 'er last rooster! All the chickens, they killed, one by one, in order to survive! One day she saw this German army sergeant, standing outside her back yard, eyeing the rooster, and asking when he could come to Sunday dinner! Well, the next day, Saturday, she choked the rooster to death, plucked it, and cooked it. She says, tough as that old bastard *was*, he made a banquet! She says *J'ai mangé ça – comme un morceau d'élastique*! She says she ate that old bastard chanticleer – With a piece of elastic! You understand? Like a piece of elastic!'

Other French jokes trundled through the night. One, concerned the *entire* German Army, on the beaches of Dunkirk, being commanded by Adolf Hitler to *walk* to Dover. First, they had to drink the English Channel. Apparently, they were doing very well, on each command – 'Drink!' the English Channel was markedly receding. Then, it seemed to rise again, even while Hitler was yelling 'Drink! Drink!' It was all called off when a carrier pigeon arrived, courtesy of a 'Fifth Column' spy on the cliffs of Dover. The carrier pigeon's message was opened, and the message read to Hitler. 'Stop! Winston Churchill is on the beach below. He has the entire British forces on the beach! He is commanding them – 'Piss! Piss! Piss!'

Another joke was about 'Le Munique Conference'. It had to do with Hitler, Chamberlain, Daladier, and Mussolini. Each was accosted by a French reporter, as he left the conference. Each was confronted with, 'Monsieur, do you know you are covered in *shit*? (This, variously, as 'Shit above your ankles . . . Shit above your knees . . .' etcetera. Finally, it was, 'Herr Hitler, do you know you are up to your *neck* in *shit*?' And the reply, 'I, Herr Adolf Hitler, am standing on the *shoulders* of Mussolini!'

Today, Pete made the observation that once you understand that *all* French jokes concern the natural (*and*, unnatural!) body functions, you will understand the French. . . . One thing I noticed, last night, when *we* refer to the Germans as *Huns*, the French still call them *Boche*. *Les Boches*. They pronounce it as 'Lay Boshay!'

We drifted back to the airfield not much before daylight. Officially it is called 'Lille Nord.' Unofficially it is called 'Bondu', as in 'Le Champ d'aviation à Bondu.' How we got back is a mystery. We staggered back, and had a terrible time finding the cut in the wire fence. I venture to say that we were all sick, one after the other. We were challenged at the fence by our guards, and we were lucky we were not shot. We *all* came back together, clutching each other for support. All, but Zhilbare. He went home with one of the French ladies.

September 14th, B.57, Lille

This is a fully operational aerodrome. The runways are usable, in spite of some very unsafe soft spots, which are fill in from bomb craters. Dispersals have real bays, in which the airmen can run engines up to full boost, without blowing dust and grit all over the place. Each dispersal is shaped like a big letter 'C', with a grassy mound over five feet in height. On the grassy outer ring, we can lie back in relaxed position.

So we were this morning, with grey clouds, from which a North American Mustang – P.51 dropped out – dropped *in*, and landed.

The pilot was a young USAAF lieutenant, who apparently lost his squadron in cloud, high up, and decided that discretion is the better part of valour. For some reason known to control, he was directed to our dispersal area, which is next to the dispersal of 331 Squadron. Wingco Rolf Berg happened to come by us, and joined us, sitting, on the grassy knoll. He was wearing his Irvin jacket, so no sign of his rank was showing.

This Yank pilot parked quite near to us, switched off, and walked over to us. He was still wearing his flying helmet, goggles up. Why he didn't leave *that* in the cockpit, I cannot fathom. His Mustang was bright, shiny aluminium, with bright yellow and black checker-board squares over the cowling. He was wearing one of those beautiful shiny leather flying tunics, with two silver bars, one on each shoulder epaulette. He was wearing high-heeled boots that looked suspiciously like cowboy boots. He was wearing short leather gloves, too, remarkably similar to Wingco Berg's own pig skin gloves. Their eyes met, I would say, as the lieutenant pulled his helmet off.

'Hi!' he said.

'Hello, there,' said Wingco Berg. 'Sit down, won't you?'

The lieutenant sat down. Whatever the fellow needed, certainly was *not* verbal encouragement. Unabashedly, he entertained us all with exploits which would fill a volume as big as a dictionary in the public library. He took us through the flak of Berlin, Hamburg, the entire Ruhr Valley. He took us into dogfights with Me109's, FW190's, Me262's, Ju88's, and so on. In fact, it was one running dogfight that seemed interminable. After forty minutes or so, a 30 hundredweight pulled up. Out stepped a squadron leader from ops. We *all* looked at him in grateful anticipation, at being rescued from this Yankee hero of the skies. The squadron leader saluted (he was saluting Wingco Berg) and the young lieutenant answered the salute! He thought the salute was for *him*! The squadron leader advised the lieutenant that he would be well advised to take off, weather permitting, and return to his base in the United Kingdom. . . .

We watched the young lieutenant taxi out for take-off in his shiny silver Mustang. (This, after a number of unnecessary handshakes and good wishes to each of us.) He waved as he taxied by. He was out of sight, as he was on the end of the runway, but then we could see him clearly as he lifted the wheels – *too soon*. He skidded along the runway, wheels *up* – in an array of sparks, for a hundred yards! There were two instant reactions from our small group. Shock, from the suddenness, the stupidity. Laughter, from the reaction of seeing this braggart get his come-uppance.

Among the 'Oh! My God! Look!' exclamations, there was one 'Wow!' – a 'Serve the bastard right!' and from Sandy Powell, the all purpose 'Fuck his Irish luck!' There is not one of us who does not want to do a 'splitarse' take-off, with wheels up – at about five feet. We are fortunate, in that we have to change hands, to retract the undercarriage with the right side of the cockpit. Maybe it was *not* an oversight, that Mitchell designed the Spitfire that way.

We took the gharry over to the aircrew mess tent at about eleven forty-five. Our young 'lootenant' came in – shaking his head, at a loss for words. Wingco Berg was with us. He took off his Irvin jacket, revealing his three bars on the épaulettes of his tunic.

'I'm sorry I fucked up your runway – *and* a new P.51,' said the 'lootenant'. Wingco Berg said, 'It happens. I would say that your haste in departure was not served well, by *gravity*. Neither was your *aeroplane*!'

The Yank nodded his head. I saw his face go pale as he realized that Wingco Berg was not just another pilot. 'Sir,' he said. 'I apologize for all of my bragging over there at dispersal. What it'll cost me, probably, is a court-martial. Am I correct, sir, in assuming that you are *in charge*?'

Wingco Berg simply nodded. Then: 'Certain nameless people have decided that I be given command *of*, and responsibility *for*, a wing of four squadrons.'

The 'lootenant' looked as though he wished the ground would open up, and swallow him.

We have two new pilots. They are Flight Lieutenant Feltham, and a non-com – Larry Hyland.

September 15th, B.57, Lille Nord

There have been some rumours running about since the day we arrived here. They have to do with an explosion in Antwerp, which came without warning. There were no sirens, no bombers, no buzz bombs. The explosion was put down as a gas main explosion. Nobody would have given a second thought about this – except that the fellows on 66 Squadron, who were in Antwerp, on their way back from leave in London, heard all about it. They were puzzled, because *two* such explosions occurred in London *three or four days before*. The circumstances were the same – no warning – and so was the explanation: 'Gas mains exploded.'

Today, all of our pilots were called to a special briefing. There were a couple of senior spies, squadron leaders, but we didn't know them, and in any case the briefing was all Brad. He was never more serious.

He told us that the big explosion in Antwerp was not a gas main explosion, any more than the two other reported gas main explosions in London recently were gas main explosions. He explained that *all three* explosions are the result of a very new Hun weapon, a stratospheric rocket. Just as the buzz bombs which still terrorize Antwerp, and the South Counties are officially dubbed – V-1 – so this new rocket will be called a V-2.

These rockets are supersonic, so they cannot be heard. Brad says you can't hear them, until after they explode. Then, he says, you can hear an enormous rush of air. The authorities are very worried. We don't know how many of these rockets the Hun has, although Lancasters and Fortresses have flattened the main place they are supposedly made, a place called Peenemünde.

There is a real fear that, even at this stage of the war, that if our troops get wind of this, that an unseeable, unstoppable, *no defence* against, rocket *exists*, that they could panic and desert.

Therefore, effective immediately, every one of us pilots will become involved in censoring letters written by our ground staff. This is an unusual command, because only officers are usually detailed – or trusted with this irksome duty. I don't think anyone but a snerd would get any pleasure out of reading other people's love letters. We were told by Brad that we must scrutinize every letter carefully, and we must scissor out any and every reference to questioned explosions, rockets, new weapons and so on. Not only *that*, but if we *do* scissor, we are to save the clipping and take note of the airman who wrote it. Some mouthy airman could well earn himself a court-martial over this. Brad also said that whoever he might be, he could expect no sympathy from anyone.

It was a very sombre briefing. The subject is viewed as very serious. I think that all of us NCO's who haven't censored letters before will feel like a fourth form *sneak*. Still, we will have to do it.

September 17th, B.57, Lille

There has not been much action to speak of. This, mostly due to rain, and morning mist. Every opportunity is taken by *all*, to catch the trolley into Lille, for two things, estaminets and women. There doesn't seem to be any shortage of make-up. The women plaster it on like – plaster! Larry Hyland seems to have 'palled up together', as they say, with Paddy Crozier. They get on well together, and they had some real stories to tell, this morning, about two young women they met. They apparently had picked up the girls in a bar. What was funny was that Larry got the girls to take them to the girls' flat, and went to a closet without asking, to hang up his tunic. The other three were apparently in the small living room, sharing a bottle of Dubonnet, which Paddy had bought on the way. As Hyland hung his tunic on a hanger, he saw a Luftwaffe tunic hanging on the adjacent hanger. On the shelf above, he found a matching forage cap. Both fitted. He walked into the living room, and Paddy almost died of fright. Then, they all had a good laugh. Through the rest of the evening, the girls apparently convinced our boys that the Luftwaffe pilots are just like *us*. 'They said – except for the uniforms, you couldn't tell any difference between the GAF and the RAF. She said *they* are every bit as fun-lovin' as we are. Now, isn't that *nice*?'

Hyland is a very intelligent person from Manchester. Like many of us born in common to poor surroundings, he has taken proper advantage of the school system through scholarship and Grammar School. Still, he has on occasion a harsh tongue and an accent (Manchester) that irritates as a bad piece of chalk on a blackboard. His classic warning, whenever his dander is up, is 'Ah'm tackin' umbrage, *now* so watch tha' fookin' mouth. Kip tha' fookin' teeth clenched, will tha' now?'

Zhilbare is almost nowhere to be found. He only shows up for briefings, sometimes, suddenly, as if he is hearing special callings to show up. He comes and goes, and answers all curious questions either with a silent wink and a smile, or a repeat of the question. 'You ask me where I was last night? Let your imagination take *flight* – you may find that you were with me!' Or – 'Where do I get thees money? Where do I get thees money? There is *much* money to be found, eef you know where to find eet. Eet is like *love – everywhere*! But you 'ave to know where to look. When I find eet – I say *Merci* – an' I put eet in my flak jacket.'

His 'flak jacket' is a thick canvas belt, worn above the waist, with pockets packed with currency. The belt must be five inches wide. He never takes it off. About a week ago – or less – he disappeared. He was gone for two days; he got a leave pass to London, ostensibly to visit Free French HQ. He came back the next day, carrying two parachute bags full of coffee beans. He had such a weight of beans that it was a wonder that the bag handles didn't simply rip off. Zhilbare said the aroma of the coffee made every passenger's nose lift high in the air. There were some Army colonels and majors on board, and Zhilbare was expecting to be unmasked and gaoled on arrival. Still, he was smiling, and unphased. A man who has been through what Zhilbare has gone through is not likely to panic at being caught with a cache of coffee beans.

Lille is an exciting city, even though the shops are pretty empty. Only the bars and night clubs are full.

I did two ops today. Both were dive bombing the harbour at Wemeldinge. The first was not very successful, so they sent us back. 'Second Time Lucky.' This, I wrote in my log book. Very little flak.

September 19th, B.57, Lille

Today, flying was scrubbed for bad weather. Still, we did not get our release orders until mid-afternoon. We all decided to go into Lille, (what else to do?) and Doc came along with us. He said he wanted to keep an eye on us. We thought that that was a joke, but later on, during our pub crawl (what else to do?) he told us he hoped that we would soon move up to another airstrip. The reason, he said, was that many of the airmen are reporting sick with clap, and not a few with syphilis. Doc says that the Norwegian erks have the largest number of cases. He said there is more truth than over-reaction to Lady Astor's supposed statement to Montgomery, 'Your syphilitic army of the Nile.'

Lille is a city sharply divided between extreme poverty and unexplainable wealth. Of poor ladies selling their bodies for cigarettes, and card-carrying prostitutes who do it only for *new* French francs.

Zhilbare said, today, (he joined us today for a change) that many thousands of men and women haven't missed a thing by being occupied by the Germans. He says that for proper financial consideration, the Germans turned a blind eye and a deaf ear to the transport of eggs, bacon, butter, mutton and even beef, between France, Belgium, Holland, and even Denmark. This has been a real revelation to Zhilbare, who suffered so much while he was in prison,

Mark IX Spitfire

(*Left*) Reg Eckert at Grimbergen. He is wearing the Irvin jacket that belonged to 'Dinger' Bell. (*Right*) Peter Coxell

The author in front of his Spitfire

courtesy of the Vichy government. He is *disgusted*. Perhaps this is why he has become a black marketeer.

We got back here about 7 p.m., too late for tea – and what passes for supper. As I was coming past the squadron tent, Corporal Turner said that Squadron Leader Bradley wanted to see me. It was a very short meeting, but a happy one. Brad (I couldn't *call* him *Brad*, as Gollins and others do!) produced a pair of warrant officer's crowns. (These are known as 'treacle tins' or 'Tate and Lyles,' because the Royal Coat of Arms is emblazoned on Tate and Lyles' syrup products.) He said, 'Smith, I thought you might be able to make use of these. Your warrant rank became official last week. I signed the acknowledgement. Why don't you get them sewn on.' It was a small gesture, but to me – significant. I thanked him for his thoughtfulness. He went on to say, 'You are doing all right. I'll be trying you out as a section leader, some time *soon*. That's all, Smith.'

I felt as if I could jump over his tent! I have become a warrant officer, and I *will* become a section leader – soon. And, on top of *that* – today, I became 22 years of age. No, I did *not* tell anybody that it is my birthday today. I will celebrate *that*, when I get home on leave, which should be *soon*.

September 20th, Lille

I got another letter from Bill Williams, today.

It bucked my spirits up today, as it always does. I can only presume that his reference to Rex North, who writes for one of the Pictorials, is alluding to an impending marriage. Fact is – that there is no enclosure, so I will probably never know what 'Rex Norf' wrote about Bill. I will show the letter to Pete tonight, who will probably crease up with laughter. Pete thinks of Bill Williams as a celebrity doing the most dangerous job in the Second TAF. I happen to subscribe to the second part, because rocket-firing Typhoons get no break at all, from that one hazardous job. They go in at a chosen trajectory, and there is no turning back. Flak is decimating our old Tealing mob. 'Hoppy' – Ken Hopley – my old 'oppo' from OTU never had a chance. He blew up the Tiger Tank – but flak blew a wing off at low level – at over 400 miles an hour. Dicky Peters baled out by a miracle. Starboard wing blown apart at the pull out. Three upward snap rolls, and he ejected as it stalled. When his 'chute' opened, they say he wasn't more than one pendulum swing from the ground. And Dicky is *lucky*. May luck stay with you Bill – if only for 'The piss-up-in *Smoke*'. . .

567 W/O. Williams, S.L.
247 Squadron
RAF
B.L.A.

Watcher Spiv,

I hoffer me regrets at not scribblin' a few lines to yer before this I 'ave been a busy man but 'ave now got the copper on my side. I'm glad to 'ear that you are goin' along alright and not having any bovver wiv anyone and fanks for the tip orf abart me 'errin' bone suit and I'll give that cowson what for when I sees 'im. As regards me own 'elf all I kin say is, I gottit, but I might as well get a stretch in the Scrubbs for all the 'appiness I gets 'ere.

Abart leave cock, seein' as 'ow I've got a few in (Ahem!) I'ad leave about free weeks ago but we 'ave 'ad a lot o' lorses since and the way it works art I should be on leave in about 5 weeks time and I will get the exact date and if you or me can fiddle to 'ave the same week as the 'over it will be bobs yer – uncle.

While I was 'ome I tried ter find yer 'ouse as I'd lorst yer haddress but went wiv wot Oppy told me but no bleeding luck. I fort I'ad farned it at first cors I went darn a street wot 'ad farsands of kids in it and I fort I saw your ol' woman on the doorstep nagging to someone's ol' China next door but when I asked 'er she said, ever so Marble Archish "Hi beg yer par'on." Gor blimey.

Er ol' man cime along then and 'e was a coalie darn the worf. I 'ad a couple of pints wiv him in the 'Lonsdale' and asted 'im he'd done time lately, and you could er knocked me darn wiv a fevver cos 'e'd never been in a' all!

Me sister in law wos rarned 'ome wen I got back on the bleeding 'earole agin.

Says me bruvver, the young one Charlie was on probation fer a 21/2^{d} job darn Fenchurch St. Soppy Sod. I tells yer these kids ain't got no idea, 'ave they. Just like I says to the ol' lady 'Fings ain't wot they used ter be.'

I 'ave henclosed a bit of orlright art of the paper wot me campaign manager Rex Norf wrote and don't take the piss iever cos it's true and I 'ave been 'ome and told me uvver bit of grumble that she's 'ad it. Boy is this one an eye full for the lads darn the Windsor make some ov them bleeding 'ores darn there fink, I bet.

But serious for a few moments this is really on the level and I do intend to marry her although the reqd. bumph is in its early stages at the moment but I will keep you posted of all the Gen and I am sincerely hoping that this war will soon finish out here and we will have the times of our lives in *Smoke*.

Ol' Brarnie and me 'ad a shot 'ot time while we wos at Brussels but we ain't there anymore they 'ad to move us it got too 'ot for me & 'im but when I gits a day orf I always goes back there.

Well China there ain't any real news to tell so I'll close and I'll write agin in a few days time givin yer the date of me leave so until then I'll say Cheerio.

Always yer Pal.

Bill

I had better write to Bill tonight.

September 22nd, Lille

The make up of the squadron, today, as opposed to a month ago, is a remarkable improvement, in morale. We have spent a lot of time on the ground, due to weather, but that has been good for those of us who haven't spent every last sou in the bars. A casual check among us today assures us that every single one of us has dipped into his escape money, the 200 crisp French francs which we were issued before we came to Normandy.

McNally has been released from the 'burns' hospital, so we are told. However, they have sent him somewhere on a 'rest,' we don't know where. They say it takes a while to recover from his type of 'flash' burns, even though the flesh remained intact.

Zhilbare is planning another trip to the United Kingdom *soon* – but he won't give the details. He has bought a 'putt-putt' motorcycle for himself, quite without permission. When we asked him what the boss, Bradley might say about it, he just shrugged his shoulders and finally said, 'If you fellows don't tell heem – he will be none the wiser, *n'est ce-pas*? Then, if he *does* find out, I will pretend not to know what he is talking about. After all, we say – 'what the eye does not see, the 'eart does not grieve over.' We have the feeling that Zhilbare will probably produce a story and a request, from Free French Air Force that will get him to the UK and back in one day. We do know that he has a cache of coffee beans, somewhere in London, and he has told us that they are unroasted beans, so that it won't be as risky as the last time, when the pervasive odour of coffee almost begged his arrest.

Among the officers, Peter Hillwood, 'B' Flight Commander, is, like Covington, a Battle of Britain survivor. He is dark-haired, with a moustache that has a bit of a droop. He takes a very good picture, as I have seen from his escape photograph. He could be easily mistaken for a film actor. I am sure that he's as approachable as the next officer, but I think we NCO's are a trifle awed over two things. First, it is natural for us to be a bit intimidated by *any* Battle of Britain pilot. Second, he has this very upper class way of speaking. He can draw out a word like AC-TU-ALL-EA so that it sounds like a sentence! ('ack-chu-alle-a No-o-o-o-o!') He is a very skilled pilot, and an excellent leader. His timing, on making turns, is so precise that we, formating on him, hardly have to make throttle adjustments beyond a touch.

Bradley, totally fearless, is ever pushing us to fly better, press on-attacks, strafe lower, bomb lower, more accurately. He has a captivating way of speaking to me. His Wiltshire brogue reminds me so much of my uncles Ron, Art, and Doug, who are all Wiltshiremen, as is of course, my grandfather – 'Gramps'. I spent part of every summer in my youth in the Roman village of Mildenhall. It is pronounced 'Mine-all' and its Roman name (55 BC and all that!) is Cunetio. It is only about seven miles from Pewsey, where Frank Bradley grew up. Back to the brogue. It is very comfortable, as it is spoken by Bradley. It is *not* public school.

'Desert' Officers: McNally, Asboe, Ted Doyle (Canadian), Gollins (NZ), Flying Officer 'Dicky' Lloyd (Australian), Flight Lieutenant Shillitoe, Flight Lieutenant Truscott, Dave Fyfe. Almost all of them are close to tour-ex. I'm not sure about Flight Lieutenant Gordon Richardson, but he is Australian, and a hell of a good scout. Len Feltham is also a good Joe, and he has a grand sense of humour. Sammy Roth is another good one. I think we NCO's measure the officers by the way they act towards us, not so much by their flying skills.

Of the NCO's, since Dinger was shot down, we only have one desert type left, and he is Ron Reeves. Ron is pretty much a lone wolf, as they say. He is affable to all, and he tells many amusing stories about desert squadron types who are no longer with us, who are real characters.

Eckert and I took off on our own, last night, to visit Roubaix, which is the other side of the river to Lille. Roubaix is an industrial city, and we only found working people. Roubaix is very drab, compared to Lille. We found a good hotel, and we took wine up to our room. The room had two beds and a bidet, Eckert had never seen or heard of a bidet until then. I had read about them. When I explained what it *did* – Eckert creased up with laughter. He thinks it is hilarious that the Froggies would produce a sit-down water closet to do what you can do as easily with a wet flannel. We got a good bath at the hotel. We had to share one piece of soap, no bigger than half a crown.

I am going on leave in two or three days. I can't wait for my mum's cooking. Somehow, Dad is still able to get, despite rationing, eggs, bacon, and chicken livers. I wonder if there will still be tomatoes to fry. I expect I will be able to shoot a big line, and be a temporary hero at the Fox and Goose.

Extracts from the Operations Record Book 127 Squadron, RAF, 132 (Norwegian) Wing

B.16, 1st September, 1944: The day broke fair and promising but it was not before 1152 that twelve aircraft were off on an armed recce in Area 'F' landing back at Base at 1314 with a score of one tank – two MET and one Ambulance destroyed. One MET probably destroyed and eight MET and heavy duty vehicles damaged.

The last mission of the day was an armed recce in Areas 'E' and 'F' and towards Lille in conjunction with No 332 Squadron – The claims for the squadron were one MET destroyed – one MET probably destroyed – twelve aircraft took off from Base at 1955 landing Lympne at 2130. Unfortunately in landing at Lympne, F/Lt McNally and F/Sgt Housden collided. Both were burned. F/Lt McNally not seriously – in trying to extricate F/Sgt Housden, who died. It is hoped that F/Lt McNally will be back with the squadron in two or three weeks' time. F/Sgt Housden had only been with the squadron three days and it was his first operational trip with the unit.

B.16, 2nd September: The squadron returned from Lympne via B.3 on an armed recce without having fired their guns. The weather was exceptionally cold with the wind at gale force all day.

B.16, 5th September: Only one show – a fighter sweep Brussels and Boulogne area then on to Manston to refuel and rearm, as this operation was uneventful the Squadron returned to base direct. 'A' Party off at 0700 hours – arriving at B.33 Camp Neuseville (our new Landing Ground) at 1830 hours. Pilots were briefed by G/Capt Morris about the new Landing Ground B.33 at 1600 hours.

B.16, 6th September: The squadron arrived at B.33 between the hours of 1100 and 1300. At 1420 hours a request for close support was received over the VHF and 332 Squadron and 127 Squadron were to attack a Radar installation outside Boulogne – Operating in section of four aircraft with fifteen minutes intervals over target. The squadrons must have done an excellent job for the Army sent a letter of thanks – worded in the most glowing terms, which was appreciated by all who took part.

B.33, 7th September: 127 Squadron three sections of four aircraft took off 1638 landed 1736. 'B' Party left B.16 at 1415 hours. The airfield was unserviceable throughout the day owing to heavy rain – Squadron released. 'B' Party arrived at 1000 hours.

B.33, 11th September: A fine day and the runway at last serviceable. Operations were restricted, however, by lack of petrol and long range tanks. The Wing carried out armed recces over the islands of the Scheldte Estuaries.

The squadron's turn came at 1100 hours when twelve aircraft took off. They sighted a lot of shipping and barges in the harbours and equally as many moving between Breskins and Flushing. They were given a pin point and ordered to attack, which of course they did in spite of the very intense accurate flak they experienced. Unfortunately after the third attack WO Bell, (Aus) was not seen again – A very sad loss to the squadron as he occasionally led a section in flight. The remainder landed at Base at 1305 hours. G-Capt Morris landed at 1600 hours from Lille/Nord (B.57) and after tea, briefed the pilots on the new location. Squadron took off at half hourly intervals from 1730–2000 hours.

B.57, 12th September: The first day at Lille/Nord was a fine one. The squadron took off on an armed recce NE of Antwerp at 1400 hours landing at 1605 hours. This operation proved uneventful. 'B' Party left B.35 in batches of 20 vehicles, the first starting off at 0930 hours for B.57.

B.57, 13th September: D.647 and N.6716 – Another fine day but the squadron's turn did not come until 1600 hours, when eight aircraft were detailed to attack machine gun posts at H.2576, which it is believed they did successfully, landing at 1720 hours. F/Lt Feltham and F/Sgt Hyland arrived from 84 GSU on posting.

B.57, 14th September: Owing to thick ground mist no flying was possible until late in the morning and it wasn't until 1158 hours, that eleven aircraft of the squadron took off on an armed recce to attack MET which had been reported west of and in the Breda Area. They returned at 1340 having damaged two MET's and observed hits on five loaded barges on the canal at Breda, and ground defences and buildings strafed.

B.57, 16th September: Weather reported as excellent all day, little if any cloud and good visibility. However the morning proved quiet, and it was not until 1325 that twelve aircraft of the squadron took off with 500 lbs. bombs to bomb a narrow neck of land carrying a road and railway at approximately D.5621, scoring four direct hits – two near misses on target and three hits on road at D.6621. Reporting on their return at 1432 hours a large concentration of troops on the quay side of Terneuzen harbour – Some forty to fifty barges at the quay sides, three barges leaving the harbour and four merchant vessels of approximately 1500 tons West towards Flushing. GCC apparently acted immediately on this information for squadrons of Typhoons and Spitfires were sent to attack this target, our turn coming at 1705 hours when twelve aircraft took off led by W/Cdr Berg and including G/Capt. Morris. One direct hit was seen on the quay and a number of near misses on shipping in the harbour. Aircraft landed at 1800 hours.

B.57, 17th September: DD.757 – Owing to the alteration in the clocks – it was expected that operations would start early – However, the weather prevented this as a heavy ground mist made flying impossible before late morning, in fact it was not before 1308 hours that twelve aircraft of the squadron were off to dive bomb shipping with No 66 Squadron. They landed at 1425, reporting only moderate results, the best of which was a direct hit on a road at Wemeldinge (D.4131). DD.774 – At 1610 hours saw twelve aircraft off again to bomb shipping and returning to base at 1700 hours with better results, having scored direct hits on a harbour.

B.57, 20th September: First light saw an improvement in the weather; however, a ground haze prevented a really early start. D.796/Bol.7 – By 0925 hours twelve aircraft of the squadron were off to dive bomb gun positions SE of Calais and landed at 1820 hours, reporting three direct hits and four near misses on the target. Unfortunately, the weather clamped again early in the afternoon.

B.57, 22nd September: Weather improved during the night and although some ground mist prevailed in the morning – 127 Squadron together with 332 Squadron were detailed to dive bomb enemy strong points two miles SW of Calais. Twelve aircraft of the squadron were off by 1130 hours and landed at 1240 hours, reporting that results of the bombing were not observed as target was partly obscured by cloud – but bombs were seen to drop in target area.

B.57, 22nd September: Second Operation – D.846/W.Y.I.2 – The squadron (twelve aircraft) were off to dive bomb a fort NE Antwerp at 1455 hours and landed at 1610 hours with their bombs – The operation having proved abortive owing to weather.

B.57, 23rd September: D.866/XPE 6. – After heavy rain during the night the day broke very overcast – however, twelve aircraft took off at 1615 hours to dive bomb gun positions at Antwerp. They were to be assisted in this instance by the Army who had arranged to lay red smoke over the target area – But owing to unknown circumstances the smoke was not on the pinpoint and as there was some uncertainty of position, bombing was poor. All aircraft landed at 1720 hours.

B.57, 26th September: DD.904 – Again heavy rain during the night which affected the airfield, but the weather cleared quickly, nevertheless the squadrons turn did not come until 1650 hours when they were detailed with 332 Squadron, to provide escort cover to Mitchells and Bostons of 2 Group who were bombing Cleve, east of Nijmegan. The mission went according to plan and the squadron reported good bombing. Twelve aircraft of the squadron took part and landed at 1825 hours.

B.57, 27th September: For a change the weather in the morning was very good and allowed the Wing to commence the day according to schedule.

D.923/CCL.2. Twelve aircraft took part at 0715 hours to dive bomb and strafe gun positions in the Antwerp area and landed at 0825 hours well satisfied with the job, having scored ten direct hits and one near miss on the target, which they well and truly strafed after bombing, including a chateau, and had the pleasure of seeing an Ammo Dump go sky high.

D.962/MJC.2. – Eleven aircraft were off at 1700 to dive bomb and strafe gun positions and strong point at Calais, landing at 1750 hours. The results of the bombing in this instance were not as good as in the morning – only two direct hits were claimed – however the target was well strafed.

Signed: C.F. Bradley
Squadron Leader, Commanding
No. 127 Squadron, R.A.F.

IV

October

October 5th, Lille

I have just returned from leave. Since I have been operational, I find that each seven days of leave is a repetition of the last. First, the simple thrill of having made it home – one more time. Then, there's the luxury of clean laundry, clean sheets, pillows that are *not* rockhard, and soft white blankets. My mother's marvellous cooking – always high on my list. This last time, they had a real gammon rasher of ham, for my first meal. I had three eggs with it – God knows how my Dad provided them. The first trip, to the Fox and Goose, is always new, and refreshing, as is, the next day, to the Park Royal Hotel – and The Abbey. These are our local pubs. If I am lucky, I see old pals I haven't seen for too long. *Oh*, it seems, everyone is in uniform, and there is a sad sweetness to meeting grown airmen whom I remember as school kids, emphasis on the 'kid' part. Surely this war has gone on too long, to see them in RAF blue, following the path taken by Bob Bode and me, and Dave Clayton, Mickey Cross, Lennie Silk, and Eric Bryant. . . .

It is always exciting, in the first three days of leave, to catch the train at Park Royal, and be in Piccadilly in thirty minutes. Of course, the Yanks *own* Rainbow Corner – but London, or 'Smoke' as we call her, is big enough for *ten* armies. . . . Of course, as 'aircrew on ops' Bob and I *have* to visit 'Shepherds', in Shepherd's Market, Mayfair. Shepherds is crowded on both sessions, seven days a week, with Allied aircrew. It fills up with bemedalled heroes and some of the most beautiful ladies in London, within twenty minutes from opening. A genuine sedan chair is just inside the door, converted to serve as a telephone kiosk – and it is always occupied; from opening to closing. It is almost impossible to get through the body mass to the bar, so orders are shouted from five rows back, and the beers and shandies are passed, backwards, from the bar to the later arrivals. Many officers' caps and raincoats are left behind by men who go on to other pubs, and forgot them. Oscar, the Swiss who is 'Guvnor' of

Shepherds, has, literally, a room full of coats and hats. Any officer in the know can simply go to Oscar, plead his case, and pick a new cap or raincoat from the room.

My parents are always putting my pals up – those I brought home from training in Rhodesia. Their largesse, to Aussies, New Zealanders, and Rhodesians, is reflected in an empty larder, and in them being relieved, when such leave is over. . . . There is a weariness in meeting my parents' friends, because they never fail to greet Bob and me with 'When are you going back?' Thus, on the fifth day, a remorse sets in with me – and fear of the uncertainty of my return comes with it. Those feelings *build*, through the next two days. It is not easy, saying goodbye to Mum at the front door; she, with our dog, Sally in her arms, and tears welling up in her blue eyes, and spilling over. We both know the reality – that an 'on time' Dakota or C47 can get me back to 127, and in a Spitfire cockpit before the afternoon is waning. . . .

Bob did it *again*. He got leave coincidental with mine. He is on rest, following his second tour as navigator, on Lancasters. He was with me, when I experienced my biggest coincidence of the war. If I had been alone, I would not believe it happened. It was that *unreal*.

We decided to go to Fulham, to visit a crew member from Bob's first tour. Our timing was off: Bert the mid-upper gunner, had returned to camp the day before. It was a nice day, so we decided to take a long walk along the Brompton road. The idea was simply to kill time, waiting for the pubs to open. As eleven o'clock marked our trail, we found pub after pub closed with notices on the door giving various licensing times. All notices began with 'Sorry, no beer.' As we were literally in sight of Knightsbridge, we were as well resolved that we would be 'bricky dry', at least to Piccadilly, where they never run out of beer.

Bob pointed across the road, to a pub which was set back from the road. It was, in fact, an island, since a narrow alley preceded the front entrance, with a narrower alley on each side. We walked across Brompton road, and saw that it had no sign on the door. We walked inside. Nobody was at the bar – and there were no signs of life. We stood by the bar for a while, wondering where the landlord or barman had gone. Finally, he emerged through an unmarked door that apparently led to the cellar. He told us that the only beer he had was ginger beer, so we had a glass of that. We were alone with him for at least twenty minutes. He was very much impressed with

Bob's DFM and his DFC. Then, he turned to me and asked me what I was doing, and where I was based. When I told him, he became interested immediately, because he said his son-in-law was flying Typhoons. He reached behind the bar, and produced a large photo of a graduation flying course, in Canada. There must have been 50 or 60 sprog pilots in the photo, and the individual heads were no bigger than a sixpence. He asked me if I could find his son-in-law, which I thought was rather preposterous. Then the man offered me an inducement which I could not refuse. A drink of some sort, for nothing, if I could point out his son-in-law. This is exactly what happened:

I took the photograph from him, first scanning the faces over four rows, then, poring over it. Two minutes went by.

'Well?' he said.

'I only know *one* of them. He is here' – I stabbed a face with my index finger. 'Second row. His name is Ken Brown!'

'Say that again. Go on. Say it again.'

'Ken Brown. He's the only one I know.'

The man looked at me in wonderment. Then he hooted. He stepped off his bar stool. 'Well – I'll be buggered! You know what you've done? You picked out my son-in-law! My Gawd! What a turn up for the books! 'e picks up my son-in-law from – well – count 'em! Dozens! All right then – for the best bloody Scotch whisky in the 'ouse, then – tell me where Ken Brown is – right now!'

I paused, 'Ken Brown is on 247 Squadron, Typhoons, somewhere in Belgium. Or Holland,' I added.

'Well, I'll be buggered! What a turnup! What's yer name? – No, let me get my special Scotch! Let me lock that bloody front door – to 'ell with business!' We left an hour later, not very sober.

I will write a letter to Bill Williams tonight. Perhaps I can borrow the adjutant's typewriter. Then I can put a carbon paper in it – and *surprise* Ken Brown. . . .

October 6th, B.57, Lille

It has been raining for three days now, and I have been in dark humour, with not a little touch of mordant, superstitious fear. The reason is that the first piece of news I got, on my return from leave, is that poor bloody Whittington got shot down. He was last seen flying towards our side of the bomb line. He was first posted as 'missing', which meant that they hadn't found his aircraft or his body. It was certain that he was a goner, because he was going down, flaming like a torch. Everyone fears being a flamer, being trapped inside a flaming cockpit. This is a most personal agonising that is mine, to share with nobody. Not even Pete. Weeks ago, when Pete and I were given our 'escape' or 'chop' pictures, somehow, I also got one of Zhilbare, and also, Whittington. Both pictures are between the pages of my log book. Here, Whittington looks at me as if he is about to smile. I look at him, he looks back. Yet for the life of me I cannot hear his voice. I have forgotten how he spoke. I can close my eyes, and I can hear Dinger's voice. I can hear McNally, Asboe, Hillwood, Pete, Sandy – and even Griffin. I cannot hear Whittington.

I think I have this depression and fear because of superstition. There is this superstition that you are prone to getting the chop, most, on the first op you fly, after a leave, or some other time off. (Just like my fear in Scotland, when I came back from the tonsillectomy, and found that the whole hut was deserted.) Bob tells me that bomber crews hate the last day of leave, and become despondent until they have come back to base from one more operation. Here, with me, it has been three days of duff weather, and haven't even been called for an air test.

I won't get rid of this numb feeling until I go through the nervous ritual of another briefing. While each briefing is different from the last, there are common elements to each. Unless it is a simple call to armed recco, or an escort job, there is always anticipated fear. When the Wingco – or chief spy says, 'You will be carrying one 500-pounder and two 250's with eleven-second delay fuses' you can sense the fear, all round. The words tell you that we will be going in low, because the fuses are set to give us time to swoop in and swoop out, so that we won't blow each other up. Some of us are addicted to writing words on our left hand, above the knuckles, in indelible ink. These are things like wind direction and speed, barometric pressure, course to target, and map coordinates. I do it myself, I don't know why. Am I going to pull off my gauntlet and my silk lining glove off, in freezing cold, just to see what I should have remembered in the first place? Of course not. I suppose we do it for some kind of assurance – such as 'If I lose everyone in cloud, at least I won't be lost!'

When the briefing ends, we get back in the three tonner, and people start telling the same weak jokes we laughed at, yesterday, and last week, out of politeness. Back at dispersal, our mechanics have put our parachutes in our cockpits, and have laid out the harness straps neatly, for an easy, quick take-off. We always hope for an immediate take-off. Delays, which are sometimes dictated by weather info, make us all nervous. Cigarettes are at least as important to post briefings as they are supposed to be to the victim of a firing squad. They are in profusion. Some of us chain smoke, even lighting a new one from the butt of another. We talk about food, films, and the other 'F'. We never speak beyond the *now*. Nobody *ever* says things like 'When we get back' or 'Let's do it tonight' – or even refers to the end of *this* operation. Why? Because superstition is rife with us. That's why. It is simply wonderful when there is no delay. We simply run to the cockpit, climb in, strap in, start up, taxy into herringbone – noses inwards, take off in pairs, close up formation – open to battle formation – and set course. We are the fighters who finally are in the ring, and the bell has rung. No time to anticipate fear!

I can't wait to get airborne again, so that I can get back, and relax again.

October 7th, B.60, Grimbergen, Belgium

We got here yesterday, and it is another real airfield, with proper runways, with many bomb hole patches. The GAF must have left in a hurry, because they did not even have time (or inclination?) to take the camouflage bunting down from the blast bays at dispersal.

All of us NCO pilots (we are nearly all warrant officers now!) are in civilian billets now. That means goodbye to tent life – at least, we hope, through the autumn, and winter. How those boy scouts can put up with tent life I will never know. The inside of a tent is never dry. The ground is always squishy, and there is always mud on your boots. In this civilian billet, there is Eckert, Pete, Sandy Powell, Paddy Crozier, Zhilbare, Griffin, Ron Reeves, and Larry Hyland. That is, nine of us. The house is not a big one. We are all packed in two rooms, but at least it can't rain on us. We are all sleeping on our own cots, these little orange canvas 'camp' cots. We are never further than six inches off the floor. The house is owned by an elderly couple, Louis, and Louise. They are Belgian people who are called 'Walloons', which means that they are more Dutch than French, and they speak Flemish, primarily, a language that we know – *not a word*. Thus, we have to converse in French, and it is very painstaking for both sides. It calls for a lot of patience. Today, for example, Louis, sitting by the stove, which is used for both cooking and heating, explained part of his youth, which had to do with his courting of Louise. It went something like this *'Moi-heinh? Moi-comprenez vous? Moi? Quand – Je mais jeune – et Louise. Louise – comprenez? J'ai une by'cyclette. Ca bycyclette – avec – un grand – et – une petite. . . .'* This took a long time, and since Zhilbare was off on his motor bike, Pete had to do the interpreting. Louis wanted to tell us that when he was *young*, when he was courting Louise, he went to visit her riding an early bicycle – the 'Ordinary,' also known as a 'Penny Farthing' because it had a huge front wheel, and a very small rear wheel. . . .

Louise is much more lively. She seems delighted to have so many young men in the house. I have the instant feeling that without knowing a word of English, she has the general drift of everything which we are saying. Louis and Louise have known tragedy. Their grandson, Pieter (or Petta?) lives with them. He is not more than seven years. His father was sent away to Holland or Germany by the Germans. His mother simply pined away and died. She died of a broken heart. The boy is both *pale* – and frail. We will have to steal from the mess. We have all agreed on that. Today, Eckert faced up to Hyland and told him to keep his yap down. Larry has been quiet this evening.

October 12th, B.60, Grimbergen, Belgium

We are making the best of our billet; with Louis and Louise. They are no trouble at all, but the problem is – *we* are. Today we had a council of war, as it were. Let us take our camp cots down every day, so at least the rooms are not so cluttered that we can't even walk around. Put small kits away, so that the one small bathroom is not one big dumping place for shaving gear. Let's keep our voices down, particularly at night. Let's try to keep the language down, so that Louis and Louise don't think that the only predominant word in the English language is 'Fuck-ing'. Let's not stink up the bathroom. Shit when you go down the flight, in our own bogs. And if you can't wait, use the outdoor crapper which is down the garden. No – repeat *no* bloody horse play. We don't want Louise and Louis to think that we are savages, and we don't need any more broken bones, for sure. Paddy Crozier put it best. 'We sound like a bloody Irish Parliament *in session*. Everybody talkin' and nobody listening!' We have done a nice job of thieving for Louise's larder Many packets of powdered eggs, tins of cheese, about three pounds of tea – too bad that L and L are coffee drinkers (they'll have to change their ways!) Powdered milk. (Canadian KLIM) Tins of bacon – tins of sausage. Larry Hyland, looking very pregnant, opened his tunic when he came in this evening. Out tumbled five loaves of bread! Paddy said, 'Too bad you couldn't have managed two tins of Jack salmon, Larry! You could have done the Sermon on the Mount!' The reply was 'Frost th' fookin' gonads, wha' doesn't?'

Louise is wonderful. She has a wonderful, wonderful sense of humour. She does imitations of Eckert, mimicking his walk, the way he cocks his head and his sometimes mock baleful facial contortions. 'Hey! Smit!' she says, '*Regardez! L'Australie!*' She does a wonderful head-shaking imitation of Hyland, who has a head of straight reddish hair which resembles a mop. She ends this one with 'Fookin', Fookin', Fookin'.' Hyland will be red-faced if he sees her do it. I think our presence (and our presents) have given Louise a new lease of life.

Finally, I was airborne today. Two bomb and strafes. Same target. Gun positions east of an aerodrome on a peninsula among the Dutch Islands – such as Overflakee. The 'drome is at a place called Woensdrecht. The targets were separate, but in the same area. The first target, we surprised them, coming in low from the sea. The second target responded with some twenty mill, flak. Nobody was hit – and I was beginning to wonder if something was wrong with me.

Pete and some others went to Brussels today. They said it was 'Wizard'.

October 13th, B.60, Grimbergen, Belgium

In spite of the potential chaos in our quarters with L and L – we actually seem to be closer and this includes our daily association with the officers. We are more open with each other than in the beach head days. I am sure that Dinger Bell's death has had a lot to do with it. We should have been prepared for it – we find we were not. Resilient as we think we are, some of us cannot get over the simple fact that Dinger was tour-expired – *and* the fact that he had his termination leave pass in his shirt pocket when he went into the drink. As somebody said – he was on borrowed time. The impact of losing Dinger could only have been eclipsed, if we were to lose our skipper, Bradley. We have had the very good fortune to have had some dammed good times together in Lille – and Brussels will be even better. Pete is very vulnerable. He gets very lachrymose when he drinks. Not that he drinks much. Two or three beers make him

Year 1944		Aircraft		Pilot, or 1st Pilot	2nd Pilot, Pupil or Passenger	Duty (Including Results and Remark
Month	Date	Type	No.			
		—	—	—	—	— Totals Brought Forwa
OCT	12	SPITFIRE IX	9N-E	SELF	—	BOMBING AND STRAF GUN POSITIONS WOENSDRE
OCT	12	SPITFIRE IX	9N-E	SELF	—	BOMB & STRAFE ON GU POSITIONS EAST OF WOENSD
OCT	13	SPITFIRE IX	9N-V	SELF	—	PATROL ANTWERP
OCT	14	SPITFIRE IX	9N-C	SELF	—	LOW LEVEL BOMBING GUN POSITIONS NORTH OF WO DRUME – STRAFE
OCT	17	SPITFIRE IX	9N-P	SELF	—	WEATHER RECCE MAASTRICHT AREA
OCT	17	SPITFIRE IX	9N-P	SELF	—	DIVE BOMBING – GERM
OCT	18	SPITFIRE IX	9N-R	SELF	—	BOMBING-RAILWAY JU NEAR VENLO - SHORT S
OCT	20	SPITFIRE IX	9N-R	SELF	—	LOW LEVEL BOMBIN STRAFE ACHTERBROE
OCT	21	SPITFIRE IX	9N-T	SELF	—	AIR TEST

Grand Total [Cols. (1) to (10)] 1298 Hrs. 50 Mins

Totals Carried Forwa

SINGLE-ENGINE AIRCRAFT				MULTI-ENGINE AIRCRAFT						PASS-ENGER	INSTR/CLOUD FLYING [Incl. in cols. (1) to (10)].	
DAY		NIGHT		DAY			NIGHT					
Dual	Pilot	Dual	Pilot	Dual	1st Pilot	2nd Pilot	Dual	1st Pilot	2nd Pilot		Dual	Pilot
(1)	(2)	(3)	(4)	(5)	(6)	(7)	(8)	(9)	(10)	(11)	(12)	(13)
0.50	1032.10	11.10	6.55	72.20	64.30		14.20	7.35		22.45	49.20	15.00
			SQDN MOVED TO B60 GRIMBERGEN									
	.40			NO OPPOSITION								
	.45			OPPOSITION 20 MILL TRACER								
	2.05		PATROL FOR V.I.P. H.M. THE KING									
	.45			STUBBORN BASTARDS!!!								
			15th F/O GEOFF DAVIES MISSING-ON FIRE. SAME TARGET									
	1.05			FIRST TIME INTO GERMANY								
	1.15				TRAIN BOMBED LITTLE OPPOSITION.							
	1.15				LITTLE OPPOSITION							
	.50			WONDERFUL PARTY-LITTLE 20 MILL OPPOSITION								
	.20		S/LDR BRADLEY POSTED ON REST. F/L MILLWOOD AWARDED D.F.C.									
.50	1041.10	11.10	6.55	72.20	64.30		14.20	7.35		22.45	49.20	15.00
(1)	(2)	(3)	(4)	(5)	(6)	(7)	(8)	(9)	(10)	(11)	(12)	(13)

very sentimental, and he goes from that mood into a morbid phase. He has talked too often, for me, anyway, about getting the chop. His sister, who lives with an aunt, and an uncle who does not work, is very much on his mind. He begs me – or anyone else around, to *understand*. 'She is only eighteen – and she has never had a date. *Imagine* that. . . .' This is the general drift. He is fearful, as we all are, of death; but he is saying that this is because of leaving his sister unprotected. After he has slept on it, he is again the practical, enthusiastic Pete; a veritable spark plug who relives every solid strafe – every accurate bomb drop. What the Yanks call a real cheer leader.

Now that we are in proximity to Brussels, we all hope to get together more often. We also enjoy being with some of the fellows on 66 Squadron. Though not, according to Pete, with Mike Larson. Pete says Larson is 'scabrous'. I don't know what that means, but I don't need a dictionary to 'gen up' on it. I think I have a fair idea.

The Norwegians are mostly wizard in the air, and they have good leaders. Major Ryg is one of these. He was my flight commander at 61 OTU Rednal. God! That seems so very long ago! It is difficult to have the same kind of camaraderie with 331 and 332 pilots. While they can use English as well as we, they go into Norwegian, often in the middle of a one-on-one discussion. They are very good at butting in – a third party – without as much as an 'Excuse me'. It is very rude, and all of us resent it. Are there no manners left?

We did one op today. Sixteen aircraft, in fours, at intervals. This was close cover to one transport, which landed at Antwerp. The transport was carrying King George, but we didn't know about it. All we were told was to identify ourselves clearly to the pilot, by steep turning away, so he could see our invasion stripes under the sings. There was a tremendous explosion on the ground, south of Antwerp. Smoke pall rose to a great height. When this came out at de-briefing, our spy, Johnson, said, 'No comment. I repeat – *No* comment.' He said this so pointedly that it begged questions. We all wonder why?

October 14th, B.60, Grimbergen, Belgium

Zhilbare is still putt-putting around on his motor bike. He carries his thick money belt – his 'flak jacket' – on his body at all times, even on ops. Covington, who despises Frenchmen, anyway, says, 'Typical that he'd rather let the fucking Huns get their hands on his money if he gets shot down.'

Pete has spent more time with Zhilbare than anybody. Pete knows more French than any of us, even though he speaks it with an appalling cockney accent 'Pardonnee mwa – sill voo play. Zher-dayzeer – dashtay – les crayons – kelker shose. . . .' etcetera . . . (French men and women tend to look at Pete in wonderment. They recognize the words, but they are not prepared for the accent, which is, indeed, *alien.*)

Notwithstanding, he has taken on, the task of getting Zhilbare's story, piece by piece. Gilbert (Zhilbare) Morisson, born prior to World War I, somewhere near, or *in*, Marseilles. He joined the French Air Force at nineteen, applied for flying training, and became an average, pre-war, fighter pilot. A year or so prior to the outbreak of hostilities between France and Germany, he was posted to French North Africa, possibly Algiers. When France fell, after Dunkirk, Zhilbare and other comrades decided that they would not respond to the urges by 80-odd-year-old Marshal Pétain, to be unified under the Vichy Government. They deserted, and unified themselves into one of a number of resistance fighters' cells, apparently somehow incommunicado with de Gaulle's Free French Forces in London.

Following some hazardous adventures of a cloak and dagger nature, Zhilbare was captured. He had previously been captured through a betrayal, wherein he had been interrogated, identified, and finger printed. This was in a police station, from which he escaped by throwing himself through the second storey window, glass and all. It was already documented that he stole an aircraft from his old airfield in broad daylight. Out of two aircraft standing together, he apparently stole the one that was almost empty of petrol. He ran out of fuel, crash landed, walked away from the wreck, and got away free. He was finally apprehended in what was ironically determined to be a 'safe' house. Zhilbare and a half dozen *collaborateurs* were plotting their next step in the downfall of the Pétain government. The house was surrounded by a body of policemen and a garrison of sharpshooters. They were transfixed when a voice boomed from a loudspeaker from a truck in the street. They were given the choice. Come out in single file with your hands on your heads, or be shot or burned to death. They gave themselves up. In the weeks he was waiting for a court martial, Zhilbare was shown a 'dead or alive' poster with his picture on it. He learned that a copy of the poster was posted on the side of his parents' house.

His mother, he says, became a white-haired old woman, *overnight*.

Zhilbare was sentenced to death. He was incarcerated for two years in solitary confinement. He tells Pete that, as a political prisoner, it was the order of the day that he, and his comrades, were treated as lower than animals. He says he had to battle maggots for his share of the daily ration of rancid food. He says that if he stripped the mould from his bread, there would not be enough left to survive. After two years of solitary confinement, he was re-tried with a second court martial. (He believes the system was responding to Vichy reasoning that if Germany were to lose the war, the Vichyites would be held accountable for the deaths of the Resistance people.) Zhilbare was again found guilty – but the death sentence was commuted to life imprisonment.

Months went by. Then, as Pete tells it, Zhilbare was whispered a message, even as he was in a circular prisoner march in the prison yard. The message *was – get into the infirmary* . . . Louis – *D*. . . .

He had the scrapings of two cigarettes in his pocket. He mixed them with the last of his cup of water. After half an hour of tobacco saturation, he drank the water. He was, of course, violently sick, with agonizing stomach pains. . . . He cried for help, and he was carried to the infirmary. Louis *D* – his oldest friend in the Resistance, who was, himself, very sick, told Zhilbare his news. In three days, all political prisoners were to be taken to another prison, by train. It was even rumoured that they might be put in a concentration camp. There might be one chance for Zhilbare to escape, bearing in mind that the transferees would all be wearing civilian clothes. The prisoners were not to be leg-shackled, or wearing handcuffs. Zhilbare was well prepared. The prisoners to be transferred were taken by truck to within a few hundred yards of the railway station. As they entered the station they were told to act like civilians. They were also told that if they attempted to escape, that they would be shot – aimed to kill, civilians present, or not. In the station, Zhilbare sat down, as he noted a family of four approaching. A man, his wife, and two young girls. He smiled at the girls, and got engaged in conversation with the man. A simple request, sir, I have not had a cigarette to smoke for over two years. I am going to a place – God knows where. Two cigarettes. Just two cigarettes. Oh – *merci, merci, Monsieur. Merci bien!* No, no match needed now, sir – I'll smoke these later. I assure you – I will think of you – and your generosity, etcetera.

On the train, they were directed to sit on the floor, and were handcuffed. As he had been instructed, he pushed the ratchets tight on his cuffs. He twisted his wrists, so that they were abrased, and soon, swollen. He begged the guard to give him some relief. He showed his swollen wrists. He begged – *please.* At least until the train started. He won the point. The guard released the handcuffs. Zhilbare says he shredded the two cigarettes of tobacco. From each, he made a ball of paper. These, he slipped into the cuffs. If he were lucky, he would make the paper ball fall into the ratchet. The ratchet would appear to lock, when, in fact, it would ride on the paper ball. Miracles never ceasing, one worked. One wrist would be free of the handcuff. Now, each carriage was fitted with a handrail, in the centre of the car, which ran the full length of the carriage.

At the propitious moment, Zhilbare released the 'cuff,' leaped up, grabbed the handrail, and launched himself out of the window, kicking the glass out as he went. He says the train was moving very fast. He still remembers the shocked faces of civilians as they saw his body flash by! He rolled down a steep bank at speed. He thought he was breaking every bone in his body – but his head. When he picked himself up, it was limb by limb, checking toes, feet, ankles, knees. . . . The train was long gone. Zhilbare ran, jogged, limped and walked, until darkness. He moved only by night. Days later, he ran into *Les Americains*. The Yanks were about to shoot him as a spy. Why not? Ragged civie clothing. . . . the handcuffs saved him, at least until they found a French-speaking interrogator. When his story was believed, they could not do enough for Zhilbare. It was canned fruits, peaches, apricots, pears, juices. It was canned vienna sausages, meat balls, spam. Zhilbare gorged himself, to make up for three years of deprivation. He broke out in body boils. His system went into fever. He almost died of – gluttony.

He got to London. More interrogation. He was transferred to the Free French Air Force. He became totally disgusted, when he learned that his bête noire – the Vichy-appointed governor of his prison – was investitured with Medaille de Résistance along with Zhilbare, at the same ceremony! Zhilbare asked to fly with an RAF squadron. *Any* RAF squadron. So that's how we got Gilbert Morisson.

We did another show today, right after breakfast. It was where we kept on going – gun positions. Bergen Op Zoom. We came in from the sea, at deck level, balls out, to gain the element of surprise. We didn't. It was very intense – tracers zipping past us, and very dicey. I was flying on Brad's port – about fifty yards port and to the rear. This was on the second pass, strafing. In one of those 'Oh! God! Spare me!' I was certain that I saw flak hit Brad, between his port leading edge and engine cowling. We went straight to the deck. In minutes, as Brad called us to re-form, climbing, he confirmed it. 'Monty Red Leader to Monty Blue Leader. I've been hit. Temperature going off the clock. Take over – I may have to prang.' 'Monty Red Leader. This is Monty Blue Leader. Wilco – out.' Longbow control broke in – told Brad to switch over to 'C' Charlie. I was very scared and then very happy to get back and land. Did we really go through all that shit in 45 minutes, take off to landing?

October 17th, B.60, Grimbergen, Belgium

Pete, Eckert, Sandy, Zhilbare and I all went into Brussels after Geoff Davies bought it, and we all got pissed as newts. We took the trolley car, which is very close to our billet, only about half a mile walk. Unlike English trams, which only run in built up areas, these Belgian trolleys run over fields and countryside, buzzing back into small hamlets, until they reach the outskirts of the city.

We hopped off the trolley at the bottom of a long rise. This was the poor end of Brussels, where the *estaminets* are so run down that they repair holes in the floorboards with discarded shoe soles! Here, a glass of Belgian beer costs only five francs. As we made our way uphill, bar to bar, we got pleasanter and pleasanter. The cost of drinks got even more expensive, as the bars got more attractive – not only by decoration, but by the class and dress of the clientele. We made the Sacré Coeur our focal point. This is where the constant flame burns, to the honour of the Unknown Warrior. How many bars we went in, I do not know. By sheer luck, we crossed a busy street, and were almost run over by a three ton truck. By sheer luck, I mean that it was our own (127) truck. We climbed in, and one by one fell asleep, as Covington, Gollins and company were already in alcoholic somnia. I am glad that we had no ops yesterday, so we had a whole day to get over our hangovers. I shudder to think what trouble we might have got into, if we had not had Zhilbare with us. He is a wonderful interpreter.

I flew into Germany twice today. The first trip was a weather recco, with Shillitoe. The second was quite a party. We bombed a railroad line, in front of a train. We bombed a factory in Grefrath. We strafed until our guns were empty.

We had a very pleasant surprise this afternoon. McNally came to visit. His face still looks very red, but all the swelling is gone. We relived the entire Lympne experience, where Sergeant Housden was killed. We all agreed that it was something of a miracle that Mac was not blown to bits when his and Housden's planes blew up. Also, that nobody was killed by cannon fire, when the guns were fire-detonated. Alas, McNally won't be staying with us. He, and Asboe, and Gollins are posted, UK, tour-expired. Gollins had a bottle of gin, so we had a horrid tasting, lively little party. Gollins carried on his old bullshit, 'Christmas dinner with me Grandmuvver, roast lamb, green peas, new potatoes – die, green wiv envy, you bastards!' . . . Then he made a special announcement. 'Smitty – you can 'ave me blankets. Think of me, while I'm on me way back to God's country, little 'ole New Zealand. Don't worry, sport – they've just been fumigated.' I thanked him, and will pick them up tomorrow morning. Paddy Crozier was browned off. He expected to 'win' Gollie's Irvin jacket. Gollie also promised it to Geoff Davies. When Geoff didn't come back, he promised it to another officer. Paddy was livid! I suppose we won't hear the last of it. Paddy being *still* without an Irvin jacket.

October 18th, B.60, Grimbergen, Belgium

We bombed and strafed a railway junction today, near a town called Venlo. We bombed from angels eight to three, and the flak was negligible – just a few 88's, a few, too late. We got eleven out of twelve bomb loads right on target, and made just one strafing run after it, getting the signal boxes. We all felt that it was a good show.

Today, it was confirmed that the very large explosion which we reported on the south side of Antwerp, when we escorted the plane carrying King George, was, in fact, a V-2 rocket. These rocket bombs do make a very big bang. As Sandy Powell said, 'Bloody sight bigger than a Boy Scout Rouser, Sport!'

We learned, at tea time, that Ron Reeves has been declared 'tour-expired'. He is very good type, and I think we will miss his sense of humour, and his cartoon jokes. He affected to be sorry that he is posted off ops, 'Since I've got to know all you bastards' – but you can't kid me that he isn't relieved. (Relieved, to be relieved!) He is the last non-com pilot from Nicosia and all that. Eckert says, soon there won't be any desert sand to kick around any more.

October 20th, B.60, Grimbergen, Belgium
Last evening, Sandy Powell came into our billet with a whole lot of ears of maize, or Indian corn. These were the first I have seen since my training in Southern Rhodesia, where we had it regularly. Five of us, cooks, par excellence, watched for the first ten minutes of boiling. Then we tried one, Larry took the first bite, burned his lips and pronounced it 'Too fookin' tough.' We put it back with the others, and cooked for ten minutes more. We let them cool awhile, and coated them with margarine. They were still tough. Shame! I remember how tender the African variety was. When we finally had dinner, it was very dark outside, and we had no inclination to go anywhere. We resorted to our own supplies, actually Louise's. We had tinned soy sausage cuts, greasy tinned bacon, (how do they find bacon rashers with no meat on them?) and surprise! a tin of English marrow fat peas. For dessert we had slices of bread, stolen from the mess, thickly laden with margarine, chunks of awful tinned processed white cheese, topped with supposed apricot jam. We got it *down*. We are always hungry.

Speaking of food, a funny thing happened on the Grub line, today, at noon. Mike Larson, 66 Squadron, didn't think it was a *bit* funny. Big Mac McLeod was the provocateur. . . .

We were standing in line together, 66 and ourselves, and Mac was by my side. We had our mess kits with us, oblong metal containers with handles for carrying. (They can handle a pound of M and V). Mac said, in a too loud voice, I think, 'Where d'you go last night, Teddie? We took our truck all the bloody way to your billet, and the old lady said there was nobody there.' 'That must have been early on,' I said. 'We were released later on, six o'clock. We stayed home. Cooked some corn, we couldn't eat. Where did you go?'

'Ah, we took our truck to Brussels. Wanna guess what we did? Well, we went into an exhibish! What a bloody sight! We were all pissed as Christmas puddins by then! God! You shoulda *been* there! First, three old French beetles danced on this little stage doin' a strippo! One was a contortionist – she licked 'er own arse. Then, some other harpie came out. She danced and pranced around, pickin' up artificial roses between the cheeks of 'er arse. Then she pissed in a cracked cup, from four foot, three foot, and two foot. She did this in short squirts. Hit the cup, spot on! Boy! was she an educated pisser! Then, she did an exhibish which I won'd even *describe*, with an Alsatian dawg! Then, later on, Mike Larson, dirty bastard, cosied up to this dirty bitch, went upstairs with her, and didn't show up today till eight o'clock! Hey! M-I-K-E! Has it dropped orf, yet?'

Larson was standing a few feet behind us, wearing, as he seemingly always does, rubber boots. He followed Mac's every gesture, with hateful observance. Then he said, 'You bloody bastard! You bloody big-mouthed bastard! May the who-ores o' Hell piss on you forever!' It was a good exchange. Everyone thought it was very funny. Everyone but Larson.

We bombed and strafed a place today called Achterbroek. It was a good show. We hit it, *bang on*. Not much flak – only twenty mill. Nobody got hit.

Brad – Squadron Leader Frank Bradley – has been posted UK tour-ex. We will miss his leadership. I wonder if he doesn't find it timely, inasmuch as they found his range, the other day. Everyone's luck runs out, some time, so they say. Our war is stepping up. It seems to be bomb and strafe – every day. When did we last fly a cushy escort mission? Ages ago, it seems. Rumour says that Bradley will come back, sometime, after his rest, as Wingco. Who knows? A Squadron Leader Lister is posted to take over 127. Nobody knows who he is, beyond DFC. We will just have to wait.

Peter Hillwood is awarded DFC. About *time*, the older bods think. Battle of Britain survivor, after all.

October 22nd, B.60, Grimbergen, Belgium

Louise is irrepressible. She now has mastered the mannerisms of most of us, and can mirror them so that they become very recognizable caricatures. She is very funny. She is very alert, very lively. Night before last, she got some eggs from *somewhere* – and she made pancakes – for all of us – whether we wanted them or not. She calls them 'kookembackers.' (I think it is all one word.)

We were on our way to Brussels (we got the three-tonner for a change, and took a number of our airmen). I am always amazed at the transformation of our ground crews, from seeing them at work, oil saturated, lace up boots and all; well pressed, with shiny brass buttons and belt buckle. It was this ability to 'shine' that got so many of them into fist fights with the army, right after Dunkirk. . . . '*We* were on the beaches. Where was the RAF?' From then on, the army dubbed us, every man jack, as 'The Brylcreem Boys'.

Well, we tried to get by Louise to get to that lorry, but she insisted that we eat a couple of kookembackers, soaked with Tate & Lyle's Golden Syrup. For whatever reason, she missed Reg Eckert. He came in after she had long since gone to bed. It was natural, in view of his late partying, that he overslept. He was either on the board for a show, or was wanted for Pink Section. Sergeant Wills came up to the house for him, driving the thirty hundred weight. Rushing for the back door, unshaven, and still buttoning his battledress blouse, he had no chance to escape the two very cold kookembackers pressed into his hands by the concerned Louise. Probably the last thing Eckert's queasy, hangover stomach craved was cold kookembackers. He rushed down the rear garden path of uncemented red bricks, almost tore the gate off its hinges, and ran through the no-man's land of twenty feet of bushes that screen the sandy road where the truck was parked. Eckert's hands were above his head, and in one movement he pirouetted, intent on hurling the kookembackers to his vision of eternity. To his surprise, he saw the blond mop and fresh features of Louise's grandson, Pieter, standing before him. He simply pirouetted again, and again, brought his arms down, swung his arms behind him, his hands now, carefully holding the kookembackers, and bowed, eloquently to young Pieter. Eckert said he was so embarrassed at being caught in the act that he stuffed the kookembackers in his mouth, gave Pieter a greasy handclasp in passing, and leapt into the back of the gharry.

Yesterday we bombed and strafed a railroad at Maasbracht. Then we found a Hun truck and we all had a go. Nobody mentioned flak, but that doesn't mean it wasn't there. Not all 20-mills are mixed with tracer. Also, there could well have been small arms fire.

There was enough anticipation, anyway, to make me sweat, particularly in the crotch. When I got to de-briefing, the itching was *unbearable*. I could hardly keep my hands away.

I went to see Doc Blanchard. He examined me with his examination flashlamp, the one with the eyepieces. 'You've got yourself a nice mess of crabs, and scabies,' he said. 'Who's the lucky girl – or do you know?' I flustered. I felt atrocious, *dirty*. I swore my virginity. Gradually it came out. 'Gollins' blankets! He said he had them fumigated, Doctor!'

'So, he *did*. Now, you mustn't blame Gollins, because I happened to be there when they were fumigated. Gollins' blankets had a red border, and I passed them on, personally, to one of the new officers. *Many* blankets were going through, so somebody undoubtedly moved some from 'pre' to 'post'. Practically, Smith, we are dealing with the fact that you've got the *lot* – as they say. . . .' He handed me a bottle of white, creamy liquid. Almost a quart, it was. He gave me a tin of ointment, and a scrubbing brush, with stiff, skin-abrasing bristles.

'Ointment is for pubic and underarm hair. That's for crabs. This liquid, Benzyl Benzoate, is for scabies. It *smarts*. Hot shower, scrub body till *red* – apply liquid. Imagine that you're doing the Mexican Ritual Fire Dance! Do it twice a day. And – Smith?'

'Yes, sir, doctor.'

'Bring those blankets back, for fumigation. Please? *Today*!'

'Yes, sir.'

Benzyl Benzoate, on a scrubbed body, is like being doused in 100 octane petrol. In the vernacular – it burns like a bastard.

October 28th, B.60, Grimbergen, Belgium

It has been seven days since we were last able to 'leap into the air' as an instructor at OTU used to say. We have had some small time off, but mostly we've spent the days on 30 minutes or 60 minutes' readiness. We, the NCO's have tried to stay away from our billet, except to change clothes and shave, mostly in the evening, before bashing off to Brussels. L & L's house is much too crowded even when weather is good. When the weather is rain, and it has been very misty, also, we are gloomy in spirit, and we all forget that we bring mud in, on our flying boots. We wear our boots every day. The only time we put on dress shoes is when we go to Brussels.

We have spent much of the last seven days in the flight hut, and all I can say is, the cards go round, and round, and round. I never learned poker, in all the bad weather at OTU – or in Tealing, Scotland. Just hearing the game calls and postulations is more than I can fathom. 'Spit in the ocean, with one-eyed Jacks and black deuces wild.' This kind of jargon seems to give allusions to cowboys in Western saloons, sailors, at sea, and convicts where convicts usually are. There might have been a time when I could have mastered it – because I do know the values, from poker dice in flying training, in the bars in Bulawayo. I suppose the final deterrent when I heard the players, a few weeks ago, complicate it all with 'High-Low'. This is more than I need to learn, I think. In any case, I do not think that I can relax myself in this atmosphere, because I know that I get small comfort out of looking out at the rain. The only real consideration is not the weather, *here* – but the weather at the target – whatever target it might be. You cannot bomb and strafe something you cannot see. Landing and take-off is a *detail*. (I heard one of the Wing Intelligence officers say that.)

Today, I flew on two operations. The first was low level dive bombing, 1,000 pounds, each. Wingco Rolf Berg led us. It was an island strongpoint, Gravenpolder. We strafed after bombing. It was a good long strafe. I must have come within a few rounds of emptying my guns. There was 20 mm opposition, but nobody was hit. It seemed strange, not hearing Bradley's voice, or seeing his spinner with the black ring. Wingco Berg flies his own Spitfire, with the call letters marking RAB (Rolf A. Berg).

The second op was into Germany, east of Roermonde. This was, potentially, a real bastard. Peter Hillwood led us. He is wearing his DFC ribbon. I suppose the adjutant has a supply of ribbon for gongs such as the DFC. I think he was glad that we noticed it. At de-briefing, Spy Johnson asked how was the flak, and Peter said, 'They threw up everything they had but the kitchen sink!' That was about it. Flying Officer Jack, Sammy Roth, and Truscott were all wearing holes from flak, but none was a direct hit. I was very glad to get home from this one. Sweat ran down my back, and then it got very cold on the way back. Maybe I should get the electrically wired kimono.

We have been discussing the mail censorship – though we are not supposed to. Gordon Richardson (Aus) said that he has read of a running feud between one of our corporals and his sister. It seems as though the sister is engaged to a Polish airman. The corporal is imploring her to break it off. *She* says he is prejudiced, simply because he (her fiancé) is Polish. Gordon says the latest letter says, 'For God's sake, don't you read the papers? Didn't you read about the Polish airman who just got a five year sentence for biting his girlfriend's nipple off?' We had a good laugh over that.

We learned two things today, one good, one bad. Sergeant Macey is definitely a POW. Flight Lieutenant Whittington's plane was found, and what were his remains were confirmed by his identity tags. One of these is impervious to fire. The other is impervious to sea water. *Confession.* I do *not* carry my ID tags on ops. I think I would be tempting fate. Pete says I am stupid, and 'stupid-stitious'. I do not have a will, either. I have nothing to leave anybody at home, and nobody to leave it to, beyond my parents, and my sisters. What have I, here, that didn't come from the stores? My Irvin jacket could go to Crozier. *That* would shut him up. Whoever said Paddy will be the last to go home with an Irvin jacket?

October 30th, B.60, Grimbergen, Belgium

I was vaguely aware of Corporal Turner's presence in our room, at about first light, today. Quiet as he is with his wake-up calls, his shoes give him away. I drifted back to sleep, with the comfort that goes with *not* being on the show. Eckert, Griffin and Hyland *all* crossed my bed space, but I was not even aware. We have a rule not to dress in the room, and certainly not put on our flying boots until we get downstairs to the kitchen. I didn't wake up until eight o'clock, when I heard noise from downstairs. The 30 hundredweight came to pick us up at nine. We *knew* something was very much wrong when the boys flew over us. *Three* missing. On the ground, spy Johnson already had part of the story. I have never seen Pete so agitated. He kept saying, 'What about Eckert?' Johnson was not clear on the detail. These things are always sketchy, when they are relayed by Longbow Control. Longbow has to construct detail from pilots' voices on RT. Johnson told us what he could, and asked us to be patient. It wasn't ten minutes later that the boys landed. Faces were very grim. Dicky Lloyd, Covie, Griffin, Jack, Larry Hyland, Sammy Roth. Perhaps even more disconsolate – Freddie Lister's oppo, Harry Lea. It was an armed recce, Dordrecht. The flak was ready for them, even as they went down diving from three to zero. Freddie, shot down, bullet wounds or flak, crashed near Ghent. Eckert, last words were, 'I'm going down. I'm going to have to pancake.' They reformed, in a fashion, and called off names by section. Captain Fosse – Belgian, did not respond. Hyland thought he saw him going in, blasted by flak. Three planes in one sortie. Macey, Malone, Whittington, Housden, Geoff Davies – now, Fosse. Fosse, Freddie, Eckert. Three down in one sortie.

An hour later, Wingco Berg came by. He was genuinely concerned. Eckert crash-landed okay, and had bread and cheese for breakfast with some Belgian farmers. The nature of Freddie Lister's wounds are not known. Condition, *serious* – whatever that means.

Captain Fosse, marked down N.Y.R. (Not Yet Returned). This almost always means, the chop.

We simply cannot believe it. Was last evening with Fred Lister, Harry Lea, and all, a *myth*? Did the party happen? Did we dream it? Harry Lea has taken our new Jeep to Ghent, to visit the hospital. Eckert got a lift on a courier's motorbike. He has a rip in the left knee of his battledress, from hitting the instrument panel, or the switches. He was bruised, hungry, and happy to be back.

We will all be shit scared on our next op. Let's hope we do one, *soon*. The sooner the better – to get our confidence back.

Extracts from the
Operations Record Book, 127 Squadron, R.A.F., 132 (Norwegian) Wing

B.57, Lille/Wambrechies, France, 2nd October 1944: Twelve aircraft of the squadron took off at 0720 to dive bomb gun positions landing at 0830 hours. Operation D84/JWM – One gun position at D.9231 – one 1556. On this mission six direct hits were scored on the target area. Area well and truly strafed after bombing. Weather – 3/10ths. at 6000 feet. Storms enroute. Visibility good except during storms.

Ten aircraft were airborne at 1050 enroute to dive bomb gun positions in area D.94/GRJ.2, landing back to base at 1210 hours. Six bombs were seen to hit the target area, which again was well strafed after bombing. One aircraft category AC the pilot F/Lt Whittington missing.

B.57, 6th October: Twelve aircraft led by S/Ldr Bradley took off from B.57 at 1000 hours to bomb and strafe shipping at Norwhal. Results were good as smoke indicated that several bombs had dropped on the target. A large fire was started and when the squadron left; it was going extremely well. Target area well strafed after bombing run. Ground haze up to 4000 feet, above that height visibility ten miles. Intense light flak in target area. Twelve aircraft landed at new location B.60 (Belgium) at 1125 hours.

Twelve aircraft took off from B.60 at 1305 hours to bomb and strafe barges in the Bergsche area. Results were only fair, a few direct hits being scored on the target, while a number of near misses were also observed. Twelve aircraft landed base at 1355. Weather – Good.

B.60, 7th October: Twelve aircraft of the squadron were airborne at 1310 enroute to bomb and strafe gun positions east of Knocke. Four hits were scored on target – two houses were set on fire. Target area strafed four times after bombing run. Intense heavy and light anti-aircraft fire from Breskins area. Weather – clear – visibility excellent. Twelve aircraft landed 1410 hours.

Eleven aircraft led by W/Cdr Berg (132 Wing) took off from base at 1620 on an armed recco over DD.227. Eleven 500 lbs eleven seconds delay fuses were dropped in a dive from 9000 to 5000 feet. Eleven near misses on target at E.2354. Ship 300 tons, strafed at E.2153 – Twenty to thirty covered barges seen and strafed at E.0150. Aircraft landed 1710 hours.

B.60, 12th October: Twelve aircraft took off at 0810 on an armed recce in the Rotterdam–Breda–Gurtsgenbosche–Utrecht area. They also carried twelve 500 lbs bombs which they dropped on a concentration of barges at D.7265 several hits being scored. A convoy of approximately forty MET were sighted at Beesd (E.3568) an attack was made resulting in eight being destroyed and four damaged. Moderate accurate light flak from E.2568. Weather – Cloudless – Visibility excellent. Aircraft landed 0920.

Nine aircraft took off at 1100 hours to bomb and strafe gun positions at Woensdrecht eight 500 lbs. .025 second delay fuses were dropped in the target area, causing debris to rise to a great height. One bomb temporarily hung up fell at D.668218. Gun positions strafed after bombing run. Meagre inaccurate light flak from target area. Weather slight haze – Visibility twelve miles above haze. All aircraft down at 1140.

Eleven aircraft took off to bomb and strafe eighty-eight millimetre gun positions SE of Bergen. Ten 500 lbs. GP.025 seconds delay fuses were dropped on the target indicated by red smoke – One temporarily hung up. Results of the bombing not observed owing to red smoke screen. Target well strafed after bombing run. All aircraft landed at 1625 hours. Target area – Slight accurate light flak – Visibility good.

B.60, 13th October: Sixteen aircraft took off in sections of four to patrol Antwerp from 0915 to 1600 hours. This mission was air cover to His Majesty The King on his visit to Antwerp. This patrol proved uneventful. The only incident seen was a terrific explosion south of the town (J.6791). Smoke was seen to rise to 1500/1600 feet. Visibility good.

B.60, 14th October: Twelve aircraft took off at 0830 hours to bomb and strafe gun positions south of Bergen Op Zoom, landing back at 0915, having managed to drop eleven bombs in the target area, results of which were not observed owing to haze. Target well strafed after bombing. One Spitfire hit by flak Cat AC pilot S/Ldr Bradley uninjured. Intense accurate light and medium flak from target and wood adjoining. Cloud 9/10ths to 1000 feet, above that height visibility eight miles.

B.60, 15th October: Twelve aircraft took off from base at 1215 to bomb and strafe Bergen Op Zoom again. But unfortunately the results fell a lot short of the previously carried mission. Three near misses were claimed. One aircraft was apparently hit by flak. It was last seen making towards our lines of fire. Pilot 152115 F/O G.W. Davies (missing). Medium and heavy flak over target. Medium and light flak from vehicles parked along the road side at D.6323. All aircraft landed base 1300 hours.

B.60, 17th October: Twelve aircraft took off at 0925 to bomb and strafe target DD.413/68 but owing to bad weather and low cloud it could not be located, so the squadron went on to the Grefrath area. They sighted two trains at A.0605 moving north. Eleven 500 lbs, eleven second delay fused bombs were dropped from 7000/4000 feet. Two direct hits were scored on the railway line in front of a train. One 500 lbs was dropped on a factory in Grefrath. Both targets were strafed after bombing runs. Aircraft landed base 1040. Visibility fair.

F/Lt McNally, F/O Asboe and Gollins were posted – Tour expired – after having spent over twelve months with the squadron.

B.60, 18th October: Twelve aircraft were airborne at 0930 en route to bomb and strafe a railway junction near Venlo. The mission proved to be highly successful as eleven 500 lbs bombs were delivered on a railway junction at Viersen F.0697, all the bombs falling in the target area. Target strafed after bombing. Aircraft landed back at 1040. W/O Reeves posted to UK (tour-expired).

Twelve aircraft led by W/C Berg (132 Wing) took off at 1535 to bomb and strafe railway bridge near Venlo. Twelve 500 lbs. bombs were dropped over target. One direct hit was observed on the line and one near miss was also observed. Target area well strafed after bombing. Very intense accurate flak over target – Believed flak rockets used. Aircraft landed 1620 hours. Visibility good.

B.60, 19th October: Operation DD SSO – Twelve aircraft took off at 0855 on a low level bomb raid. They dropped twelve 500 lb bombs on Esschen (target area). This area was also well and truly strafed after bombing. Intense accurate light and medium flak was experienced NW of Achterbroek. (D.7516).

Operation DD.549/13B. Twelve aircraft led by W/C Berg (132 Wing) took off at 1400 hours to bomb and strafe a railway junction at Utrecht. Twelve 500 lb bombs were dropped from 5000 to zero feet, at least one direct hit was scored on the track east of Bridle – other results not observed. One MET flamer towing two trailers in area E.2865 was completely destroyed. Aircraft landed at 1500 hours. Intense accurate light flak from target area. Weather – Good. S/Ldr Bradley posted to UK tour-expired –

having been commander of the squadron for just over twelve months. S/Ldr Lister DFC posted from 84 GSU as Squadron Commander.

B.60, 20th October: Twelve aircraft of the squadron led by W/C Berg (132 Wing) took off at 1114 to bomb and strafe targets in the Breskins area. Twelve 500 lb bombs were dropped eight hits were scored on the target area, two on the quay in Breskins, causing a terrific explosion and large fire. The results of the last two bombs were not observed. Meagre inaccurate light flak experienced in the target area. A 300 ton ship NW of D.1917 was strafed.

B.60, 28th October: Twelve aircraft of the squadron led by W/C Berg (132 Wing) took off at 0740 hours to bomb and strafe gun positions at Gravenpoldre. Eleven 500 lbs eleven seconds delay fuses were dropped, one hung up. Target well and truly strafed after bombing but unfortunately detailed results were not observed. Visibility good.

Twelve aircraft of the squadron led by F/Lt Hillwood DFC took off at 1515 hours to bomb and strafe railway at Rheidt and Roermond. Two aircraft returned early, one as escort and the other with mechanical trouble. Six 500 lbs were dropped on first target and three on the second. One hung up. Results were not observed owing to haze. Intense flak was experienced at FO 385. Visibility fair.

B.60, 30th October: Twelve aircraft took off at 0815 hours on armed recce enemy strong point near Dordrecht. They experienced intense, accurate, medium and light flak. S/Ldr Lister DFC was shot down, and transported to hospital with wounds caused by flak or ground fire. Another pilot, Capt Fosse (Belg) is missing from this mission. W/O Eckert forced landed (aircraft category unknown) pilot unhurt. This was S/Ldr Lister's debut mission with the squadron. A bad show. Results unreported.

V

November

November 2nd, B.60, Grimbergen, Belgium

Our new skipper, F.W. 'Freddie' Lister, is going to be okay, according to Harry Lea, who was able to visit Freddie, but not for long. For Freddie, his first op with us could well have been his last. According to Harry Lea, Freddie knew he had been hit, at the split second something came ripping through the starboard side of the cockpit. Whatever it was – small arms fire or flak, it severed his microphone cord, possibly an inch from his throat. His R/T went dead, even as he was trying to give the order to re-form out from the target area. His plane was not flying correctly, and he began to have real fears that elevator control wires might be severed on the starboard side. Then he noticed that the instruments began merging together, and he felt a great lassitude. His throttle hand seemed to weigh very heavily. He lifted his gauntlet to look at his hand, and was surprised and shocked when a shower of blood poured out of the gauntlet sleeve. He pulled the throttle back, fishtailed down to the deck, saw that he was over green fields, cut the switches and pancaked. He remembers being pulled out of the cockpit, and that is all.

Eckert is no worse for wear. He says the cheese and bread were quite good. One of the Belgians tried to get him to drink Calvados, but he remembered it too well from an encounter with it at B.16. Captain Fosse is a *goner*.

Yesterday was the invasion of Walcheren Island. We had a breakfast show, led by Rolf Berg. I had my second start as section leader. This is a very exciting development, because you are faced with more exacting flying standards. All sub-section leaders and others only have to concentrate on formating on one other plane at fifty yards, in battle formation. In leading a section, you have to concentrate on the other section leader, at 200 yards. Battle formation must always be loose enough so that every individual pilot can steep turn into an attack from the rear. However, battle formation, too loose, is enough to bring disciplinary heat (threats of action!) from Red Leader. A section leader must *anticipate* turns, because few CO's call the turns on R/T.

There has been fierce fighting in the taking of the Dutch Islands along the coast. Today's operation was the bombing and strafing of heavy field artillery and crews. We dive bombed, and we were right on target. At the end of the day, the show was confirmed a success. Wingco Berg was well satisfied, and he is not easily well satisfied. We were told that our target was overrun by our assault troops. They reported that we destroyed six out of nine heavy guns, and over 130 personnel. That's 130 Huns that won't kill our troops.

We were told today that we will soon be flying new Spitfire Mark XVI's. Nobody is very clear on their performance. Just as the Mark V was a big step up over the Mark II, and the Mark IX was a huge power boost over the V; we hope that the XVI will be something to write home about. (Figuratively, only, of course!) About the only thing we *do* know. A few XVI's have been designed with airframe changes to allow the crank-operated bubble canopy. The 'bubble' has made a tremendous difference in the (P.51) Mustang.

I am going on leave tomorrow. I wondered whether the loss of Fosse and Freddie would make us too short-handed. However, both Peter Hillwood and Harry Lea said, take your leave whenever you can. Big Mac McLeod, New Zealand, 66 Squadron, is going on leave at the same time. He is only guaranteed two or three days' accommodation in whatever hotel New Zealand House has control of – so I have invited him to come over and spend some days with my family. I know that Mum and Dad won't mind, as long as Mac can put up with whatever bed is vacant. I can hardly wait to get away. These ops *are*, as Paddy Crozier said, getting too bloody 'fraught' to challenge rational reason. He ended his tirade to Larry Hyland, with 'Press on, regardless? – *Bull-shit*!'

November 12th, B.60, Grimbergen, Belgium

When I got back from leave, two days ago, I was told the news, during my absence, in one sentence, by Eckert. He said it, matter of factly, even quietly, but it had as much shock value as if he had screamed it. 'Dick Lloyd and Dave Shillitoe both got the chop.' Further questioning from me brought forth the facts. Dicky Lloyd was as close to tour-ex as was Dinger Bell, when *he* bought it. Dave Shillitoe was not far behind him. Dicky Lloyd was hit, and he crashed. Apparently it was not a crash landing. He was still alive when they got him to hospital. He didn't get through the night. Three days later, Dave got it, strafing a train. The boys bombed from very low level. Somebody, or more than one saw Shillitoe's wing fold back at low level. The very thing, next to *fire* – that we fear most – is a direct hit like that. You don't have a Chinaman's chance at high speed, low level. And our 'work' seems to take us lower, every single operational day. Eckert says all the boys took it badly. Eckert says the boys are moody, irritable. Morale, as a Yank I know would say, is 'lower than whale shit, and that's on the ocean floor.' I wish that I could get in an op today. Not a flak-ridden 'hit, suck in guts, and shit' op – but any op which will get me over this 'back from leave', fear. Superstition and imagination are two of our enemies. You cannot fight the *one*, and you are probably *born* with the other. I am at the point where I can listen to the facts, and imagine *me* – in the cockpit.

It is pissing rain. Two new NCO bods joined us today. A Flight Sergeant Wade, and a Sergeant Harris. I just heard about it.

November 15th, B.60, Grimbergen, Belgium

The poker game, down at flight, is interminable. It loses players, it adds players, it loses *them*, and the others get back in again. All the matches they use for betting have been lighted. They *all* have one burned end. The rain keeps falling.

Mac McLeod, 66, has been telling everyone about the 'shit hot time' he had (his words) with me and my family, in 'Smoke', and at the Fox and Goose. My father does miracles with rations. He can still get chicken livers, about four pounds each week, from a pal of his who is a poulterer in the West End. Actually, I think, Alec works in Smithfield market. Chicken livers are a delicacy today. Mac just loves London, loves beer, loves pubs, and particularly loves the Fox and Goose, and my mum and dad. My oldest pal in all the world, Bob, managed to work it again, so we did have fun. A sad note was that among our pals around late school days, Jim Blanchard is missing. Navigator, Stirlings. This follows Dave Clayton, flight engineer, shot down. Also, Stirlings. In both cases Bob predicted that they *would* be shot down. I believe that Bob has made this prediction on seven or eight pilots and air crews that we have jointly known. In all cases they have got the chop. His predictions are uncanny, and frightening.

Well, I suppose we won't see F.W. Lister back as skipper. We have a new CO today. His name is Smik. Squadron Leader Smik. He is a Czech. He's a very affable type. He has a most creditable feat (if you want to call it that) to his credit. He is one of only very, very few who have escaped from POW camp. All the camps are a long way into Germany, and to be able to hide, to *survive*, and to walk all the way back, even with good underground contacts, is practically a miracle. Perhaps the best reason is that he speaks Czech, German, some Dutch, French, and, pretty good English. He is apparently a superior pilot, which was mostly proven air-to-air. He says he will have to learn 'the niceties' by *doing*. He was talking about *our* ops, bombing and strafing. Sandy Powell said, later on, 'Well, the poor bastard hasn't got a clue about air-to-ground and *we* are the poor bastards who've got to fly behind him! Fuck *our* Irish luck!'

We also have two more new bods, both NCO's, Flight Sergeants Wallace, Scotch – 'Jock' – and Peter Coxell, an ex-Kittyhawk pilot, shot down in Italy. Harris is a sprog to operations, Wade is a Canuck.

When will the rain stop? When will the runway be serviceable again?

November 18th, B.60, Grimbergen, Belgium

We finally got operational today. My fears of being rusty from so many days, and the overall fear of the first op after a lay-off were put to rest.

Perhaps I have been dreading another armed recce, for I could have jumped for joy when I learned that it was escort to 36 (B.25) Mitchells. We escorted them into the target area to Viersen. These bomber boys really draw the flak! As has been said so often, Jerry lays a carpet of 37 mm that you could *walk* on. They were six boxes of six, and as usual, they try to fool the flak gunners by flying seemingly past the target, then suddenly swinging back in a dogleg which becomes the bombing run. Only the first box may fool Jerry, because the sky is full of grey and black puffs as mathematically set by the time the second box goes in.

It was bitchingly cold. Rendezvous at angels eighteen is no bloody joke in an unheated cockpit. You feel like the centre of a tub of ice cold water. Feet freeze, and you change from one rudder pedal stirrup to the other. Knees go dead, because *they*, like the right hand on the control column, have maximum exposure. Beat the right hand on the knees, having set the throttle, temporarily, and switched the throttle hand to the spade grip on the stick. Beat, beat, fist on left knee, now on right knee. The knees do not react. They are simply – frigid. Blood comes back to the right hand. It is very painful. I tell myself that I *should* get the electric kimono. My other side says – How many escorts do you fly? How many times do you go above angels, eight? Remember – you may have to bail out in a bloody hurry – *that* comes with *armed recce* – and a kimono means you've got to disconnect three plugs – not two. Oxygen, r/t, are enough. Three disconnects are one too many.

I am glad we got operational today. Smik did very well. He is a good air-to-air pilot. He is also a very amiable chap, with no upper school bullshit – to coin a word.

November 21st, B.60, Grimbergen, Belgium

It just occurred to me, today, that Eckert, Griffin, Crozier, Pete, Sandy and me are all *old hands*. With Ron Reeves gone, there are no 'desert type' NCO's. What brought it to mind was the new infusion of Harris, Wade, Coxell (another Peter) and Wallace (Jock). In a way, I should include the ubiquitous Zhilbare Morisson, but he is not an oppo, in the sense that Eckert, Pete and Sandy are my special oppos. Larry Hyland *almost* qualifies, but then, again, Hyland is, well, more like a *person*. It used to be that most squadrons were comprised of mostly officers, and the officers led the sections. As it is, to date, most of us old hands, are section leaders *and* sub-section leaders. I was really scared about leading a section – but it was the same as the fear I had when I joined. That is, the fear of failure. This can be just as negative as that overall gut-rambling fear of getting flak blasted, and getting the chop. (The bomber boys call it 'going for a Burton' as in deference of leaving *permanently* to get some brew in the sky. Ergo: 'Billy Goodwin? Billy went for a Burton last night.' Bob Bode, my oldest, dearest pal, says the bomber boys refer to Air Marshal Harris as 'Butch'. This is short for 'Butcher'.)

I do not think there is one of us who would rather be somewhere else. At least, until it is all over. Flying is all a thrill to me, and I think being airborne is what every one of us loves. Take-offs, formations, diving down steep – watching the airspeed indicator go up as the altimetre winds down . . . and, of course, that last wide turn, all the way down to the runway – or strip. Finally, getting out of the cockpit, jumping down to a beaming mechanic, bullshitting about the sortie, all the time gazing in awe at the lovely lines of the most beautiful aeroplane ever built.

We are almost all flying Mark XVI's, now, and we are thrilled, only that they are, literally, new from the factory. (Factory, to 84 GSU to here). Only three, that I can count, have the bubble canopy. Now we hear that the bubble is an expensive addition, because it means change in fuselage design. So the XVI has no more power than a IX, and the engine is Lend Lease, made in the USA. It is a Packard Merlin 266, as opposed to the Mark IX's Rolls Royce Merlin, 66.

Another thing which does not amuse us, is that there is no automatic pitch control. We have been 'babied', I suppose, with the Mark IX. You take off with pitch full fine, and after safe take-off, wheels and flaps up, you pull the pitch control lever back to automatic. From then until final approach, the pitch is automatically set by the throttle. Another thing that Pete was the first to discover. While this Yankee made engine is identical to the Merlin 66 – it has different *beat*! We argued like fools when Pete first made a point of it, but most of us agree. It simply does have a different beat.

I did one op this afternoon. It was dive bombing on railway interdiction at Bieren, east of Arnhem. Smik led us. He is very calm, speaks very clearly on r/t, with very little accent. He sounds his tees well, as my old French teacher used to *implore* us. We had some excitement when we saw two jets – Me262's quite close. They did not make passes at us, and we would have been out of luck if they had, carrying one thousand pounds of bombs. . . . Our bombing was bang on; superb. The flak was awful. Again, we had fortune flying with us. Sammy Roth was hit, but got home, okay. Interdiction, that is, cutting railroad lines, is very important so we are told. Every time the lines are bombed means that Jerry cannot move his heavy transport. That is why they are so heavily defended, I suppose.

A letter from home today, which is rare, because mum and dad don't write much. Also, there are always some of my pals visiting our house. Mum wrote this one. She put in ten shillings, I suppose as force of habit. I can't spend it here in Brussels. She says they all enjoyed having Big Mac McLeod home. She remembers with much amusement the 'knees up' party we had after the Fox and Goose closed. Mac, who was a bit sozzled, begged for someone to join him in singing 'Ciri-Ciri-Bim' (he was funny).

November 25th, B.60, Grimbergen, Belgium
I am beginning to know how the bomber boys feel when they are ready to go out on a hot target, only to have it cancelled – or worse – *postponed.* Bob always says the bomber crews build up a certain enthusiasm, or a nonchalance, depending on the make-up of the individual. He has told me that a postponement, on a Hamburg, an Essen, or a Berlin, first brings a relief – and then comes back to fear that is there to build all night; then to be followed the next day, right up to take-off.

The first time he went to bomb Berlin there was, he said, much concern before and after briefing. (He says, yes, they had reason to fear the briefing because, as usual, somebody *talked.*) The operation was postponed. The crews had a whole day to sweat it out. The next night, they arrived with a bomber's moon, a break in the clouds, and very little flak. They found that their fears were groundless. They had been victims of their own imagination. Ironically, they were sent out the following night, and in the 24 hours' interim the Berliners had brought in some hundreds of flak guns, and the crews felt they were lucky that *any* aeroplanes got in, and got back.

Anyway, now *we* know about fear building on the biggest op we have undertaken so far – The Barracks at Bussum, near Hilversum. It was postponed four times, due to weather. When we finally did it today, I was as nervous as a church man in a brothel. At the first briefing, it sounded like an exciting development, a chance to kill a lot of Germans who would otherwise kill our soldiers. Specifically, we were told that the 8th Panzer (Tanks) Division would occupy the barracks. We were told that the barracks buildings were all brand new – just completed. We were told that it would be a major target, and because of its importance, would probably be well defended by flak gunners. The project came through the Dutch underground, and it was dubbed a 'CD' target, which means 'Cloak and Dagger'. Each time we have been called to briefing the potential defences have been stressed. On two occasions we have all been strapped in our cockpits when the op has been scrubbed. In my mind, I have built it up with a fear factor as big as our attack on the radar stations at Boulogne, where I flew through an exploding 88-mm burst. My fear may have been even bigger.

We got final briefing at 11.30 am today. It was decided, earlier, that it would be a total wing effort, all four squadrons, carrying forty-eight 500-pounders and twice that number of 250 pounders.

Wingco Berg and Squadron Leader Ellis (Wing IO) briefed us. We were told that a contact from the underground was made early this morning. The message was that the barracks were fully occupied, that if the weather was right, today would be a good day. The message also suggested that since lunch was served at twelve noon, that 12.30 pm would be perfect timing.

Wingco Berg led *us*, so we were first squadron in on target. I flew Red Three behind Group Captain Morris, who decided to come with us. Two of our new bods, Coxell and Wallace, flew their first op. Rolf Berg's timing was perfect. We dropped out of cloud at angels seven, rolled onto our backs, dived down to deck level, strafing. Seven buildings, in a row, with just enough space between each, make a target impossible to miss. We must have scared the shit out of them from the moment we opened up with our guns. I believe I was doing 350 mph as I dropped my eggs. When we left, the seven buildings were a total shambles, and the smoke was billowing up through the clouds. Hot air rises! Every aeroplane got back.

Wingco Berg was very pleased. We were *all* very pleased. That will pay the bastards back for what they did to my house, my street and my London. We have another new NCO with us. Sergeant Baecke, pronounced 'Biker', Belgian. He's on the small side, below middleweight. Just a kid, by his looks. No ops experience. Well, he'll get it here.

November 26th, B.60, Grimbergen, Belgium

I flew two ops today. (Two, for the price of one!) The first one was interdiction, railways lines near Ruurlo. We saw two Me262's, but again, they wanted no parts of us, and we couldn't chase them, carrying bombs. This was the second time we hit the same target today, but we did not have anything like the luck they had on the first sortie. (Two goods trains.)

Later on we dive-bombed marshalling yards in the Utrecht–Arnhem area. Four direct hits – all the rest were near misses, but all in the target area. Anyway we *did* cut the lines. We had some fun after bombing, when we strafed a signal box, which was right in the middle of converging lines. When we finished, it was not worth scrap wood. We didn't see any bods in the signal box, but some had to be there. We all felt good at de-briefing, right up to the point where someone wondered whether there were Huns in there, controlling the traffic, or whether they were Dutch railway men. Then someone else said 'Who cares?' That seemed to make sense. The important thing *is* – nothing will be moving guns or ammo for the Huns, up or down – for tonight.

After briefing, it was time for tea. Tonight the meal was that old standby – cheese and potato pie. As usual, the cheese contribution was green-flecked old heels of iron-hard orange cheddar. The cooks (Norwegian, mostly) save up these old heels for enough weeks to make a batch. The cheddar heels almost defy the efforts to make them melt and merge with the mashed potatoes. What is disconcerting is when you dig into the pie (it has no crust!) you are as likely to spoon a piece of linen into your mouth. Linen cheesecloth is irrevocably glued to the right angled cheese heel. We did get some pound cake, probably 'liberated' from a nearby bakery. The cheese and potato pie was not worth stealing for Louise and family, but the cake was. One of the new bods stuffed a two pound loaf of it inside his khaki battle dress.

I often wonder what Louise actually thinks of us. She is so alert, so smiling when we come in the door after squadron release. She probably thinks we are 'round the bend,' and she has a right to, the way we sometimes act. Zhilbare liberated an electric iron for her from God knows where. The sad thing is that one of *us* is using it, most of the time, to 'press up' and 'dog-out' for Brussels. One thing certain, we *will* be leaving here sometime, and maybe soon. As always, the new location will be secret until we climb in the cockpits and fly there. Louise probably looks at us as participants in a game. It is most fortunate that not one of us billetees has been shot down since we arrived. I am not sure how dear old Louise would take it if it were, for example, *L'Australie* (Eckert) it would certainly shake her. Of all of us, she likes *L'Australie* the most.

To Brussels. Sixty-Six has got the gharry for tonight.

November 30th, B.60, Grimbergen, Belgium

We came a gutser, day before yesterday. Our skipper Smik and Flying Officer Taymans (Belgian) both got the chop. We have been 'shook rigid' as the airmen say, ever since. There were eight of us NCO's on the show, and we could not even eat lunch after de-briefing, we were so shaken. Why Smik took us down to bomb and strafe Zwolle marshalling yards, we certainly will never know.

We were out on a simple armed recce, patrolling Arnhem-Hengele-Zwolle. We had plenty of petrol, each of us carrying a sixty gallon belly tank. Why we didn't continue patrolling until we found some MET's or even a railway train in a siding, is a good question – to which there will never be an answer. Even as Red Leader came in on r/t, I found myself saying, silently, 'No, shit, no, no, no! *Not* the marshalling yards, for Christ's sake!' What he said was, 'Monty Squadron, this is Monty Red Leader. Jettison tanks – arm bombs. We are going in. Count five, and in we go.'

I could feel my face freezing, as if from a dentist's hypodermic. Hell, we hadn't jettisoned half the drop tanks when the flak guns started firing. The heavies had our height and range immediately – twenty, thirty black mushroom puffs from 88's. Before half of us rolled over for the dive, the 37 and 20-mm tracers came arcing up from all around the yards.

I was fourth in, flying number two to Eckert, and even as I started diving I saw they had my range, too. I was following Eckert, making sure that I would not shoot him in the dive, then the tracers flashed below and above my wings, like fireworks. I was perhaps 300 feet, pressing the bomb tit, when I saw one gigantic red-yellow streak flash across the yard rails for perhaps two hundred yards, and I knew immediately that someone had bought it. Did I *see* – or imagine – out of the corner of my right goggle, a cartwheeling mass of Spitfire wing, like a broken boomerang, at ten, twenty feet, crossing almost every shiny rail to the starboard side? Now I was down to the deck, very conscious of the flak zipping past me, braced for the hit that would surely come. I suddenly realized that I was below the power-wire pylons, and I had to pull up to clear them. To my quiet horror, I saw a Spitfire cross my beam from starboard, and I realized it was one of Yellow Section – and he hadn't even seen me. I watched him pull up, rudder pedals obviously kicking madly, and I saw the tracers literally snapping at his arse.

Then, stupidly, I stole a glance in my rear view mirror, and saw whatever was shooting at *him* was happening to me. Self-preservation was telling me, 'Pull up! Pull *uppp*!' and my logic said, 'Stay down!' I was flying across Zwolle, rooftops just beneath me, seemingly for a minute, but actually a matter of seconds.

It took us minutes to re-form at angels eight, far away from the gunfire. There were still traces of black (88) smoke as we climbed. I saw no bombs explode, though they must have done. Then, it was the clear, accented, calm voice of Peter Hillwood Blue Leader. 'Monty Squadron, call off by position, angels eight. This is Monty

Blue Leader.' 'Monty Blue Two.' 'Blue Three.' 'Monty Blue Four.'

'Yellow Section?' 'Yellow Leader' – etcetera. 'Monty Red Leader – are you with us – *over?*'

There was just – silence. Peter Hillwood must have known. 'Monty Squadron. Form up on me.' He waggled his wings, steeply, left, right, left right. We know what to do. Leave the missing planes as holes in Red Section. 'Setting course. Longbow Control – this is Monty Squadron. Coming home. Over.'

'Roger, Monty – Can we help?'

'Actually, Longbow, no.'

I have never been as wet with sweat, or as shivering cold, as I was on the way back. When I jumped down from the wing's trailing edge – I thought that my legs were gone – had given out. I could barely stand.

De-briefing went on and on. Many questions, few answers. I wanted to make an emotional outburst. More importantly, I needed to relieve my bladder. The bladder won, in the circumstances.

Today, I flew on a show, low level bombing and strafing gun positions at Dunkirk. Though we did not see much flak, Griffin got a hit in the engine. He got back okay. In a way, it was a wizard show. We started fires, and the smoke covered the target even before we left. We got a 'blue ribbon' bulletin just before squadron release. It read, 'The following message has been received by 84 Group from SHAEF via TAF to be passed on to 132 Wing:

> THE ARMY WAS MUCH IMPRESSED BY THE WING'S EFFORTS THIS MORNING'S TARGETS – KEJ1, KEJ2, AND KEJ3.

Commendations do not come every day. I have lifted a copy from the adj's office to stick in my flying log book.

I hope to God that we never go down again on a Zwolle. I will remember Zwolle.

Extracts from the
Operations Record Book 127 Squadron, RAF 132 (Norwegian) Wing

B.60, 1st November 1944: Twelve aircraft led by W/Cdr Berg (132 Wing) took off at 0910 to bomb and strafe the neighbourhood of the sea front at Walcheren. They met with considerable success eleven 500 lb eleven second delay fused bombs were dropped along the sea wall and on the south side of the town. All bombs fell in target area. One hung up. All aircraft landed base 0955 hours. Visibility good.

A further twelve aircraft once again led by W/Cdr Berg took off at 1535 hours to bomb and strafe gun positions in the Domburg area. Ten 500 lbs bombs were dropped in the target area, with one near miss and an overshoot. The wood, north of Domburg, was also well and truly strafed. Slight inaccurate light flak was experienced from the target areas. All aircraft landed at base at 1645 hours.

B.60, 3rd November: Twelve aircraft led by W/Cdr Berg (132 Wing) took off at 1110 hours to attack interdiction targets at DD.735/I.B. Primary target not located. Squadron was then vectored to Klondert where considerable success was achieved. Eight 500 lb bombs were dropped in the town, the remaining four falling outside the target area. Town well and truly strafed after bombing run. Two MET destroyed in the town. Battery west of Klondert and town full of Hun. Moderate accurate light flak from target area. All aircraft landed at base at 1210 hours.

Twelve aircraft again led by W/Cdr Berg (132 Wing) took off at 1405 to bomb and strafe enemy MET in the Klondert area. Targets were numerous – the following hits being observed – four on defence positions at D.782454 fires afterwards seen – Four on defence positions at Doudestoof, a further two on defence position at D.772455 – One severely damaging a bridge over the canal at D.793455 – leaving one not accounted for. Targets well strafed after bombing. One MET flamer and three MET damaged at D.759464. F/O R.O. Lloyd (Aus) was seen to crash SW of Tilburg – He was admitted to hospital in Antwerp but unfortunately died that evening. A sad loss to the squadron as he had served with the unit in the Middle East, England, and France. F/O Taymans landed at D.70 owing to shortage of fuel. All other aircraft landed base 1500 hours.

B.60, 6th November: Twelve aircraft under F/Lt Shillitoe took off from base at 0900 hours on railway interdiction between Arnhem and Utrecht. All aircraft dropped one 500 lb MC bomb eleven seconds delay in a dive from 1000 to 100 feet, and the line was cut at two places. E.6979 and E.5983 by two direct hits. In addition the line was probably cut by three near misses at E.6482. No movement was seen on this line and all bridges appeared to be intact. The squadron returned to base at 1010 hours.

Bombing Arnhem–Utrecht. At 1145 hours twelve aircraft took off from base (at B.60) to bomb a bridge at Groep. Several near misses were scored when eleven bombs were dropped in a dive from 6000 to 1000 feet and the bridge was possibly damaged. One bomb hung up but was accidentally dropped safe south of Antwerp. A convoy of ten plus vehicles were sighted at 1225 hours at E.4387 moving north. The squadron landed back at base at 1245 hours.

Ten aircraft with F/Lt Doyle leading were airborne at 1510 hours to attack a concentration of trains on the line between Zwolle and Harderwijk. A stationary train of twenty plus was attacked at Z.5514 with bombs in a dive from 4000 to 50 feet after which it was strafed with cannon. Two direct hits and five near misses are claimed with two wide, and as a result the train is considered completely out of action. Meagre light inaccurate flak was experienced F/Lt Shillitoe's aircraft was seen to lose one wing and dive in and he is believed to be killed. The squadron returned at 1620 hours.

Escort to VIP to Eindhoven – Two Spits led by F/Lt Lea took off at 1528 hours on an uneventful escort and returned at 1628 hours.

B.60, 12th November: Weather recce Arnhem–Utrecht. Two Spitfire XVIs took off at 0850 on the above weather recco. Landing at base at 0935 hours.

9/10ths at 1200 feet. Above 7000 feet frequent showers. Visibility below cloud three to four miles. In showers 300 to 400 yards.

F/Sgt Wade and Sgt Harris arrived from 84 GSU on posting.

B.60, 13th November: Bad weather prevented any form of operation. F/Sgts Wallace and Coxell arrived on posting.

B.60, 14th November: Duff weather still continues. S/Ldr O. Smik (Czech) arrived from 84 GSU to take over command of the squadron.

B.60, 18th November: A considerable improvement in the weather – 331 Squadron together with twelve aircraft of 127 Squadron were airborne at 1240 hours as target cover to thirty-six Bostons.

The wing was led by W/Cdr Berg. Owing to other Bostons in the area at the same time only the last six bombers were seen over the target but otherwise the escort was uneventful. Intense heavy inaccurate flak was experienced by bombers over the target area. The squadron landed back at 1410 hours. Weather 9/10ths thin layer at 5000 feet. Visibility good.

B.60, 19th November: Twelve aircraft of 127 Squadron led by W/Cdr Berg (132 Wing) were airborne at 1020 hours on railway interdiction between Amersfoort and Apeldoorn. All 500 lb bombs were dropped in a dive from 5000 to 100 feet, as a result of which three near misses are claimed on the track just west of Zeumeren (E.5498). The remaining bombs fell in the target area. A staff car on the road at E.5299 moving east was strafed with cannon fire and left in the flames. Trucks and buildings in the goods yard at Zeumeren were also strafed. A smoke trail was sighted in the Hague area at 1054 hours heading south towards Antwerp. The weather in the area was very good 3/10ths cloud at 6000 feet. The squadron landed back at base at 1125 hours.

The squadron was again led by W/Cdr Berg when eleven aircraft took off at 1350 hours, each aircraft carrying one 500 lb bomb. G/Capt Morris (132 Wing) was also flying with the squadron. The operation proved abortive owing to weather, and due to shortage of petrol, landing was made at Antwerp (B.70) at 1525 hours. The squadron returned to base at 1655 hours.

B.60, 21st November: F/Lt Hillwood led a section on a weather recce taking off at 1410 hours. The two 500 lb bombs which were carried were dropped in a dive from 8000 to 3000, on a factory of EDE (E.5884), scoring two Direct Hits on the north-east corner of the building. Moderate inaccurate light flak was encountered from the factory. Motor Transport activity was observed on the road from Ede to Arnhem. The section landed at 1515 hours. Weather base to River Maas 10/10ths. 1000 to 10,000 feet with heavy rain, moving north-east. Further north 5/10ths. Scattered cumulus at 5,000 feet. Visibility below cloud 10–15 miles.

Nine aircraft led by S/Ldr Smik (OC 127 Squadron) were airborne at 1530 hours on rail interdiction between Hengele–Zutphen–Arnhem. Nine 500 lb bombs eleven seconds delay were dropped in a dive from 4000 to zero feet, scoring three direct hits and one near miss on a railway bridge and junction near Dieren (E.8885) and one direct hit, hit a bridge, which was seen to collapse. Intense accurate light and heavy flak was met within this area. Three Me262's were seen flying south-west to north-east in the area E.75 at 6000 feet and losing height. The squadron returned to base at 1645 hours. Visibility two to three miles.

B.60, 25th November: Bombing enemy occupied barracks near Bussum. All four squadrons were detailed for the above operation and 127 Squadron with thirteen aircraft led by W/Cdr Berg and with G/C Morris also flying with the squadron took off at 1205 hours. They were the first squadron to attack, diving from 7000 feet to deck level and letting go with all bombs (each aircraft carried one 500 lb and two 250 lb bombs). All bombs fell in the target area and direct hits were scored on five out of the seven buildings. The targets were well and truly strafed after bombing. No flak was encountered and the squadron returned to base at 1315 hours.

B.60, 26th November: The squadron was engaged on rail interdiction between Zutphen–Ruurlo. Eleven aircraft were airborne at 0810 hours, under S/Ldr Smik, but one returned early due to late take-off. Two goods trains were sighted east of Vorden 300 yards apart and converging. Ten 500 lb and twenty 250 lb MC eleven seconds delay bombs were dropped in a dive from 2000 to 1000 feet and both trains stopped. One locomotive was blown up by a direct hit whilst a direct hit or very near miss is believed to have destroyed the other locomotive. The two trains were strafed after bombing by cannon and machine gun fire, flames and smoke were seen issuing in two places from tarpaulin covered trucks. A train at Emmerich was also strafed and strikes were seen. Due to flak the squadron became split up in cloud and owing to shortage of petrol only two aircraft landed back at base at 0935 hours. Six of the remainder landed at other bases but two made crash landings as a result of which two aircraft were Cat E and F/S Wade was slightly injured.

At 1510 hours twelve aircraft of the squadron were again airborne under

S/Ldr Smik on rail interdiction between Zutphen–Ruurlo. Twelve 500 lb bombs were dropped two miles north-west of Ruurlo (A.1088). Two near misses on the railway were claimed with the remainder in the target area. Two V-2 contrails were seen at 1330 hours in the Amsterdam area. Moderate light inaccurate flak was experienced from the wood north of Ruurlo. The squadron landed at 1430 hours.

For the last operation of the day twelve aircraft were up at 1550 hours on a rail interdiction mission between Arnhem–Utrecht. The squadron was led by S/Ldr Smik. Two 500 lb bombs were dropped on a level crossing six miles east-south-east of Utrecht (E.3088) scoring four direct hits, while the remainder fell in the target area. Both up and down lines are believed to have been cut. There was intense heavy and light accurate flak in the area north of the river Waal, batteries of 88 millimetres flak dual purpose being observed along most roads in this area. The squadron landed back at base at 1655 hours.

B.60, 27th November: Weather duff – preventing any form of operation taking place.

B.60, 28th November: At 0940 hours twelve aircraft led by S/Ldr Smik were airborne on an armed recce between Arnhem–Hengele–and Zwolle. Fitted with long range tanks and each carrying two 250 lb bombs.

No rail or road movement was seen so the squadron went down in a dive from 5000 feet to deck level to bomb the goods yard at Zwolle. An intense barrage of accurate heavy and light flak was encountered, and only two very near misses are claimed. Unfortunately S/Ldr Smik (Czech) and F/O Taymans (Belgian) are missing as a result of this attack. One aircraft was seen to hit the ground and explode but the fate of the other is still unknown. A sad loss to the squadron, particularly as the CO was a good leader and a friend of all his fellow pilots. The remaining ten aircraft returned to base at 1112 hours.

B.60, 30th November: Squadrons 127 and 332 led by W/Cdr Berg were detailed to bomb and strafe strong points at Dunkirk, twelve aircraft of the squadron took off at 0835 hours. 127 Squadron went in first and dropped twelve 500 bombs in a dive from 5000 to 100 feet. Eleven of the bombs were well concentrated amongst the four strong points. One temporary hang up was dropped in flooded country to the south of the target. Sections then went down and strafed. Only meagre light inaccurate flak was encountered. Smoke and flames covered the target when the squadron headed for base, landing at 0950 hours. Weather – 4/10ths, thin layer at 5000 feet. Visibility seven to eight miles.

(Signed)
Commanding, No. 127 Squadron
Royal Air Force

VI

December

December 3rd, B.60, Grimbergen, Belgium
We got a commendation of sorts today, from Group, regarding the wing's bombing of the barracks at Bussum. I happened to be passing Corporal Turner's desk, and I saw him typing it. I did some sweet talking and I got him to put a carbon in his typewriter and I got him to type it ten times or more. I have put mine in my logbook. It reads as follows:

MESSAGE FROM G.C.C. 3.12.44.

> Ref. Target C.D.14 New Barracks at Bussum Panzer troops occupied barracks on 24.11.44. and were there when bombed by 132 Wing 25.11.44.

That is all it says. Only yesterday at ops room we were shown the stereo-optigon pictures, from line overlaps taken by a photo-recce Spitfire. We had no idea how well we wrecked those seven buildings. The roofs are literally torn off, and there are no complete walls standing. The photo process is shown three-dimensional. We would be surprised if many Hun troops got out alive.

We got a reprieve today from what seems to be relentless bombing and strafing. We are all sleeping very badly these days. I often wake up shaking, and when I fall off this silly little cot, and realize that I am only six inches above the floorboards, I find it difficult to fall off to sleep again. Lately I have even been having this recurring dream that I am being woken up by Corporal Turner. In the dream, I am *dreaming*. The subject is not clear, but I am in a pleasant frame of mind. Then I feel a hand shaking my right shoulder, and Corporal Turner says, 'Wake up, Mr Smith, there's a show on.' I wake, I sit bolt upright, and then I realize it is a dream. The room is in total darkness. I am alone with the sounds of heavy breathing, and one, perhaps, snoring.

Today we got a respite, escort to B.25 Mitchells, bombing in the

Venlo area. They did a good, brave job, as always. As usual, we took our box of six Mitchells into the target, right up to their final run. (This was Griffin and me, two escorts to a box.) Then we steep turned away, throttled up to full boost, and climbed above the bombers to avoid the flak. Discretion is the better part of valour in bombing escorts. We know the ground gunners will concentrate on the bombers, because it represents a much better opportunity than re-setting altitude calibrations to try to clobber a handful of Spitfires. As we look after our own safety, we make sure that our box of bombers is not, itself, attacked by Jerry fighters.

Again, today, we saw a few Me262 jets. They were way above us, and they elected not to come down to our bomber's height. It was a good show. The bombers did well, and we got a rewarding, if freezing cold, relief.

December 7th, B.60, Grimbergen, Belgium

It is going to be a cold winter, a far cry from the weather in Honolulu. (That's a reference to the fact that, for the Yanks, this is Pearl Harbour Day). I, for one, am very much appreciative of my sheepwool Irvin jacket. Those of us who have them wear them everywhere but in the cockpit. You cannot wear them in the cockpit because they are simply too bulky. You can just about utilize the cockpit space wearing battledress with an aircrew sweater. Nowadays, the stores are only issuing Irvins to the bomber crews. Bombers are the only aeroplanes with *both* – lots of cold, and enough *room*. There is hardly a week goes by without Paddy Crozier opining that the *world* would be a better place if he had an Irvin – even though it be mine, or Pete's, or Eckert's, which formerly belonged to Dinger Bell. Generally, Brussels, on time off, has become a bore. Simply, too many of our own troops. Brussels is like a gigantic camp for the combined armed forces. A couple of the boys have had luck with meeting girls who have taken them home to their familes, and got a good meal. Mostly, though, the women in Brussels in the bars are mascara'd *beetles*. 'Old mutton, done up like spring lamb,' my sisters would say. I had a show two days ago, escort job to Mitchells, east and north of Aachen. They (the Mitchells) went through a ton of flak. They bombed from sixteen. It was simply, bloody freezing cold. Larry Hyland claimed he saw a Spit Mark V making a move toward the bombers. He claimed he chased it, and it made a getaway going east! He was vehement about it – though he never made mention of it on the r/t. At de-briefing he told Spy Johnson that he thought it was a re-built, captured and flown by Jerry. Flying Officer Johnson gave him a sort of wry look.

December 8th, B.60, Grimbergen, Belgium

Yesterday was a day that started off badly, but ended well with six of us getting electric shavers. We flew an armed recce in the Munster area, and the weather was most foul. We were carrying two 250-pounders, each, and the sky seemed like one great circular black wall. Peter Hillwood never told us he was lost, but I know by his square search that he was looking for a spot to identify. It was terribly turbulent, and we were bouncing all over the sky. Finding no train or other target, and being given no help, target wise by Longbow Control, we headed home and ran into almost impenetrable rain and sleet. After stumbling all over the sky for too long a time, somebody got the word to Hillwood over r/t. 'Airfield, eight o'clock below, Monty Red Leader.' We proceeded down to land. Here it was, morning, and it was as black as midnight. Nearly all of us had trouble landing, as there were many filled potholes from bomb damage (very big potholes for very big pots!) Every repaired bomb hole was water filled, every huge puddle at least six inches deep. Such torrents of water gushed over the wings that I was certain my flaps were damaged. (They weren't.)

We all got together. The aerodrome – B78 – was on the outskirts of Eindhoven. We knew that we would be stranded for at least a couple of hours. Then, the name Eindhoven struck a magic chord in Zhilbare Morisson. 'Aha! Fellows! Dees plahce. Ein'hoven, 'appens to be the *home* (you say home, yes?) of the beeg Fabrique, Phillips! They make rahdios, they make light bulbs, they make all electrique. . . !' We were there within an hour. Zhilbare waved some guilders at a truck, and the driver stopped. The entire factory is just back in operation. The boss of the Phillips factory speaks French as well as he speaks Dutch, so he and Zhilbare got along like long lost twins. We were shown all through the plant, and the Managing Director, Van de Kuyver, translated a sign for us that was huge, and hanging down from a high rafter. In Dutch, it said, 'Attention All Workers. Under the Occupation, Phillips encouraged you all to appropriate radio parts to make your own wireless receivers, in order to listen to BBC and Allied broadcasts. Now that the emergency is passed, it is hoped that you will be encouraged to disassemble the receivers and bring the parts back to us. *The Management*. . . !'

We were allowed to purchase Phillips goods, and we bought a communal wireless set, and individual electric shavers. These are four inches long, tube shaped, black. At one end is the electric cord, and at the other, a round chrome screen which you hold against your face. Under the screen is a jagged cutter with many sharp teeth. It is an odd looking affair, but it does shave the face. Zhilbare bought out the store at the factory. Among other things he bought a dozen light bulbs, three wireless sets and half a dozen shavers. Undoubtedly the whole purpose was for re-sale. On the way back, (he kept the driver waiting) he had us making a detour. Going into a house near the aerodrome, he emerged with a dozen eggs, and two kilos of Danish bacon. Back to his Spitfire he drew a screwdriver from his pocket and opened up the gun ammunition compartments. He stuffed all his goods in them, in the trust that we would not be called upon to do an op on the way back. (We all had two bombs with us.)

Zhilbare only missed one detail. In his rush to get to the Phillips factory, Zhilbare forgot to get his tanks re-filled from the bowser. The weather was still very duff, on the way back. Zhilbare lost us, in cloud. He ran short of petrol, pranged, 500 feet short of the B.60 runway. When he opened the ammo panel, he found his wirelesses and shavers swimming in egg yolks and whites. Every light bulb was smashed, as were the hydraulics on his landing gear. Thank goodness he didn't belly flop. He was called before Rolf Berg, who was all set to tear him off a strip, when he saw the streaks of egg yolk, over Zhilbare's hands, on his tunic, around his mouth, and even in his Gallic black hair. It stopped Wingco Berg, *cold*. Then he laughed, and told Zhilbare to make himself scarce. Don't tell me that Rolf Berg doesn't have a sense of humour.

The other team got airborne today. I don't know all the details but Griffin and Pete shot an Me109 down today.

December 12th, B.60, Grimbergen, Belgium

Seems like we are having an invasion of Canucks, and we also have a new CO. He is Squadron Leader R.M.P. Sampson.

Three Canadian officers came from GSU the other day. Flying Officers Round, McCallum, and Nolan. The next day, an NCO – Warrant Officer Mallandaine. This more than makes up (Canadian-wise) for the tour–ex posting of Ted Doyle – though only in numbers. Ted Doyle is a bloody good leader, and we can't make up his kind of operational leadership very easily.

We all shared in and rehashed a bottle of Johnny Walker when Ted got posted (he hasn't gone yet!) and rehashed the 'Gollins goin' *down*' incident, which had happened on a sweep over Dunkirk, Frank Bradley leading. It was a 'no action' sweep, and though we were vectored onto 'twenty plus' bandits, they turned out to be shiny Mustangs, on their way to escort B.17s.

We had been about to turn for home, at about angels eighteen, about five-tenths cloud cover, below. Nobody had used the r/t for some minutes. Then, Gollins broke in, in an anguished voice. ''ello Monty Red Leader, this is Monty Red Four. I'm goin' *down*! My engine's cut!'

Bradley: 'Monty Red Four. This is an order! *Stay* in formation!'

Gollins – more anguished: 'I *can't* stay in formation! I'm goin' *down*! My engine's *cut*!'

Bradley: Monty Blue Four. You will *stay in formation*! That's a bloody order!'

Gollins – panic: 'I can't stay in formation! I'm at eight thousand fuckin' feet!'

Ted Doyle, leading 'A' Flight. *Very* Canadian accent. 'Mon'y Red Leader – Mon'y Red Four *cannot* stay in formation! He has a *dead stick* – a *dead* stick! His engine's dead! Do you *read me*? (The last, was yelled – strength twenty).

Bradley: 'Oh, I'm sorry Red Four, I thought you'd said you're goin' down – you'd *seen a* truck! Good luck Red Four. . . .'

Gollins, ecstatically: 'Monty Red Leader, this is Red Four. I got it started! I'm okay! I'm goin' 'ome!'

It turned out later, Gollins had an air lock, which developed when he changed tanks, drop tank back to mains.

We all admitted that we had all laughed, silently, on a return trip that was in radio silence until we came over base. They said that Frank Bradley enjoyed it, most, when we got to de-briefing!

We got a 'good conduct' citation today, from Group. Once again, I have filched a copy for my log book.

MESSAGE OF APPRECIATION

The Air Officer Commanding has received the following message from Lt. Gen. G.G. Simonds, CB, CBE, DSO, Acting GCC – in – C 1st Canadian Army

> Would you please express to your staff, Wing Commanders Pilots and Ground Staff, the appreciation of the soldiers for the invaluable assistance given by 84 Group RAF in the Battles for the Schelde Estuary.
>
> Because of the whole hearted cooperation which the Army has received every day, we have all come to take it for granted. Though this perhaps may seem unappreciative, in reality there could be no higher compliment to the support which 84 Group gives to us. We have, I know, been freer in our expressions of thanks for support when it has come from Groups other than your Command, not so closely associated with us. This is because such support represents the notable exception rather than the daily rule, which is always characteristic of the support we receive from 84 Group.

December 13th, B.60, Grimbergen, Belgium

We met Squadron Leader Sampson for the first time today. He has a DFC and is obviously a seasoned campaigner. He is dark-haired, cultured, kindly man, who probably should be wing commander by now. I mean, that's the feeling we had after meeting him. (That's the funny thing about 'Getting to know you.' The new CO comes to a meeting to find out about *us* – and *we* are the ones doing the evaluation!) We told him, frankly, that we have been set back by the losses. I don't know whether we expected sympathy or not. While we were waiting for him to show up in the new jeep, we discovered that Zhilbare was nowhere to be seen. Peter Hillwood, who has been acting CO, was embarrassed, and then browned off. He sent the 30 hundredweight up to our billet. No sooner was it out of sight, than up came the jeep, with Squadron Leader Sampson driving it. We were introducing ourselves all round, and shaking hands, when along came Zhilbare on his putt-putt motor bike. Apparently he passed the truck which was sent to fetch him. He had been balancing a slice of bread and jam on the petrol tank, and as he jumped off the bike, he crammed the jammy bread into his mouth.

Hillwood gave a contemptuous look to Zhilbare, and said, 'Er, this man, sir, is our Free French pilot – Gilbert Morisson. He is a warrant officer.' Startled, Zhilbare took the jammy bread from his mouth (it was most of a slice) then transferred it to the other hand. Jam was all over his right hand as R.M.P. Sampson proffered *his* right hand. Zhilbare shot his hand out, thought better, and put it to his mouth, licking his fingers. Then he grabbed the CO's hand, transferring his spit. The CO now, looked startled, and did the only thing he could do. He *laughed*! Then we all laughed, and the tension was broken. It was all too funny.

Anyway, we had the rest of today to get to know each other. It has poured rain all day long. No ops today.

December 16th, B.60, Grimbergen, Belgium

Rain and more rain. We had a brief respite yesterday, for about two hours. Of all the escorts I might want to fly, this was *it*. Escort to Mitchells to bomb Zwolle marshalling yards. The only thing that would have given me more satisfaction would have been cloudless skies. I would have loved to have seen every detail of those railway yards. I would have loved to have seen every bomb explode. As it was, it was about six-tenths cloud, so I could only see some of the bombs go off.

Wingco Berg led the squadron, and R.M.P. Sampson flew as his number two. (A good way to break in our new CO.) I know that Rolf Berg appreciated the operation as much as we did. At de-briefing he said, '*That's* the way to take care of Zwolle – with 36 Mitchells – not twelve Spitfires.' Whether or not this was deprecatory, deliberate, to Smik, I don't know. I'm sure it was not anything but a statement of *fact*. Anyway, those of us NCO's on the escort got satisfaction out of seeing Zwolle 'get it hot.' Griffin, Paddy Crozier, Hyland and me.

We had a party for the airmen last night. We finally got Zhilbare to loosen up his 'flak jacket,' i.e. his canvas money belt. It has been getting fatter and fatter with his black market dealings. We have been chiding him for weeks, it seems, to 'share yer fuckin' wealth with the boys who keep us in the air' – and finally, it worked. An old van pulled up at flight, seemingly on its last legs. It was backfiring all the way. Inside, with the driver, was Zhilbare, and it was loaded to the gunnels with Belgian and Dutch beer.

Well, it was an all-male bash, of course and it lasted until the final bottle was emptied. A few of the airmen got plastered, but there was no trouble whatsoever. Warrant Officer Deems and Flight Sergeant 'Chiefie Wills' detailed other, more sober airmen to carry the inebriated home to their billets. The party turned out to be one big singing bash, and they trotted out all the repertoire of his Air Force songs. Why do Englishmen all have to sing, as long as they are 'lapping up?' First, 'Chiefie' Wills began it with 'The Zoo Story'. A well told story of a Whipsnade Zoo keeper's Spiv brother, who substituted for the zoo keeper, who was 'queer', with the 'flu and who didn't want to lose a day's work, 'Being 'as 'ow he'd done this for 25 years, and was due for the gold watch.' The brothers were twins, identical in suit size. The Spiv brother had never been inside a zoo, but armed with quick wit and cockney guile, he (as played by Chiefie Wills) gave the tour.

It went on and on, and the boys were often in helpless laughter. Some stanzas: ' 'ere my friends re-gar-day the Camel. He feeds on hay, shits bricks – triangular arse-hole – Hence! The pyramids!'

'This is a fine example of – The Spotted Leopard. Three 'undred and sixty-five spots on 'is body – one for every day of the year.' 'What about leap year, Mister?' 'Look under 'is tail, sonny!'

' 'ere my friends we 'ave the Rhino-Sore-arse! Rhino meaning money, sore-arse, meaning Piles – Piles o' bleeding money!'
Then came the songs:

Oh, we're leaving Khartoum
By the light o' the moon.
We're sailing by night and by day.
We're all so *dead beat* –
And we've nothing to eat –
And we've thrown all our rations away!
Shine, shine, Som-er-set Shire!
The skipper looks on 'er with pride.
He'd have a *blue fit*.
If he saw any shit.
On the side of the Som-er-set Shire.

I have wondered about the savage irony of the first two lines of 'The Big Wheel' since I first heard it, three years ago.

An airman told me, before he died.
(I don't know if the bastard lied!)

Well, song after song was trotted out, and the beer bottles were turned into 'dead soldiers'.

The party was very good for all of us. None of us, except the CO and flight commanders have their own allotted mechanics. We share them, as they are work detailed. And, of course, *they* share *us*. We, the pilots, have our favourites among *them*, and they have their favourites among *us*. It pays, very much, to have and share 'good gen' with your mechanic. It pays to tell them, not only how much you *do* appreciate them and their work, but also to spend the time telling them all you can about the last show. As they have their favourite pilots, so they share the sadness when that pilot or this pilot goes missing, or outright gets the unarguable chop. I am sure that there are times they wonder 'if the kite performed'.

The rain continues. The cards go round. 'High,' 'Low' and 'Split the pot' are heard, all day.

December 19th, B.60, Grimbergen, Belgium

I am going home for leave, tomorrow. Since it is Christmas leave, we consider it very special. We could only spare three people, and there are six of us close enough to qualify, so we drew straws, and I was one of the winners.

A rotten thing happened today, and I would have done anything to prevent it. The trouble with horseplay *is*, it can get out of hand. It was a silly misunderstanding. Pete, Sandy, Eckert and Larry Hyland were 'muckin' about' is the way it was. Pushing, pulling, and a lot of giggling. Eckert was pushed, once too often, so he retaliated, as he has done with me. He had Sandy and Larry tied, within two minutes. This was at Flight. Eckert, with his immense strength, can grab the sleeves of an aircrew sweater where they extend over the wrist openings of battledress sleeves. He tugs them so hard that he can stretch the sweater sleeves to about ten inches. Then, quickly, he ties the sleeves in one big knot. Eckert had Sandy and Larry hog tied, as they say, or you might say – 'strait-jacketed.' It was funny, because neither of them could free the other. Then Pete came out of the hut with a waterpistol, which he sprayed on each of us in turn. He had just got his aircrew sweater back from a laundry near our dispersal, which has only recently gone back into business. (They got a load of German 'liberated' Persil.) Here was Pete, all gleaming white, spraying me. I grabbed the pistol, ran away to the side of the hut, and filled it from a mud puddle. (They are *everywhere*.) I sprayed Pete. He looked down at the black, slimy stain on his clean sweater. 'You *bastard*, you!' he said. He grappled with me, and we both overbalanced, and went down in a heap, with me on top. His back plonked into soft ooze. Then he really got mad, and started swinging punches at me. He was very, very cross with me. I know, because he had tears in his eyes. They were red-rimmed. He has not spoken to me since.

Another rotten thing happened today. Just like us, 66 Squadron had a meeting to determine who was going to get Christmas leave. It was supposed to be Big Mac McLeod's turn. He is overdue, and he applied for it at least ten days ago. He has planned with me, all along, that if *I* got leave, he would spend Christmas at my home. Then, in the meeting, they got into, as Mac says, 'A hairy-arsed *bind*.' They started arguing, and Mac was overruled because, of all shitty excuses, Mac is a New Zealander, so Christmas in England 'does not mean as much to you chaps, as it does to us.' To this, Mac says he retorted, 'Fuck orf.' It is a bloody shame. Everyone at home has been hoping we would be together.

I have packed my leave bag. I have also packed my kitbags. We will definitely be moving soon, closer to the bomb line. It is very unfair to go on leave, and to leave kit unpacked, for someone else to have to pack, in your absence.

December 27th, B.79, Woensdrecht

Mac McLeod is *dead*. What a welcome back. So much to say, not much time to write it. My leave started badly. The weather was duff intense fog, and Scotch Mist (light, thin rain).

The transport I got on was lost, over London, and we flew around forever, it seemed. We pancaked at Croydon, quite far from Park Royal between Wembley and Ealing, where I live. I and one other ground sergeant were the only two RAF bods on board. All the rest of the passengers were army –'Brown Jobs' as Paddy Crozier always calls them. They were a sad looking lot, and no wonder. The only leaves, to Blighty, for the army types, are called 'Compassionate leaves of absence' – and these are all minor or major tragedy reasons. Somebody has died, a next-of-kin has been killed in the armed forces, a wife has decamped, leaving babies unattended. All those sort of things. I was all set to walk away from Croyden and thumb a ride on a passing lorry (the Yanks always pick up an RAF type) when my progress was detained by a flying officer, Intelligence. He ushered me into a room, where I was confronted by *three* Intelligence officers, one, a Wingco. They were very stern, and they asked me – where was I going? Where had I come from? And what was my purpose in being in England?

They made me turn out my pockets, and they seized on my paybook. Since the day I was issued that particular paybook, I have wondered who toyed with it, prior to issue. Someone had speculated on my names, from the initials E.A.W. Whoever he was, he wrote Eric, Albert, and then crossed a line through it. Well, the *grilling* got very stern, and even though I kept saying 'Call One-two-seven Squadron,' I was very frightened. It really shook me up. They let me go after an hour, without so much as an apology. I was told, finally, that they were looking for a very dangerous fugitive from justice, from Palestine. Wherever he *is* – he is a member of the notorious Stern Gang.

I never saw the sun in seven days. It was a wonderful Christmas. All my family was together, and my sisters brought some Yanks home, who are stationed at Kew Gardens.

My father got a turkey! A huge, beautiful turkey. It was cooked beautifully by mum, and had wonderful stuffing. Getting the turkey was a real coup. Meat is rationed, fiercely, our butcher has about five hundred clientele, and he only had about thirty turkeys. He decided to have drawings. Every ration book was to be good for a numbered lottery ticket. Since my dad is an expert poulterer (he did that for a living, before I was born) he inspected every turkey hanging up in the shop. He noted the number on the absolute prize bird, (number 202). Then, he went outside, got on his bike, and rode to Wembley, to a stationer's shop. He bought a book of tickets, extracted the ticket with the number, 202, and rode back to the butcher, proffering it triumphantly. That is how he got the turkey. It was so good that nobody had any qualms about the poor buggers who missed out, with the right number. We had plum pudding, iced cake, and all the trimmings, as they say. It all went too soon, as always. The weather stayed the same, grey fog.

I got back today, via Antwerp, where a giant explosion occurred. Just like the one we saw from the air, when we were escorting HM The King. The lorry we were in, to take us to B.60 jumped three feet in to the air! Was it, I wonder, another V-2?

When we got to Grimbergen, we found that everyone had gone. (There were a couple of types from 66, and three from 331 Squadron.) There was no time to visit Louise's house.

We got a transport here. My first rotten shock. Big Mac went in, on Christmas day. I am in tears, and am very low. Only this morning, when I left, Mum said to me, 'Now, you be sure to tell Mac that his Christmas dinner is walking around at the end of the garden, in the chicken house.' Oh, what a bloody rotten war this is. I will never be prepared for the death of my friends. And it just goes on, doesn't it. It just bloody well goes *on*.

December 29th, B.79, Woensdrecht

Another of those days when everything starts off so well, and then turns to ashes. Peter Attwooll was killed today, and I am numb. No more Pete to chide us, laugh with us, make washing boards and wash basins from old petrol tins. I am numb, so that I cannot even be sick. I remember the Pete who was always trying to improve his flying, his gunnery, his bombing – with so many questions. Why? Who said? How do you know *that*, for sure? The Pete who took the flak as it came, never complaining, never whining. The Pete who was always willing to climb in that cockpit to 'have another go'. The Pete who did *not* get 'browned off' when he was detailed for a show a half hour prior to squadron release. I think of the Pete, lachrymose after three beers, and the fears he had for his sister – in the event – well. I think of him as I last saw him – right before lunch. It was the first I had seen of him since the fight we had, slopping in the mud at Grimbergen. He was standing with Harry Lea, Eckert, Sandy Powell, and the new Canadian bod we've just picked up, during the move. George Boudreau. They were waiting for the ops telephone to ring. Pete was staring into space, lost in thought. Then his head turned, and we saw each other, full-faced. I waved at him. His expression was quite blank. I felt very awkward, and I turned away. I thought that I would make up with him later today. How idiotic of me not to make peace, before he took off.

The day started well. I got a sudden call this morning for a show right after breakfast. Armed recce in the Dordrecht area. We bombed and strafed a train in the Scheuwens area. We had a hell of a good strafe on the second pass. I was feeling good, because I had 'broken my duck' – that is, coming back off leave, doing my first post leave show, and beating that old nemesis, superstition, again.

All day long, we have been operating in section fours, and I went back to our new hut after lunch, fully expecting to be operating again. I suppose I corked off for a while, reading a book about sailing (I have never sailed) on my new cot. I was pleased to see, on arrival here, that the Germans left their iron camp beds to us, when they left, in a rush. Lying on a real bed with real mattress biscuits after weeks on the canvas cots is a luxury.

Suddenly, I sat upright, went outside and thumbed a ride with Dave Fyfe to flight. As soon as we got there, we met Harry Lea. The chaps were actually laughing about Pete's crash landing, the way he was 'talking himself down' after he got hit. The last words he spoke were enthusiastic. 'Glycol's all gone, I think. Temps are off the clock. I've found a beautiful field here. Catch up – later.'

An hour later the adj came in, with Corporal Turner. 'We've got some bad news for you. Peter Attwooll didn't make it. He crashed and his plane went on fire. There were soldiers nearby – but they couldn't get near. He may have forgotten to cut the switches.'

That was all. We had tea together, the rest of us in 'our hut' and hardly anyone spoke during the meal. Later, I walked into the mess. (The Germans left two messes, here) and talked with some of the fellows from 66. Woody Woodhouse, Mike Larson and Johnny Turk. They said they were sorry about Pete, who was quite popular with them. I asked about Mac McLeod. Johnny Turk said it. 'If you've gotta go, sport, might as well go the way Mac went. We had a bloody tre-*men*-dous piss up on Christmas Eve. Right here. We made a connection, weeks ago. Cases of champagne from Rheims. Mac didn't leave till it was all gone. Matter of fact he took a bottle to bed with him. I saw him right before he got into the cockpit at eight o'clock. He said, 'Johnny. My poor fuckin' noggin is pounding like a fuckin' trip hammer.' He got a direct hit on the first pass. Straight into the deck. He's probably *still* pissed – *up there*.'

Tomorrow, Larry Hyland I are going to the oyster beds on the coast. It is very near here. They (the oystermen) will swap Zealand oysters, one small barrel for a carton of cigarettes. Who discovered the oyster beds? Pete Attwooll discovered the oyster beds.

December 31st, B.79, Woensdrecht

This place is as weird as its name. Set close to the sea, which is grey and green, and sometimes almost black, it is set in dark woods, with pines and firs so thick that you can easily get lost in them. Not that you'd want to go far in. They say that the Germans have mined them solidly, so that our invading forces could not take them by surprise. Outside of the snarl of Merlin engines, this aerodrome is like a sanctuary. The runway bomb holes have been repaired. It is easy to contemplate how the Huns must have *loved* this place, with warm barracks, messes, *baths*, and showers. The huts are very solidly timbered, and the windows have green shutters, of solid steel. Each hut is surrounded by a two feet thick, brick wall, for bomb blast protection.

How many times did we bomb and strafe this 'drome? It must have been six, or seven times. Maybe twenty times, if you count the efforts by all of us, 66, 331 and 332. It was *here* that Larry Hyland claimed (and still claims) that he saw black uniformed SS officers manning the gun pits when we strafed them. I can *still* see the approach we took, with Bradley leading, coming in at sea level, and surprising them – *not at all*.

Harry Lea led us on a bomb and strafe show this afternoon. Bombing Hun strong positions at Drongelen. Nearly every bomb found the target, and when we left, there were big fires, and spreading. No flak that I saw, but you never know.

After de-briefing, the adj asked me to drop in and see R.M.P. Sampson. I *like* Sampson. He came right to the point. 'Ted, would you do me, and the rest of us a big favour? Now, before you say "Yes" – it could be a painful experience. I'm asking you to go with Warrant Officer Jackson to Breda tomorrow. Your friend Peter Attwooll is to be buried in the cemetery, and since you were the closest friend he had, I wonder if you wouldn't be too upset to perform this sad duty?'

Of course, I said I would. I did not jump at my answer, saying I would be happy to go, because I am *not*. The very thought of funerals makes me very sad. My last school, Ealing Modern, was not far from a cemetery, and I remember, at fourteen, crossing the street where there was a funeral in progress. I would shudder at the women's black clothes, and veer away, in case I met the mourners' eyes with my own.

Tomorrow, Breda. Also New Year's Day. There will be no party tonight.

Extracts from the Operations Record Book 127 Squadron, RAF 132 (Norwegian) Wing

B.60, 3rd December 1944: Led by S/Ldr Easby 66 and 127 Squadrons were detailed as close escort to thirty Mitchells bombing a target in Kalden – Kirchen area. Under F/Lt Hillwood twelve aircraft of 127 Squadron were airborne at 0855 hours. The bombers were met at the rendezvous point over Eindhoven and escorted uneventfully to the target where the bombing was concentrated in spite of a smoke screen put up by the enemy. Intense accurate flak was encountered by the bombers. One Me262 was seen in the target area at about 25,000 feet. On the way back one aircraft with a glycol leak made a crash landing two miles south of Weert, (AC Category E) Pilot F/S Wallace unhurt. The squadron landed at base at 1035 hours. Weather 3/10ths. 5000 to 7000 feet.

B.60, 5th December: 331 and 127 Squadrons were detailed as escort to Mitchells and Bostons bombing Dremmen. Twelve aircraft of the Squadron led by F/Lt Hillwood were airborne at 0920 hours. The bombers were met at the rendezvous point and escorted to the target where the bombing was concentrated. Moderate inaccurate heavy flak from target area. A lone Spitfire V 'C' was seen at 0940 hours west of Aachen. It made several circuits round the bombers and when bounced by one of our aircraft made off towards Germany. The markings appeared to be friendly. Aircraft landed back to base at 1040 hours.

B.60, 7th December: 127 and 66 Squadrons were detailed for an armed recce in the Munster area. Twelve aircraft of 127 Squadron led by F/Lt Hillwood took off from base at 0930 hours. Two aircraft returned early owing to R/T trouble, the remainder carried on the operation but the mission proved abortive due to bad weather, landing at B.78 at 1045 hours. Taking off from B.78 at 1630 landing at base at 1650 hours, all aircraft carried two 250 lb bombs. F/Os McCallum, Round and Nowland (all Canadians) arrived from 84 GSU.

B.60, 8th December: 66 and 127 Squadrons were detailed to carry out an armed recce in the Enschede–Munster–Dorster area. Eight aircraft of the squadron were airborne from B.70 under F/Lt Doyle at 1125 hours. Each aircraft carried two 250 lb bombs and was fitted with a long range fuel tank. After sweeping uneventfully in the area, the squadron attacked a factory and railway at Neede (A.2394) and dropped their bombs in a dive from 7000 to 1500 feet.

Three direct hits were scored on the factory along side the railway line and a tall chimney was seen to collapse. There was also one cut on the railway line. The target was also strafed. While the squadron was reforming an Me109 attacked Blue four from behind, but was himself shot down and seen to crash to the ground near Neede, the claim is shared by F/S Griffin and F/S Attwooll. The Spitfire flown by W/O Morisson (Free French) (Blue four) was damaged but landed at B.80 safely, pilot uninjured. Intense accurate light flak was experienced by F/S Griffin in the Neede area, when he followed the Me109 down to see it crash. The Squadron landed back to base at 1300 hours. WO Mallandaine (Canadian) arrived on posting from 84 GSU.

B.60, 12th December: Two Spitfires took off at 0850 on a weather recce in the Arnhem/Utrecht area landing at base at 0935 hours. Weather 9–10/10ths at 1200 feet, above 7000 feet frequent showers, visibility below cloud three to four miles.

S/L RMF Sampson DFC arrived on posting from No 84 GSU. He took over command of the squadron effective 10.12.44. replacing S/L Smik who was reported missing on 28.11.44.

B.60, 13th December: Slight rain and thick haze prevented operations.

B.60, 14th December: Another day of 'ropey' weather. F/Lt Doyle posted tour-expired. He is the last but one of the old Middle East campaigners to be disposed of as tour-expired.

B.60, 23rd December: Four aircraft under F/Lt Covington carried out an uneventful armed weather recce in the Amersfoort–Zwolle–Enschede area, taking off at 0820 and landed at 0930 hours. The weather was reported suitable for flying with 3–4/10ths. at 8–9000 feet.

66 and 127 Squadrons were detailed for a fighter sweep in the Aachen–Trier–Bonn area. Eleven aircraft of the squadron under S/Ldr Sampson were airborne at 1350 hours and patrolled uneventfully in the area. The only item of interest was the sight of snow on the ground in Germany. The squadron landed at 1545 hours.

Two aircraft under F/Lt Covington carried out an uneventful patrol off Flushing for midget submarines which had been reported throughout the day. They took off at 1435 hours and landed back at base at 1555 hours.

B.79, 24th December: Two aircraft were airborne at 1110 hours on a fighter sweep to Northern Holland, S/Ldr Sampson was leading. Two trains facing north were seen at Zwolle at 1145 hours but were too close to the Marshalling Yards to be attacked. Soon afterwards five barges were observed on the canal near Kampen Z.7543 and it was intended to attack these on the return trip but, by then, they had disappeared. The area north of Kampen and Meppel appeared to be deserted and no movement was seen. The squadron landed at 1240 hours.

Twelve aircraft under S/Ldr Sampson were airborne at 1520 hours to cover the withdrawal of heavy bombers from the Aachen–Cologne area. The squadron was diverted for Huns reported north of Essen but nothing was seen and the patrol was uneventful, landing back at base at 1655 hours.

B.79, 25th December: 66 and 127 Squadrons were detailed for a fighter sweep in the Twente/Rheine area with W/Cdr Berg leading. Eleven aircraft took off at 0855 hours. A train with approximately ten wagons was attacked with

(Right) Squadron Leader F.W. Lister, DSO, DFC, who was shot down on his first mission with 127 (30th October 1944), survived and came back to lead 127 until its disbandment on 30th April 1945.

(Below) Spitfires being armed, December 1944, Belgium

Arming Spitfires, December 1944

from the feet end of the blanket. The Dutch civilians stepped back with gasps of horror. He couldn't listen to the chaplain any more, he was crying too much. He told himself that fighter pilots didn't cry, but he couldn't stop till it was all over. He did not make much noise, crying. When he got back to the airfield, he told the rest of the squadron pilots, and some of them had moist eyes, too. They thought that was a hell of a way to get buried, and said so.

Three weeks later he went back to Breda with a sergeant photographer to take pictures. It rained on the way. When they got to the grave they found it piled high with horse manure. The wooden cross lay on the ground. He left the sergeant while he went to borrow two shovels. They cleared the dung off and made a smooth mound. They replaced the cross, and he walked round the graveyard to find the best wreaths. He borrowed four, and they placed them on the grave. Then they took pictures.

When he went home on leave, he took the photos to Pete's sister, who was an orphan of eighteen, who lived with an aunt and an uncle who was incapacitated. Eckert was on leave, too, and went with him. Pete's sister was very brave and proud, and she said how well kept the grave looked. He said yes, and the funeral was as you would have wanted it. He was glad he had taken the pictures.

January 4th, 1945, B.79, Woensdrecht

We were talking about the move from B.60, today.

As usual, it was all quite quick. One minute, all personnel are around, everything normal. Night falls, and in the morning, the ground crews are decimated. One third or more, advance party, went off in the night. Pilots are briefed, seemingly last, because all that eighteen of them do is climb into a cockpit and fly to the new venue. The boys tried to mask their getaway from Louis and Louise and Pieter until the last minute, but somehow dear old Louise could not be fooled. She made kookembachers, and she made little rock cakes, and she made tea, and tinned pink salmon sandwiches. The boys had to sit down in the spacious cold old kitchen, and have tea.

Zhilbare was first to get up, and was surprised when Eckert stopped his passage. He opened Zhilbare's tunic, removed his 'flak jacket' money belt, unzipped it, and removed a wad of guilders. Next, he opened his own wallet, and extracted his own 'escape money.' (I'm surprised that Eckert had never spent a sou of *his* own.) Putting them together, he took Louise's hand, and pressed the stack of money into it. She tried to give the money back, but Eckert smilingly said, 'No, no, Louise – it's for the *boy*.' He pointed to Pieter, whose eyes, I'm told, were wide, and moist.

R.M.P. Sampson asked me to do another favour today. This was, would I be good enough to write a complete report on the débâcle that was Pete's burial. Of course, I *did.* It is to go directly to Group Captain Morris. I will be very much surprised if he isn't shaken up when he reads it.

Our squadron flight hut is quite cozy. It still has fir branches tied to the rafters, that the boys brought in for Christmas decoration. I saw a telegram on the cork notice board today. I couldn't make it out, at first. It reads 'Wishing all the wonderful boys of one-two-seven a bonzer Christmas. Our hearts go out to all of you. Much love – may you be safe.' Signed 'The Richardsons.' I must have stood looking at it for five minutes when it clicked. 'The Richardsons.' Gordon's mum and dad. They must be wonderful people.

One op today. Armed recce – Zutphen, Zwolle, Amersfoort, Arnhem. Cold as hell. I froze for about an hour. Then someone on the r/t broke in – 'MET below, looks like a staff car – three o'clock, proceeding east.' Well we went down to the deck, and I got it right in my sights. Even as I pressed the gun button I was thinking, this is for Pete, you bastards. . . . Suddenly the two back doors opened and two bods flew out, while it was going top speed, one from each side. I don't know if they got hit or not, but we totally destroyed the car. It was flaming when we re-formed.

January 6th, 1945, B.79, Woensdrecht

I have been at sixes and sevens since Pete was killed. I have not been able to concentrate. I have simply not been aware. I have even made up situations that I know, do not exist. Three days ago, I even came close to telling Sandy Powell that we had better get together and pack Pete's gear, so we could send the personal stuff home. I opened my mouth, and before the words could come out, I remembered. I had participated in packing it before I went to Breda. In fact, I did the personal stuff myself – December 30th.

I was so shaken when I got back after the funeral that I could not comprehend how lucky we were that the entire wing, seemingly, was airborne, when the Hun struck. We believe this to be his last big effort. Apparently he mustered every aircraft he could find, serviceable, and put it into the air. He could not have had better weather. A day that began with frozen rain, sleet, broke into clear crisp sunlight, with about five-tenths cloud cover. He put a veritable

Balbo together, with about half of them seasoned pilots, and the other half, absolute sprogs. He hit the airfields and caught them by surprise. The Balbo never flew above fifty feet on the approaches, so they were not picked up by radar. They did massive damage on some airstrips, with our Mitchells and Bostons and Marauders, sitting ducks on the ground. We, here, suffered little damage, and our gunners knocked down an FW190. The pilot pulled the stick back and climbed to stall point, about 600 feet, glycol streaming, when he baled out. He came down right near our dispersal and was arrested by our newest pilot, N.J. 'Robbie' Robinson, who liberated his Luger automatic. He turned out to be just a kid, a green sprog, and he was interrogated by our wing spies. I was told that the kid had a folded piece of paper, typed, in his flying boot. It showed how green the GAF pilots are, today. There was a list of 'Do's' and 'Don'ts' – about twenty. The last one, (naturally in German) is reputed to have said, 'When you get back to your base, do *not* forget to lower your undercarriage!'

Naturally, everyone was full of this when I got back from the funeral, but I was in such a total, mental fog, that I simply could not take it in. It all seemed so puny, so meaningless, compared to the loss of Peter. I was so much in a fog that I only found out yesterday that Zhilbare is no longer with us. I realized, suddenly, that I had not seen him since returning from leave. I turned to Sandy and Larry and said, 'Where's Zhilbare? Did he go on leave after Eckert took him for money for Louise?'

They both broke out, laughing. 'Do you mean you haven't missed him?' said Sandy, 'Tell him how you caught him playing cowboy-six-gun, Larry!' They laughed again. It seems that the day after the boys landed here, a group of 66 pilots liberated some German machine pistols and took them to the blast bay which had been used as the Huns' ground target firing range. Zhilbare heard about it, and went there with his .38 Smith and Wesson revolver, strapped to his thigh. He gave an exhibition of quick 'draw and fire' to the boys from 66, five times. The sixth time – last bullet – things went awry. He pulled the trigger before the revolver had cleared his holster. He shot himself in the right calf. Zhilbare was funny to the last. As he was being stretcher-lifted into the meat wagon, he pulled his thick money belt from his tunic. 'Hylin,' he said, 'for God's sake! Take care of my flak jacket!'

Jerry's losses on New Year's day must have been costly. I have done two semi-sweeps in the last two days, and we haven't seen one German kite. Even the Me262's have departed. We have seen the condensation trails of a number of V-2 rockets in the last couple of weeks. They are firing them more on the port of Antwerp, rather than London. I'm glad of that. I am also glad that our heavy boys and the Yanks' B.17's and 24's bombed the hell out of Peenemünde. They say that Jerry had enough to destroy half of London.

January 16th, 1945, B.79, Woensdrecht
We have had duff weather for a week. It has rained and sleeted, day after day, turning to snow at night. We had a hell of a shock two days ago. A V-1 flying bomb 'shook us rigid' as the airmen are wont to say. We were in our big room in the hut where we sleep.

We had just been released. Hyland came in to place the last of his gear in his new bed space. He has decided to move in with us, taking over Pete's bed. Pete's old bed has coil springs, so since Eckert, Sandy, Paddy and I are too superstitious (never sleep in a dead man's bed) Larry decided *he* would defy superstition for coil springs. One by one they came into our room, to ask if we planned to go to town with the three tonner. In addition to people and beds, we had three canvas toilet bowls on wooden stands – each with dirty shaving water.

Suddenly we heard a shocking roar of engine blast, and Larry standing next to the door, jumped. 'Get out!' he yelled. 'Fuckin' one-nineties!'

Everybody charged the door, and jammed in a mass of flesh, as an enormous explosion seemed to lift the entire hut from its base. We *fell* through the door, and the big space in the outer blast wall. Smoke was rising between the pines, way beyond the officers' quarters, and the air was full of debris. It took us many minutes to deduce the cause. It was a flying bomb that had the misfortune to run into icing clouds. It had been gradually forced down by the weight of ice until it struck the trees straight and level at over 350 miles an hour. After all the excitement died, everyone went away. Everyone that is, but Gordie Richardson and Dave Fyfe. They were both in bathtubs, next door to each other, in the bath house. Both dived head down into the water as the wire re-inforced windows shattered. Both of them received minor cuts and abrasions on the cheeks of their arses. They spent the next hour or more in surgery, with Doc Blanchard picking out shafts of glass and glass splinters from their arses with tweezers. Nobody else was even grazed.

This V-1 was targeted for Antwerp, so the diversion of the bomb was probably a life saver to some troops or civilians.

One op today, a combination of escort to Mitchells, very very cold at 15,000 feet, and a sweep in the Enschede–Rheine area. The escort went well – but the sweep produced no Hun aircraft. The heavy flak, we drew was intense. We dived and twisted out of it. None of us was hit.

January 17th, 1945, B.79, Woensdrecht

Today was a blast of a day, in every way. Really socked in with sea fog, and I was not alone in hoping that no shows would develop. I felt relatively safe, since Paddy and I were on Pink Section, and we knew there was not much chance of Jerry bouncing us, in view of the weather.

It was about three-thirty when Wingco Berg came bouncing in, tugging at his yellow pigskin gloves and positively beaming. 'Hello, boys! I've got just the very thing to liven up a dull winter day. Maasluis. We're going to dive-bomb some miniature submarine pens. Let's go to briefing, right away!'

Suddenly Eckert jumped up, and grabbed the chalk eraser from the 'team' ops blackboard. With one sweep he erased his name, Blue Three, and chalked in S-M-I-T-H! I couldn't believe my eyes. 'Eckert, you bastard,' I said, 'I'm not subbing for you! I'm on Pink Section, for Christ's sake!' He gave me a sly grin. 'Not *now*, you're not, sport! Now *I'm* on Pink Section! Come on, Sport! You can sub for your old Aussie mate, can't yer? You know, me bein' close to tour-ex, and all *that.* I've decided to try to just do the easy ones from here on. You take my place, you'll be all right, sport!'

Well, it wasn't worth a fight – certainly not with Eckert. Not only is he my oppo, but he is bigger, and stronger than me.

Before I knew it I was in the lorry and over at ops. Berg opted to lead us, and I was certainly pleased that of three squadrons, we would be going in *first*. When we got back to flight, Eckert was sitting there with Paddy, playing draughts.

Harry Lea took me on one side. 'This new chap, Birbeck,' he said. 'He's back for second tour. His problem is that he's never done much air to ground, Smithy. I wonder if you'd be good enough to gen him up on the bomb switches, and perhaps, well, you know, give him a confidence boost.'

Of course, I did. I took him out to my aeroplane, and noted that the name C.R. Birbeck was painted in white dope, on the upturned collar of his Irvin jacket. 'Why are you *C.R.* Birbeck, when you ask us to call you *Joe*?' I asked.

'Frankly,' he answered, 'I don't like the stiffness of either of my two Christian names, so I am just C.R. for RAF records.' It seemed simple enough. I went over the switches procedure, which switches arm bombs, the real difference between fuses (11 second delay versus .025, which is just shy of instantaneous, and must not be used for very low level bombing). We chatted awhile, and I did my best to assure him that he would very soon get used to air to ground. (I don't think I ever will.)

The weather was foul. Only good flying brought the three squadrons over the target at precisely the right moment. It was snowing heavily over the target, and the turbulence was cruel. We were bouncing in the air like rubber balls. Visibility was so bad that it was even hard to read the RAB markings on Wingco Berg's fuselage. As always, Rolf Berg was as cool as a cucumber. 'This is Monty Red Leader. Target ten o'clock below. Echelon starboard.'

Harry Lea, Blue Leader, throttled up and steep turned, dived slightly and slid over the starboard. We followed, one, two, three. I was flying Blue Three. 'Monty Squadron. Arm bombs. Going in, eight to three.' The ground was covered in snow, and the target was unmistakable, seven long flat roofed buildings, probably concrete, parallel to each other, right on the water. On the ground, they knew what we had come for. Black 88 puffs appeared all round us, even before we rolled over for the dive.

'Monty Squadron. In we go.'

The flak looked as shit-scaring as Zwolle, I took great lungfuls of oxygen as I sighted my aeroplane on the centre building, in an almost vertical dive. My entire body went freezing numb as I pressed the bomb tits as radio silence was broken. It was a halting, hesitant, voice, trying desperately to sound calm. 'Hello (pause) Monty (pause) Red – Leader. Monty – Red – Two. I've been (pause) badly hit.'

'This is Monty Red Leader. Bail out! Bail out!'

'Red Leader – I will try . . . not much –' And that was it.

There was no second strafing pass. The flak was so thick it became almost every squadron, every section for itself. We were in the teeth of a blizzard, and Blue Two lost Blue Leader. I felt that very strange feeling of elation – the second that I knew we had cleared the flak area. Blue Two formed up on my port side as we flew back. Again, the sweat was turning cold on my back. I knew my back was saturated. I never knew a more welcome sight than our runway. On the final approach, with canopy opened, I was half blind from the driving snow on my goggles.

I landed, and taxied into dispersal. I could barely discern the other pilots who had landed – *all* running for shelter from the snow.

I switched off, unlocked the halfdoor, and climbed down. *There*, not five feet away, was Paddy Crozier. He was wearing an Irvin jacket, collar up, his head half buried. On the collar I read 'C.R. Birbeck'. That beautiful Irish voice, consoling. 'I heard it was a really bad target, Smithy.'

'It was.'

'Poor Joe. Got shot down on his – second show, was it?'

'It was.'

'Eckert and I were playin' draughts – you know – and we got the news on the red telephone. You know, Eddie, of all the bloody callous men there are – Eckert takes the cake! The red phone rang, and Eckert picked it up. Someone from ops must have asked him a question. He turned his head to look at the readiness board. 'Red Two is C.R. Birbeck.' Then, he said, '*Oh.*' That's all he said. Then he walked across the room to the wooden plank seat, and picked up Joe Birbeck's Irvin jacket. He said, 'Paddy. This is *your* lucky day, sport. Birbeck got the chop. You get his jacket.' 'Isn't, that callous, Eddie? Is *that – not* – callous?' Then, suddenly, he *beamed*. 'It fits me very well, don't you think?'

There will never be another Paddy Crozier.

Group Captain Morris has issued an order. No pilot from 132 Wing is to attend the funeral of any other pilot from here on.

January 18th, 1945, B.79, Woensdrecht

I do not believe that I will ever be more afraid, or more depressed. I could not sleep a wink, and I am haunted by the words of Joe Birbeck. We have all discussed it, those of us who were on the show. Was it – what we *heard* – or was the hesitation due to a short in his r/t?

We will never know. There was a report, unconfirmed, that he was seen 'limping' away, somewhere over Overflakkee. Spy Johnson says *someone* thought Birbeck baled out. There is no evidence of this. The only thing certain, as Eckert says, is that Paddy has an Irvin jacket.

I had a verbal fight today, with two of the cooks. It happened because I turned left instead of right, immediately following lunch. I found myself at the rear of the mess hall, where the wide doors were open. There must have been 25 Dutch children queuing at the doors, and the sight brought me close to tears. They were standing in the cold, blue, pinched faces, clothed in threadbare garments, with holes in the elbows, socks, bedraggled around the ankles with holes in the heels. Some had large, staring eyes, appearing larger because the cheekbones were so prominent, due to semi-starvation. All were carrying some kind of bucket, from slop buckets to gallon paint buckets. The latter had crude carrying handles made of wire which was looped through holes in the top. They came from the village, and they were here to get a share of our leftover food. I watched one cook ladling the food into a bucket, and I was at least, pleased that the RAF could help this very poor country feed its people. Then my eyes drifted to the tub he was ladling *from*. I was appalled. The cooks had steeped the meat course with the stewed cherries and the blancmange. I showed my anger to the two cooks in a verbal barrage, when one of them asked, what did it matter, it all goes down to the same place. I walked away, shocked. I looked back at the children and could control my emotions no longer. I walked back to our hut, crying as I never cried before. I must have cried for fifteen minutes. How I wish the Pattons and the Montgomerys could have seen those children today.

Some of the boys got the jeep this afternoon and went down to the oyster beds. They bartered Yank cigarettes for two barrels of oysters. The practice is to get bread and margarine from the mess, and to toast slices of bread by pressing them against the side of the red hot stove that is used to warm the hut.

We slather margarine on the toast, and make overstuffed sandwiches. I was given one, and was about to bite into it, when I thought of the Dutch children. I gave it back. I may not eat, tomorrow, either.

I got this letter, today. Who knows where it has been? It has been in transit since the middle of December. It tells me more in the postscript than anywhere else. I wonder if Bill Williams is still alive?

567 W/O. Williams S.L.
124 Wing
247 Squadron
R.A.F.
B.L.A.

Tuesday 12th

Dear Spiv,

Fanks fer yer letter cock and it warms me art to ear that yer O.K.

I'm sorry I aint wrote before but I jist got back orf leaf and ave ad to ave a week ter git over hit. Talk about pissed, gorblimey.

I met me mate wots a poor bleeding infantry basher, been arsole crawling and got his stripe and we was on the piss all day.

I met a smashing bit o' grumble and grunt and er china and wiv a couple of over tarts made a good gang.

On Fersdie dinner time I met Joycey art of Freds Cafe and she's bleeding well expectin agin, cor she dun arf like her little bit.

Says ole Tom got knocked orf agin taking bets darn the mews. Soppy bleeder 'es.

It got up my snout to ear abart those bleeding bits o' boys getting knocked orf agin. There ought ter be a law again those cowsons. Talking abart cowsons, that split wot 'as been getting in the Bedford Arms 'as got is lot. Some o' the Martin boys 'ad a go at im cos the bleeding copper tried ter knock young Vera orf fer oring, just as if she'd awk hers.

Yer remember Phil Lewis 'oo used ter do a bit of boxin' up the Vale well I saw him selling dog papers in the 'Cock' one night. Didn't even say wotcher to me. I bet 'es doing a bit of fiddling to make 'im all igh and bleeding mighty ey! if yer go art fer a drink any night yer 'ome go up the 'Black 'Orse' they got a shit ot band up there nar. . . .

Well I'm goin ter Kip nar ole cock so I'll say cheerio for nar, ope ter see yer soon good drinking.

Your great Pal

Bill

Ken Brown is a POW. Ken Morse and Ken Love are going strong.

January 22nd, 1945, B.79, Woensdrecht

When my cockpit canopy is closed, a small black hard rubber ball hangs just above my head. Two cable wires run through the ball, and they are run through a channel to connect with a shiny steel pin which rests in a channel at the canopy base on each side of the cockpit. I never climb into the cockpit without mentally practising three moves, the black ball, my oxygen connection, and my r/t connection. I practise, one, two, three, over and *over* and *over*. These are the three things which will get me *out*, if I have to bail out. I am assured that a quick strong tug on the ball will pull out the pins, and the canopy will fly away with a double ram of my elbows. I practise *that*, also. I have never told anyone this.

I might have had to yank the black ball today, but I didn't know about it. Had I known I was hit and the damage caused, I might well have baled out. As it was, I came back from the show, sick at heart, because Gordon Richardson, my second favourite Aussie did not come back. Harry led us, since R.M.P. Sampson has been upped to wing commander, and has been posted to command 145 Wing. Gordon must have got it in the dive, because we never heard another word from him. Will our losses keep on, until none of us is left?

It was an oxygen factory at Alblassedam. Our bombing was not all that good, from what I could see on the ground. When we reformed at angels eight, the ground 88's opened up. I saw three bursts, instead of four. My aeroplane jumped, suddenly and I could not conceive why. Harry Lea came on r/t to call off by section. That was when we realized that Gordon was not with us.

When I taxied in and switched off, Corporal Fowler stood on my port wing. I pulled my helmet off.

His words were, '*We've* been hit, sir. Are you aware?'

It sounded so odd, so very archaic. Yet I was quite touched. I climbed out of the cockpit, jumped to the ground, and clapped a hand on his shoulder. I said, why don't we take a look, together. I may well have sounded a trifle patronising, but if I did, I changed my attitude very quickly. Here were three holes, one of them big enough to put my head through. All holes which did the damage were behind the cockpit, on the underside of the fuselage. This then, was what had caused that jump – that push upwards that I had felt. Fowler got down on the ground, under the big hole.

'Look at this, Mr Smith,' he said. 'You're lucky to be alive.' I got down to his level. My elevator cables were held together, on the starboard side, by one strand of wire. Beads of sweat appeared on my forehead, and I wiped them away.

Fowler is a very good type. *All* of our ground crews are very good types. I thanked him very much for his concern.

Everyone is very glum, at the moment. With the news that Squadron Leader Sampson is posted, we are again without a skipper. A squadron is rudderless without a skipper. We are depressed, we older types, because we have got the reputation of being the 'Hard Luck' Squadron. Wingco Berg makes no bones about that. The fact is that he leads us on any mission that calls for a wing effort. Translated by 66, 331 and 332, this means we are the bottom of the pile, a notion that is simply not true. Only yesterday, we talked about it, and Paddy said it best.

I have not had a comfortable week since Bradley was posted. Somebody said Bradley is wing commander. He has also been awarded a DSO.

There are days when my feet are so leaden that I find it difficult to climb on to the port wing – let alone get into the cockpit. The thrill I once had, anticipating the start up roar of the engine, is turning into a literal nightmare. I wake up, sweating, in a room that is cold.

January 31st, 1945, B.79, Woensdrecht
It has been a most depressing 'rest of the month'. The weather has been most foul. I flew on one show on the 24th, my 55th sortie. This was a bombing show, north of Nijmegan. Cloud covered the target. Harry Lea took Red Section down below cloud, they overshot – and we aborted the mission, bringing the bombs back. My aeroplane still has them on. Nobody, including *me*, has flown it for seven days.

We have a whole new bunch of bods, and they are working out just wizard. While it seems like only yesterday that they were posted to us, Coxell, Wallace, Jimmy Harris, and Wade are all well seasoned. Both Jock Wallace and Wade have suffered prangs, and have walked away. (One was flak, one was engine trouble.) I admire Coxell's guts. He volunteered for this, after having been shot down over Italy, getting hidden by villagers for weeks, going underground, and finally walking back to our side of the lines. I think I would have had enough, by then, but after getting back to London and survivor's leave, Coxell *volunteered*. He says he did it because he wanted to fly Spitfires. In Italy, he flew Kittyhawks. Among the new bods is Bunny Bundara, Australian. He is a quiet one, but at times, very funny. He came in the Flight hut the other day, steamingly browned off. It seems he went over to the bogs for his morning constitutional and took the first cubicle, by the main door. The Germans built the cubicles without doors. Bunny was sitting on the first throne, then, when the door opened, revealing an officer from 66. Bunny looked up from the Australian newspaper he was reading, and welcomed the flight lieutenant with his usual, 'Good'ay, mate.'

Apparently the officer was not amused. 'Who in *hell* do you think you are, sergeant. Don't you know that I'm an officer?'

Bunny held the intruder's gaze, and replied, 'First of all, cobber, I'm a *flight* sergeant, *not* sergeant. Second, you can throw every page of the King's Rules and Regulations at me, and I'll never give you a salute when I'm takin' a shit! You got that, cobber?' We all laughed over that one.

We have all been closer, lately, officers and non-coms. We have been down to Woensdrecht together, even though there is not much to do. (The beer is awful, but one of the places has three billiard tables, without pockets, so one can knock the balls around.) Peter Hillwood went on leave and was posted, tour-ex. He only came back for his gear, and most of us didn't see him. Dave Fyfe is gone, same reason. Sammy Roth is still here. New officers, Alan Willis – Rhodesian – and Robbie Robinson – Australian. Alan Willis was the heavyweight champion boxer of Southern Rhodesia, N.J. 'Robbie' Robinson is Alan Willis's oppo, and they make an excitable pair. Harry Lea, who came to us with F.W. Lister DFC (Freddie) is *super*. He is a very good *leader* – no toffee-nosed bullshit – and he has a great sense of humour.

He proved it again, today, right before squadron release. He called us all down to flight. Most of us thought we were in for another bloody late afternoon show. We shuffled into the hut, which is divided into two rooms. One, our flight briefing room, and another, smaller room. (We have begun carpentry in the room, converting it to a squadron bar and lounge. The Germans left us tons of lumber.)

Harry made us sit for ten minutes, while we expected Wingco Berg to come striding in any moment, pulling on the cuffs of his pig-skin gloves, inviting us to 'Just another little show, boys!' Finally, Harry got up, rapped three times on the door to the other room. Surprise! Out stepped a smiling, though wan-faced – Freddie Lister.

Of course, it caught all the new fellows by surprise – but Eckert, Paddy, Griffin, Len Feltham, Sandy and I all *cheered*! Freddie motioned us to silence. Then he opened with, 'As I was saying, before I was so *rudely* interrupted. . . !'

There was a burst of laughter, but there was, also, a moist eye, here and there. Freddie is back! I don't know what we are going to *do* – but I know we will do it *well*.

(Left) 'Big Mac' McLeod of 66 Squadron, who was shot down and killed on Christmas Day, 1944. *(Right)* The author's oldest friend, Bob Bode, DFC, DFM, photographed on leave

Spitfire Mark XVI with rocket projectile launcher

(Left) Harry Lea, 'B' Flight Commander, 127 Squadron, with Freddie Lister, cavorting on leave in 1945.

Spitfire Mark XVIE

Extracts from the Operations Record Book 127 Squadron, RAF 132 (Norwegian) Wing

B.79, 1st January, 1945: 66 and 127 Squadrons were detailed to escort Mitchells and Bostons bombing Dasburg. Eleven aircraft of 127 Squadron led by S/Ldr Sampson were airborne at 0910 hours, and carried out an uneventful sweep in the target area. The bombing was not observed. Moderate heavy and light flak was experienced from the German salient area. Two aircraft returned early due to missing the formation, five aircraft landed at B.60 owing to shortage of petrol. The remainder landed at base at 1110 hours.

Three aircraft under F/Lt Covington were scrambled at 0940 hours for Huns in the area. They were ordered to cover Antwerp but the Huns had by then disappeared and there was nothing to report, landing back at 1050 hours.

66 and 127 Squadrons were airborne at 1345 hours on a Fighter Sweep in the Enschede/Rheine area but the sweep was completely uneventful. There was meagre, accurate, heavy flak reported from Deventer. One aircraft returned early with mechanical trouble. The Squadron landed at 1550 hours.

66 and 127 Squadrons were ordered up on Airfield Defence Tilburg/Eindhoven area. Six aircraft of 127 Squadron under F/Lt Lea were airborne at 1635 hours, but the patrol was uneventful and the Squadron landed at 1720 hours. There was one early return owing to technical trouble.

B.79, 4th January: Armed recce: Area West. Twelve aircraft in sections of four carried out armed recces in the fore-mentioned area.

(a) F/Lt Fyfe's section was airborne at 1315 hours. Two horse-drawn vehicles were attacked at Z.6406 and one horse was seen to break away and bolt. A train was observed on the west side of Zwolle and a certain amount of transport on the road Z.5508 to Z.5402. Much new earthworks were seen in the area Z.6505. The section landed at 1445 hours.

(b) Led by F/Lt Lea the second section was airborne at 1335 hours. One MET was damaged north-east of Nunspeet Z.0824–1/2. A concentration of thirty plus barges was seen in a loop of the river at E.2454 but otherwise there was little activity. The section landed at 1500 hours.

(c) A third section led by S/Ldr Sampson took off at 1355 hours and destroyed a staff car at E.6584. A small convoy of four trucks was seen stopped in a wood at Heino Z.9827 but flak prevented an attack. Trains with steam up were sighted at Zutphen. The section landed at 1530 hours.

B.79, 5th January: Two aircraft led by WO Hyland took off at 1450 hours and patrolled in the Hertogenbosch/Tilburg area. Two enemy aircraft were sighted in the distance flying north-west from Hertogenbosch at 5/6000 feet but the section was unable to make contact and landed at 1530 hours.

Nine aircraft led by S/Ldr Sampson were airborne at 1525 hours crossing the river in the Goringhem area where meagre, accurate, heavy flak was encountered, and flew on to Deelen airfield. No movement was seen here but there were a few bursts of heavy, inaccurate flak. A staff car at V.1046 travelling south was strafed and seen to crash into the ditch a total wreck. When in the vicinity of Steenwick Airfield the squadron was diverted to attack a train reported on the Amersfoort–Hilversum railway but no train was found. Three large fires were seen burning along the north bank of the river from E.1330 to E.1837 and a fourth fire at E.2555. There was a concentration of thirty barges seen at E.2454. The squadron landed at 1650 hours.

B.79, 6th January: After being recalled from a false start 127 and 322 Squadrons led by S/Ldr Sampson, got away at 1255 hours as area cover to Marauders bombing P.870777. They swept the target area uneventfully. Owing to 10/10ths cloud the ground could not be seen. One aircraft returned early with R/T trouble and another Spitfire provided escort. The squadron landed at 1445 hours. F/Lt C.R. Birbeck arrived on posting from 84 GSU.

B.79, 16th January: Four aircraft under F/Lt Lea were scrambled to relieve 332 Squadron (who were patrolling the Tilburg area) at 1245 hours in view of Huns reported in the area. The section was diverted by control to attack horse-drawn vehicles in woods heading north–east at E.8288. Four horse-drawn vehicles were destroyed and the other two damaged. No other movement was seen. The section landed at 1405 hours.

66, 127 and 322 Squadrons led by S/Ldr Sampson were detailed for a fighter sweep in the Enchede/Rheine area. Twelve aircraft of 127 Squadron were airborne at 1436 hours and swept the area uneventfully. Five to six enemy aircraft were seen on the perimeter on the east side of the field at Plantlunne, whilst two more were observed on the other side of the airfield. All airfields in the area (except Twente) appeared swept and in use. Two MET's at A.3285 were strafed by yellow section, two men who jumped out were hit but no claims regarding the vehicles are made.

On the way back there was intense accurate heavy flak from E.9462. The squadron landed at 1620 hours.

S/Ldr Sampson promoted to the Acting Rank of Wing Commander and posted to 145 Wing as Wing Commander Operations.

B.79, 18th January: Only nine non-operational trips totalling three hours and forty minutes were flown.

B.79, 22nd January: Dive bomb V2 oxygen factory at Alblasserdam. 66, 127, and 332 Squadrons were detailed for the forementioned mission. Twelve aircraft of 127 Squadron took off at 1025 hours and followed 332 Squadron in a dive from 8000 to 4000 feet. Nine 500 lb and twenty four 250 lb bombs MC .025 seconds delay were dropped with only fair result obtained. Five hits were scored in the target area and several near misses were observed. Of three 500 lb bombs which hung up, two were jettisoned in the target area and one fell off at D.8538. There was meagre, accurate, heavy flak from the target area and it is believed that F/Lt Richardson, who is not yet reported, was hit. He was last seen weaving low in an easterly direction away from the target area. The squadron landed back at base at 1105 hours.

127 and 322 Squadrons were detailed to carry out a Fighter Sweep in the Osnabrück area, which was designed to catch enemy aircraft returning back to their bases after attacking Allied bombers.

Twelve aircraft of 127 Squadron led by F/Lt Lea were airborne at 1410 hours and patrolled the area uneventfully, returning to base at 1545 hours.

B.79, 23rd January: Dive bomb midget submarine factory four miles east of Nijmegan. Eleven aircraft were airborne at 1100 hours under F/Lt Lea eleven 500 lb and twenty-two 250 lb bombs MC .025 seconds delay were dropped in a dive from 8000 to 3000 feet. One direct hit was scored on a big building on the west side of the target and two hits also obtained on other buildings. One hang up was brought back. The remainder fell in the target area. The squadron landed at 1205 hours.

66, 127 and 322 Squadrons were detailed to attack enemy road and rail movement in the Amersfoort – Opeldoorn and Amersfoort, Zwolle area. Twelve aircraft led by F/Lt Lea took off at 1420 hours and dropped twelve 500 and twenty-four 250 lb bombs .025 fusing on a road rail junction at Z.5208 obtaining three direct hits which cut the line. Two heavy duty vehicles were destroyed at Z.5302 whilst fifteen heavy duty vehicles were observed heading south-west at Z.4807. There was meagre, inaccurate, light flak from Z.5208. The squadron landed at 1540 hours.

B.79, 28th January: Operation-dive bombing and strafing Hun forward positions in dykes along the river Maas E.0851. The squadron operated in sections of four against three targets consisting of German forward positions in the dyke along the north bank of the river Maas. Twelve aircraft took off at 1525 hours and dropped twelve 500 lb and twenty-three lb bombs. One 250 lb bomb hung up and was brought back, of the remainder eighteen bombs were in the target areas and the targets were afterwards strafed. The squadron landed at 1615 hours.

B.79, 30th January: Nothing doing – S/Ldr F.W. Lister arrived from 84

GSU to take over command of the squadron, this incidentally is the second time S/Ldr Lister has been in command of the squadron.

B.79, 31st January: Duff weather – Nothing doing.

(Signed)
Flying Officer, for
Squadron Leader, Commanding
No. 127 Squadron, R.A.F.

VIII

February

February 3rd, 1945, B.79, Woensdrecht

Today is a very sad day for all of us. Wing Commander Rolf Berg – the legendary one – has gone to join the Viking Gods. He flew one show yesterday. This morning, there was a Dakota waiting to take him back to Blighty. Major Ryg, now Colonel Ryg – my old flight commander at OTU is Wingco Berg's replacement. They talked. It was early morning. One said to the other – how about doing a show together? Just the two of us. . . . They went deep into enemy territory, and they found enemy transports, parked. They went down, Wingco Berg violating his own rule – going in, in spite of the fact that he could not jettison his drop tank. What they dived down to was a flak trap. As Colonel Ryg pulled out he saw Wingco Berg, a ball of flame, hit the woods and explode.

How many times did Rolf Berg tell us never to attack a ground target unless you have jettisoned the tank? *Many* times.

Operations went on all afternoon. I was Blue Leader, Harry Lea led 'A' Flight, and Freddie led the show. It was a sweep and armed recce Enschede–Rheine–Oldenburg areas. Two hours in the air. My arse was like a ball bearing, riding on the CO2 bottle in my seat dinghy. We found no bandits, but we did find some transport. I couldn't jettison my tank. I brought the section home.

331 had an absolute field day. Perhaps it was in the spirit of what Rolf Berg represented. They found three trains, and they clobbered them good. They apparently wrecked all three.

Dave Fyfe's posting has been delayed. This is good, because he is very handy with a saw, and hammers and nails. Our bar will be completed in about one week. I wonder what we will do for beer and bar supplies?

February 6th, 1945, B.79, Woensdrecht

I flew an escort today, 30 B.25 Mitchells to bomb the bridge at Deventer. Harry Lea led it, and again I marvelled at the cold guts of the bomber boys, who just fly, straight and level, through a black carpet of 88-mm flak. They fly in boxes of six, and we, first of all desert them as they make their dog leg turn to start the bombing run. We simply push our throttles to the gate, and pitch fully fine on the airscrew so that the illusion is not four propeller blades driving us, but a mystical big disc of darkish perspex. We pull our control column back and literally hang on the propeller, twisting, turning, until there is our box – *down – over there*. We are cold, but we sweat along with the planes we guard, and the crews in them. The Mitchell is a stable platform, and is inevitably black. This is probably because they also bomb at night. We have one job to do, and that is to make damned sure that no bandits attack the bombers. It is not our job to get shot at, unnecessarily. It is the bombers' job to drop the eggs in the right spot, flak, regardless. Today, they hit the rail lines. They didn't hit the bridge. I still marvel at their courage.

The squadron flew four shows in all today, and I was glad to cop the first. I was not asked to do another sortie, and I was fervently glad.

I am going on leave tomorrow, to Blighty. Harry Lea, Larry Hyland, Eckert and me. I shall have to stop calling him *Eckert*, while I am home. My mother says it is not decent. 'His name is Reg – not Eckert. How would *you* like it?' My rejoinder, that everyone calls me Smith, Smitty, *Smit* (as in the case of Zhilbare Morisson) and even Smudge, and Smudger – cuts no ice. So, it's 'Reg' while I am home.

I am dreadfully tired. So much flak. So many good fellows dead. I have got photos of Pete Attwooll's grave, and I have to take them to Pete's sister, the other side of London. I am dreading it. Thank God that Eckert has promised to accompany me. I would despair, at going home.

I can't wait to get home again. What with the losses, the tour-exes, the crash postings and the new bods, I hardly know the faces at a Wing briefing – let alone the names. My best blues are hanging up. Will the tunic and slacks still look like concertinas when I land in Smoke?

February 13th, 1945, B.79, Woensdrecht

This chronicle of events began on the 7th, when I went on leave. On the morning, sea fog moved in, the entire aerodrome being in the state of 'clampus'. There was Harry Lea, Larry Hyland, Eckert and me. We were anxious to get in the transport and take off for London.

With the aerodrome being socked in, we were forced to play the RAF game for airmen 'Hurry up and wait'. Two hours went by, and I remember having a strange presentiment that if we didn't get away, perhaps we would be pressed into service again, and have to do another show. I even said it to Sandy Powell, who was standing by. 'Let's face it, I said. We've got so many sprog ops pilots, and you can't fly every show. Here's Harry, senior flight commander, and three section leaders. Wingco Berg is gone, and Colonel Ryg is new to the job.' Sandy said he was sure we could be spared.

About this time Harry Lea came back from a trip to the officers' mess. He said, 'Look, chaps, I've just run into an Anson pilot and navigator. They say the weather, according to control, is a wall of fog, all over this part of Holland, and all across the Channel. Still, they're willing to chance it. They will take us, if *we* are willing to have a go. Our transport may not get in today. What do you say?' We said, 'aye.'

The trip was fraught, to say the least. From the moment that the underpowered, overloaded Anson lumbered into the air, we were sightless, until we reached the English coast. Then suddenly, frighteningly, the pilot gunned both engines, and for one split second we saw the grassy tops of white cliffs, and, hearts in our mouths, we sucked in our stomachs, gratefully, as we made it over. We continued to fly blind for a good 40 minutes. After only fifteen of these, Larry Hyland looked at me, made motions with his hands, and mouthed the words 'Square Search'. It was true. The navigator, hunched over the pilot, was giving him the appropriate nudge about every three minutes to make ninety degree turns. We were facing dismal futures.

Suddenly, Larry Hyland grabbed my shoulder, and pointed out of the starboard window. As far as the eye could see, on an imaginary horizon, a neat row of pinpoint yellowish, reddish lights. It could only be Ford, or Manston. Larry got up, lurched forward, hit the navigator on the shoulder, and pointed out of the side cockpit window. The navigator looked annoyed – and Larry almost pulled the pilot from his seat. Then, the pilot made a steep turn to starboard. Within minutes, we were on the ground. Confirmed, Manston. We were saved by Larry Hyland's keen eyes, and the FIDO (Fog, Intense Dispersal, Operation). Larry had a final altercation with the navigator as we stepped down to the ground.

'Lad, tha' can thank *me* for tha' fookin' miserable gormless life. And don't forget to tell tha' little grey-haired moother!'

We hitched a Yank lorry ride to Piccadilly, and then, we split up,

Hyland going north by train, Harry Lea being dropped off in the city, and Eckert and me to Park Royal and the Piccadilly–Uxbridge underground. My oldest, closest friend Bob Bode showed up at home the next day. He had wangled it again – *coincidental leave*. I was thrilled for three reasons. One, for being there. Two, for the fact that his war is finally over. Three tours of operations – (Two heavy bomber tours, one 'Special Duties'. The latter, working with the European underground, dropping spies, CD 'cloak and dagger' people, by parachute, from Halifaxes, Lancasters and Wellingtons.) The third thrill – Bob has been awarded the DFC to go with his DFM.

So my parents' house was full. We had one tremendous leave. We pub-crawled London every day until closing – 3:00 p.m. Shepherds, the Running Footman, the Blue Posts, Addoninos, the Cheshire Cheese, the George, at the Law Courts, the Coal Hole in the Strand, the Running Footman, the Blue Posts, Oddoninos, the Cheshire after hours' club, off Wardour Street. Then, back to the Fox and Goose.

We all went to see a big musical show, a new big star, Sid Fields, in *Strike A New Note*. That was a big hit, with all of us. Very funny sketches, with Sid Fields playing King John at a 'burning at the stake.'

As always, it all ended too quickly. We got back a few hours ago. The first shocking news, Bunny Bundara is dead, killed by a trip wire mine. This very quiet, nice Australian, who only had a few ops hours needed for tour-ex. He was shot down and wounded in the Italian campaign, was repatriated to England, and posted to us, to finish his tour. It was all over a crashed Me109 in the woods. Bunny heard about it, and wanted to see it. One late afternoon, on the day after we went on leave, Jock Wallace led on the search. They were deeply in the woods when Jock stopped, suddenly. He had spotted a wire, two inches above the ground. He said, 'Bunny – that's a trip wire land mine. I'm going back.' He had not retreated ten yards, he says, when the explosion came. Bunny came hobbling back, the foot of his flying boot – one bloody mass of exposed bone. Jock got him back safely, out of the woods, and to the infirmary. Doc Blanchard pumped Bunny with morphine, and operated. He removed the remainder of the foot. When Bundara came around from the anaesthetic Doc was there. He said, 'You've got a *Blighty*, lad. You'll be going back *soon*, for rest and repatriation. Then, it's fitting you with a new foot, and you'll be walking again in no time. Your pal, Jock is here to see you. He must be gone very soon. I want you to sleep.'

Bundara said, 'Tell me the truth, Doc. Will I fly again?' And Doc said, 'Yes – you will fly again.'

Jock Wallace came back at eight o'clock the next morning. He was met at the door by Doc Blanchard. 'Sergeant Bundara did not survive the night. He died of shock. I am sorry.' And that was it.

The second news we got was *this*. The Dakota which we were supposed to catch for leave, arrived an hour after we took off in the Anson. It was near full of 'compassionate leave' soldiers. When they heard that we had aborted, the crew taxied back to the runway, and took off for England. They crashed in the fog. There were no survivors.

Harry, Larry, Reg Eckert, and I all feel funny about that. In fact, it gives me chills. We are all cut up about Bundara's death. Such a bloody shame. Everybody, with the exception of a certain officer on 66 Squadron, liked him very much. Doc Blanchard wrote on his death certificate. 'Misadventure.'

February 15th, 1945, B.79, Woensdrecht

Our Red Letter Day began at squadron release, late yesterday afternoon. Freddie Lister called us all together, and said simply, 'Great News – particularly for you older chaps. The older, wiser men of this Air Force of ours have reviewed our record, and our losses. They have decided to grant 127 Squadron – a Three Week – Rest, and Repatriation. Our next show is – Fairwood Common, which is near Swansea, Wales. Our second show will be in the bar of the Prince of Wales Hotel!' There was a stunned silence for perhaps five seconds before cheers and handshakes took over. Eckert, Fyfe, Sammy Roth, Paddy, Sandy – the old hands – were silent because of wondrous shock. Not one of us, privately, anyway, had given even remote thought that such a relief was possible. Who would contemplate such, with the war at its height? My own despondency, at all the losses, has had *this* effect. I have closed my mind to making friends with any of the new pilots. To one extent or another, this *must* be the stance of all the old hands. The new boys looked just as shocked when Freddie broke the news. I am sure they are thinking – Rest and Repatriation? I only just got here, for God's sake!

What may have made the decision was Wingco Berg's MBK, on top of the fact that we have served under five CO's counting

F.W. Lister, *twice*. (Bradley, Lister, Smik, Sampson.)

The news sent a number of people packing. Packing for the move, of course. Freddie detained some of us; notably Reg Eckert, Sandy, Larry, Paddy and me. All warrant officers, with *time* on the squadron. He called each of us into his office, which is now the bar, separately.

When it was my turn, he explained that the AOC was planning a visit to the wing, perhaps very soon. Freddie has decided that he would like all of us with warrant rank to be commissioned. As he explained it to me, he can recommend me for a commission, but I have to make the application. He gave me the form, and I have filled it out. Pronto, as a matter of fact. He was surprised, when he opened his door to dismiss Larry Hyland, the last one in, and I handed him the completed form. I hope the AOC arrives before we all go to Fairwood Common. Otherwise our commissions could be held up for weeks. I *think* that this is called 'Commissioned in the Field.'

Last night, we had a good, old fashioned piss up. I was surprised at the cache of gin and whisky we gathered from individuals. There were a number of half bottles, and less, and even one bottle of Gilbey's and one of Johnny Walker *unopened*. Then we had lots of beer, which we had secreted outside our hut, between the plank walls and the blast wall. We kicked it all off with a couple of bottles of champagne which someone had liberated. One bottle was set aside, and later on, Sandy Powell put up a terrific black, by getting well and truly sozzled. He started giggling, which is a sure sign that he has had one over the eight. Apparently he found the lonely bottle of 'champers', uncorked it, and poured it over Freddie Lister's head. It was a thoughtless thing to do. Freddie took it very well, in the circumstances, but there was no doubt that the skipper was cheesed off about it. Freddie was wearing his best blues, as a sort of salute to the work that we had accomplished in the building of the new bar. This is really remarkable. Dave Fyfe showed us his mettle in reworking the door, by drilling holes in the top and bottom, in the door's centre, and inserting a bolt. Then, using parachute elastic straps, he made the door swing back and forth. Somebody even put red curtains at the windows and got a couple of lamps which make the bar look like a lounge.

The highlight of the party was the skipper's remarkable ability to tell stories. One of his more gruesome (told hilariously) stories was from his recent base at OTU. A student flew much too low in the low flying area. A farmer was ploughing a field. The student, returning from the area, complained to Control that his oil temperature was going off the clock. Control told him to return to base, and pancake, pronto. He did. Ground crew was startled and shocked to see student taxi in with farmer's head in the Mark V air scoop! Freddie told of the panic to rush the student to the scene of the beheading in an ambulance to get to the corpse before the farmer's family did. (They made it.)

I cannot wait to get to Fairwood Common.

February 18th, 1945, B.79, Woensdrecht

The weather has been light rain and ten tenths 'clampers' for days. Sea fog, so thick we couldn't even do a weather recce.

Fortuitously, the AOC was in the area, so he drove in, in a staff car. We all had our commission interviews, and some of 66 pilots were there, notably Woody Woodhouse, Johnny Turk, and Mike Larson. Somebody was wise enough to make Mike Larson swap his perennial rubber Wellingtons for issue shoes just before the interviews began. Typically, we went before the AOC in alphabetical order, so it was Crozier, Eckert, Hyland, Powell, Smith. When it came to my turn, it was probing, but pleasant. I answered questions on the differences between the Mark IX and the XVI. (No automatic pitch control on the XVI, different beat on the Packard Merlin 266, and our disappointment that there are only two out of eighteen with bubble canopy). He asked me about dive bombing timing, strategies, and attack directions. He seemed to agree – never attack from a direction that dictates an escape into the teeth of the flak. I was almost mesmerized by the thick blue/black ribbon and two thinner ones on his uniform forearms, and the fruit salad (gong ribbons) on his left breast. If the AOC had had many more ribbons, his flying brevet would have been upside down on the back of his shoulder. The interview took twenty minutes at most. When he said, 'Well, that's about all for now' I jumped up, saluted, and made my way to the door. I grabbed the door handle, and was about to exit, following my, 'Thank you, sir,' when I heard, 'Oh, one thing more, please.' 'Yes, sir,' I said, turning back to face him. 'Mister Smith, I am recommending that you be commissioned, forthwith.'

'Thank you, sir.' My spirits were elevated. I wonder if it will come through while I am at Fairwood Common?

February 21st, 1945, Fairwood Common, Swansea, Wales
We cannot believe that our Air Force could treat us so well. We can't get over the differences between this camp and any other camp, with the exception of Paignton, Devon, where we all were posted to, briefly, on re-entering England after flying training. That was a camp of exceptional food, so that the Empire recruits wouldn't get too much of a bloody shock on first acquaintance with wartime rations. This is so superior to Devon. First of all, we are all in a huge country house. There is a kitchen here, which we can use if we have anything to cook. (There is real white bread here, not the usual wartime grey, sometimes with sawdust in it. There is real butter in the kitchen refrigerator – not margarine. Sometimes, they say, we can get black market eggs.)

There is a large dining room, and on each of the tables there is fresh fruit. There are oranges, peaches, plums, which are probably all from the Middle East, or other parts, even Gibraltar, for strawberries. There are six bathtubs in the bath house. There is plenty of soap, there are plenty of towels, and there is plenty of hot water. There are even big mirrors. Until we saw ourselves reflected in these, we did not realize how very skinny we, the old hands, are. In the German showers at B.79, I tended to think how bony the other fellow looked, now I can see how bony *I* look.

We have four batmen here, and, under Freddie Lister's orders, they are to wash the shirts and press the trousers and tunics of *all* the pilots, not just the officers. Among all of these special emoluments for graceful living is that we have the total use of a three tonner to take us to Swansea whenever we are free.

Ten pilots came here by Dakota, and I was one of them. Freddie held a final briefing at B.79 for the other fourteen who brought the Spitfires here, by way of Colerne, near Bath. Sandy Powell says that Freddie made them all laugh, and think, with his final edict before they climbed into the cockpits. It was, 'You will have to *learn*, starting now, to break old habits. When we land over there, you will *not* proceed in sections to the nearest aeroplane to piss on the tail wheel, in the daily ritual to which you have become accustomed. Many of the ground crews you will meet in the UK are WAAFS, and I can assure you that they will not appreciate bringing a petrol bowser up to three clouds of steaming urine!'

Our spirits could not be higher. Tomorrow, we begin rehearsals again for our squadron song, 'The Guardians'. Can I whip them into shape for our first performance at the Prince of Wales hotel lounge?

February 28th, 1945, Fairwood Common, Swansea, Wales
We are getting into the flying training course here with unexpected zeal. As Reg Eckert said yesterday, 'It's bloody marvellous, sport, to be flying right into a ground target, full bore with cannons and point fives, and to know that there are no fuckin' gunners waitin' to see the whites of your eyes!' It is also fun to see these funny little white 25 lb bombs hit the circle and emit a cloud of white chalk 'smoke'.

We have organized a number of categories for overall contests, best aggregate air to air shooting, best air to ground, best diving bombing, etcetera. We have sported one pound each, less Freddie, for twenty four pounds, prize money.

We are practising the chorus line of our squadron song, 'The Guardians'. All of the boys are enthusiastic, but nearly all have two left legs. How this began was two days after Freddie came back. We were having a few beers together, and for something better to say, someone suggested that we should have a squadron song. Eckert immediately came up with *his* suggestion by singing it.

> One – Two – Seven Squadron – One – Two – Seven Squadron
> All clapped out to Buggery!
> One – Two – Seven Squadron – One – Two – Seven Squadron
> All clapped out to Buggery!
> Onward! Onward! Into battle go!
> Give us Spits and we'll make the bastards know –

'For God's sake, Eckert – *shut up*!' This was from Paddy Crozier.

'It's better than nothin',' Eckert retorted, heatedly.

'Oh, to hell it is! It's not *original*! You could insert any damned squadron in there, and someone probably *has*. Besides – that shit about '*give us Spits*' is redundant! We've already *got* Spits! And apart from *that*, I don't like the tune. . . .'

As usual, one thing led to another, and finally I trotted out my version of 'The Guardians' which an old pal from Cranwell, Gerry Lilly, had written and performed. I explained that the song is an action song, and the way to perform it is to sing and act it out in a chorus line. Then I performed it, and everyone had a very good belly laugh. I got two encores, and they decided that it is different enough and funny enough to adopt it. The problem we have, is that most of us have two left feet, as I have stated. 'The Guardians' goes like this.

> (Move forward toward stage left. Jaw thrust out)
> We're The Guardians of the sky above (*point to heaven*).
> Up in the *air* – Devil may care (*Give leering grin*).
> We're The Guardians of the Land we love
> and when we're called upon to fight (*brandish fists like old time bare knuckle fighter*).
> We'lllllll (*pause*) *show* the foe our might! (*slap left hand on right bicep*).
> We're The Guardians of the sky above.
> We'llll (*pause*) drive old Jerry from the air! (*imitate two hands on car steering wheel*).
> We'llll (*pause*) blaze a trail to freedom as we're fly-ing' (produce match box, extract match and light it!)
> Up in the air! Devil may care (*repeat leering grin!*)

Of course it is not easy for 25 people coordinating all the above, together, in a simulated chorus line. Unless the boys are plied with enough 'Dutch courage' to get a bit squiffy they are reluctant to perform. Some of them find it difficult to do the match striking bit properly. Some of them look as if they have never struck a match before. Some of them are so clumsy they drop the match.

Music Hall stardom does not come easily. I hope we can perform 'The Guardians' in the Prince of Wales saloon lounge, *soon*.

Extracts from the
Operations Record Book 127 Squadron, R.A.F. 132 (Norwegian) Wing

B.79, 3rd February 1945: 66 and 127 Squadrons were detailed to carry out a fighter sweep in the Rheine–Vechta–Oldenburg and Leeuwarden areas, which proved to be completely uneventful. Eleven aircraft of 127 Squadron led by F/Lt Lea took off at 0945 hours and landed back to base at 1200 hours.

127 and 331 Squadrons were detailed to carry out a Fighter Sweep and Armed Recce in the Osnabrück, Vechta and Oldenburg area. Eleven aircraft of 127 uneventfully landing back to base at 1745 hours. Two aircraft lost the formation and returned early.

B.79, 4th February: Six Spitfires of 127 Squadron led by F/Lt Fyfe were detailed to escort Mitchells bombing target at Deventer. They were airborne at 1425 hours and proceeded to rendezvous but owing to 10/10ths cloud contact was not made and Mitchells were actually found returning from the target, and were escorted back to our lines. The section landed at 1555 hours.

B.79, 6th February: Today has been one of the squadron's biggest days for several weeks. Two aircraft led by F/O Roth carried out a Weather Recce from 0755 to 0935 hours in the Arnhem–Deventer and The Hague areas.

Four of the Wing's squadrons were detailed as escort to Mitchells and Bostons bombing railway bridge at Deventer. Nine aircraft of 127 Squadron under F/Lt Lea were airborne at 0925 hours and made rendezvous with the thirty bombers, escorting them uneventfully to the target. The bridge was not hit, the majority of the bombs fell in the town itself but the lines leading to the western approaches to the bridge received direct hits and the lines were cut in many places. There was intense accurate heavy flak from the target area. The squadron escorted the bombers back to our lines and landed at 1045 hours.

Twelve aircraft operating in sections of four were airborne at 1325, 1330 and 1345 hours to attack enemy movement reported in the Amersfoort area.

Red section under F/Lt Lea dropped six 250 lb MC .025 delay bombs on the road at Z.6825 scoring two near misses, the remainder falling east of the road. Traffic on the road was identified as civilian and was not attacked. Two bombs hung up and were brought back.

Yellow section under F/Lt Fyfe dropped five 250 lb MC .025 seconds delay bombs amongst twelve MET on the road at E.2264. One bomb hung up and was brought back. Two bombs hit the road with two on the verge. One MET was strafed at Z.7932 and set on fire.

Blue section under F/Lt Covington dropped six 250 lb eleven second delay bombs on the railway at Z.8322 claiming several near misses. Four plus MET were strafed at Z.5515 and two damaged. There was slight, inaccurate, heavy flak from Z.6723. All aircraft landed by 1505 hours. Hours flown 31.40 – Sorties 23.

B.79, 8th February: Twelve aircraft under F/Lt Covington were airborne at 0930 hours but as cloud was reported obscuring the area the aircraft were recalled and all bombs were brought back. The squadron landed at 1045 hours.

The squadron operating in sections of six aircraft each. No 1 section being led by S/Ldr Lister took off at 1650 and 1700 hours to bomb and strafe enemy foxholes in dyke at E.791620. Red smoke was laid. Twelve 500 lb and twenty three 250 lb MC 025 seconds bombs were dropped. The first section scoring twelve direct hits and six near misses and the last section getting all bombs in the target area. There was one hang up. The positions along the dyke were then strafed. Meagre, inaccurate, light flak was experienced from the target area. Due to darkness one section landed at B.77 at 1815 hours whilst the other section put in to B.88 at 1800 hours.

B.79, 9th February: Eleven aircraft under S/Ldr Lister took off at 1630 hours and proceeded to rendezvous where, at 10,000 feet, they were taken over by MRCP. Ten 500 lb and nineteen 250 lb MC 025 seconds bombs were dropped in the east portion of the town of Goch. One 500 and three 250 lb bombs hung up and were brought back. The squadron landed at 1735 hours.

B.79, 10th February: Twelve aircraft led by F/Lt Fyfe took off at 1315 hours to Blind Bomb an Ammunition Dump at Xanten. They proceeded to rendezvous north–east of Arnhem where at 10,000 feet they were taken over by MRCP control. Twelve 500 and twenty two 250 lb MC 025 seconds were dropped and all fell closely concentrated in the centre of the target. Smoke was seen but there was no abnormal explosion. Two 250 lb bombs hung up and were jettisoned. One aircraft returned early due to losing formation in cloud. The squadron landed at 1425 hours.

66 and 127 Squadrons were detailed to dive bomb German Military Headquarters at Kasteel Biyenbeek. Twelve aircraft of 127 Squadron led by F/Lt Fyfe were airborne at 1625 hours. Nine 500 and twenty two 250 lb MC 025 seconds bombs were dropped in a dive from 8000 to 4000 feet scoring one direct hit on the most northerly building and the remainder in the target area. Three 500 and two 250 lb bombs hung up of which one 500 lb and two 250 lb were brought back. One 500 lb fell off on the runway whilst one 500 lb was jettisoned. The squadron landed at 1725 hours.

B.79, 13th February: Armed recce area V. Ten aircraft operating in pairs at 15 minute intervals were airborne commencing at 1010 hours. Three MET moving north-west at A.0457 were attacked and one MET was damaged. Four trucks heading east at A.1560 were also attacked and two were left burning, and the other two were damaged. A large covered lorry was destroyed at E.9973. There was intense light flak from A.1560 and one Spitfire was damaged (Category AC) but the pilot was unhurt. The last section landed by 1245 hours.

Operating in the same area, eight aircraft were airborne at 1440 hours but were recalled due to poor weather and landed at 1525 hours.

B.79, 14th February: Operating in pairs twelve aircraft of 127 Squadron carried out Armed Recces in the area south–east of the battle area (Nijmegan). The first section was airborne at 0825 hours. Moderate inaccurate light flak was experienced from Netterden, Emmerich and AQ263. Seven aircraft landed back at base by 1025 hours whilst two went down at B.88 and three at B.80.

The same operation was continued by eight aircraft with the first section away at 1130 hours. Three MET were destroyed and two MET, a 1/2 track vehicle and a horse-drawn vehicle damaged. A marshalling yard at A.0858 containing 100 plus trucks but no locomotive was strafed at 1210 hours. No claims are made. Two barges with a platform between them were seen at A.0852 and there were two Red Cross barges stationary in the river at A.0158. Intense, accurate, light flak was encountered at A.0545. The last section landed by 1255 hours.

Ten Spitfires carried on with an Armed Recce with the first section airborne at 1420 hours. A troop carrier moving south–west at A.2863 was destroyed and there were at least twenty Hun casualties. A MET with a trailer was also destroyed and two MET damaged. Some buildings alongside the road and railway between A.0956 and A.0858 were strafed. Possible supply buildings were seen evenly spaced at 500 yards intervals in woods along the road at Z.6704. A train of locomotive and six or seven trucks were seen moving into Haldern (A.1253) at 1500 hours from south–east. Approximately ten military cyclists were also observed moving South at A.3846. Intense accurate light flak came from Ruulo, and moderate, accurate, light from Borken. One aircraft landed at B.77 and the last section was down at 1540 hours.

B.79, 15th February: Duff weather – nothing doing – the squadron should have gone to Fairwood Common today.

B.79, 18th February: Slight improvement in the weather yet not sufficient to justify the move to Fairwood Common.

B.79, 20th February: One Dakota carrying equipment and twelve passengers is Blighty bound – The whole squadron is delighted with the very thought of home service for at least three weeks.

B.79, 21st February: Fifteen aircraft with pilots arrived at Fairwood Common. What a break.

B.79, 28th February: A perfect day – twenty-nine sorties (eighteen hours) were flown. Practices in Dive Bombing and Air to Air being carried out.

(Signed M.E. Mathews)
Flying Officer, for
Squadron Leader, Commanding
No. 127 Squadron, R.A.F.

IX

March

March 17th, 1945, B.85, Schindel, Holland
I would say that it is good to be back to operations again, except it isn't. The time went all too quickly, as did our money. We had all saved a fair amount, because there is no place in Holland or Belgium to spend any money. My commission came through at Fairwood Common, and so did those of Paddy, and Sandy. Eckert's did not go through, or at least has *not*, until now. As a sprog officer, I have a new number, and this has made me flinch a bit. The number is 191525 and so I have to face the fact that my lucky omen has gone. For all my ops flown so far, I have flown with my number 1333127, and the 127 I have considered my private Good Luck charm. Now, it's gone. I got an elevation in pay. Pilot officers get thirty quid a month, which is one pound per day, on the average. I wonder whether some day in the future people will find out what we are doing, and realize that we do it for less money than any factory worker in all the UK? This is by their hourly pay, and doesn't include overtime! From what I hear, they all can do overtime, if they are on war work! Yes, and this includes factory floor sweepers. Even the aerodrome runway sweepers make more money than most pilots. This was pointed out to a runway sweeper not long ago, and he replied, 'That's *true* – but don't forget I still work all through air raid alerts!' That was in the *Daily Express* – or the *Daily Mail*.

We had a smashing time in our three weeks together. We got to know each other, and we got to like each other. It was best said by Robbie Robinson, who is Australian. We were in the bar of the Welsh Harp in Swansea. Robby said, 'I don't like to get arseholes drunk, but I like to get to the point where each of you appears to be a bloody fine mate, and I wonder why I don't see more of yer!'

We performed 'The Guardians' in the Prince of Wales saloon lounge, and it was clapped at, whistled at, cheered at, and only one man cackawed. We did two encores. I must say that we also got plenty of laughs. I think some of the boys are having dreams of glory.

They want to perform it in London, and they even dream of the Palladium. (That's a joke, of course). The camaraderie has been totally wizard. I don't think there was one night when we didn't utilize the three tonner to go somewhere on a pub crawl. There is no brother love quite as sincere as that conditioned by booze.

The daily lectures have been enlightening, though some were not instructional. We have learned, via film, how to incapacitate the enemy by kicking his shin with the inside sole of boot and in the same movement slamming the boot down hard on his instep. This, we are assured, will break the small bones in his instep, and the result will be excruciating pain and no mobility.

We have also learned how to kill a man with one powerful stroke of the hand under his nose. This is supposed to fracture the entire nose structure, and send a bone into the brain. We watched film after film of strafing. In the darkness, we confronted more trains, lorries and staff cars, all burning. This is the very thing we went on rest, to *escape* – for three weeks. Ironically, we even watched an old film of our own, which was applauded by us in full measure. We ended with a last lecture by an interrogation officer. He was very effective, very frightening, and he convinced us that, if we get shot down and give the enemy interrogaters anything more than name, rank and number, we will be guilty of utmost treason, and deserve a firing squad.

Our last evening flowed heavily with suds from the brewery, at the Duke of Wellington. We performed 'The Guardians' to a pub full of silent, stunned Welshmen. On the way back to our billet, we stopped the lorry, and we all stripped our clothes and ran into the sea for a moonlight dip. Then, having no towels, we dressed, wet, into our clothes, and froze together and separately, on the way home.

Back in our big house, Robinson and Alan Willis had a case of Brown ale, cached in a cupboard. We drank that, and we told jokes. Freddie Lister, as skipper, was entitled to take the floor for the last performance. First, he acted out an improvisation, silent, in which a first violinist in a string section copes with a ghastly smell is finally identified, the source being a dog turd which he has stepped in.

He capped this with another hilarious one, 'The One-armed Fiddler'. The climax of this was when, being one-armed, he is perplexed on how to snatch his cap from his head, and hold the cap for his tips. He has the imaginary violin clamped under his jaw. He snatches the bow with his left hand, which he jams into the stump where his right arm should be. He whips his cap off, and a finger appears through the fly of his trousers, and grabs the cap, simulating an educated dick. We laughed ourselves to our beds.

We stopped at Manston, on the way to this new strip. The boys of 66 seemed glad to see us when we landed here. They have missed us, because we *do* represent another outlet for them to converse in English. The Norwegians still speak Norwegian, most of the time.

March 18th, 1945, B.85, Schindel, Holland

No sooner back – two shows in one day. Both ops were bombing, both on the bridge at Dieren. We cut the lines, but had no direct hits on the bridge. I was relieved that we didn't run into a hornet's next of flak. We didn't need a hot welcome for the first target coming back to action.

We spent the day unpacking, getting to find our way around to the different squadron dispersals.

Freddie showed his ingenuity today, when we went to briefing. Our 30 hundredweight did not get back in time. Freddie ordered the whole team to get on his little jeep, wherever we could hang on. The jeep went to briefing and back with twelve bodies on it. Quite a coup! Our ground crew enjoyed it very much. They likened us to circus clowns.

March 21st, 1945, B.85, Schindel, Holland

A few days spent here in Holland, and we can hardly remember our three glorious if inebriate weeks in England. March winds are pretty bothersome here. We seem to be more exposed than usual, and it is all complicated by such a sand content of the soil that we might as well be on a beach. Sand gets into every nook and cranny. At night, we find it in our socks, and in our undershorts, and even gracing our armpits and private parts. When it gets into our bread and jam, it is *too much*. The sand blows into everything, and dangerously, into our engines. There is talk of finding special sand baffles such as are used in the Middle East – where there is nothing *but* sand. Unfortunately, all of the baffles are in the Middle and the Far East. Thus, there have been four crashes, between 331, 332, and 66.

The ground crews have found the cause, and it is most disturbing, because any one of us could crash at any time. In order to give us super boost, they have produced a new type of petrol. 'Chiefie' Wills says it is called 150 grade octane. It is very much infused with lead.

When sand gets into the engine, the sand and lead become fused together in the fierce heat, and glass is formed, right on the spark plug heads. It can kill an engine in a very short time, and most particularly in the case of seven plus boost – on take off. None of the four crashes killed the pilot – but all were victims of smashed faces, caused by the pilot's head crashing into the gyro gunsight.

In the last three days I have flown four shows, three which were escorts to B.25 Mitchells – to Coesfeld, Bocholt, and Borkum. Lots of flak at Borkum. The Mitchells were lucky to get through without losses. I know that some of them were hit by flak. I flew Blue Leader on two of these. The other op was an air sea rescue west of Haarlem in which I led Sergeant Baecke to try to find a pranged Walrus and/or dinghy. We did not see anything to report.

March 23rd, 1945, B.85, Schindel, Holland

I have just been away, on a 'piece of cake' trip to Blighty. Two aircraft were needed to do a VIP escort to Marshal of The Royal Air Force Trenchard. Simple enough. Just fly close enough to a shiny Dakota and see that no Jerry bandit comes close enough to shoot it down. Harry Lea knows that I live closer to Northolt than anybody else, so he gave me the assignment. I, in turn, picked one of the new boys, Flight Sergeant Norman Simpson as my number two.

We rendezvous'd 4.30 pm Antwerp, and had a good time the minute we crossed the British coast, to the minute we followed the Marshal's Dakota to land at Northolt. This was a real and proper thrill to me. A thrill, landing on this famous aerodrome, that I have dreamed about since the day the war broke out. How many times have Bob and I come here on our bicycles, just to watch the Battle of Britain boys take off and land. How many times have we saluted the ace pilots of Polish 303 Squadron as they went into the air. And here was me, landing on the same runway. We taxied in, parked, and caught a ride to Northolt's front gates. When I told the driver that I live at Park Royal, on the Piccadilly-Uxbridge line, he decided to drive us to Northolt station.

We surprised my parents, walking in the front door wearing flying boots, and me, wearing my new officer's cap that I bought in Swansea. We all went down to the Fox and Goose, and had a high old time in the Saloon Lounge. I suppose there was nobody who didn't notice that Simpson and I were wearing flying boots, so of course we had to tell them about our escort to Marshal of the RAF Trenchard. I got congratulations on my commission from the locals at the Fox, and neither Simpson nor I put our hands in our pockets all evening. We couldn't even buy one drink.

This has been a busy day, Mum cooked our breakfast, and we caught the bus to Park Royal underground. Then, train to Northolt, and hitchhike to the aerodrome. We got our routing from Control – Epsom, Dungeness, Gris Nez, Ghent, Brussels, to base. All the boys were envious about our little trip. We were just about to be released, this evening, when we were called to briefing. There is a very big operation starting tomorrow. We were told that this is Top Secret. It concerns a major assault, a gigantic dropping of airborne forces commanded by Field Marshal Montgomery. The operation has the code name 'Operation Plunder'. We will be doing air cover.

I wish that we hadn't been briefed tonight – because all I can think about is tomorrow, and *flak – flak – flak*.

March 24th, 1945, B.85, Schindel, Holland

'Plunder' began this morning and we were close cover. We flew in and out of cloud, usually at around angels seven. The cloud cover, about six tenths, made our job twice as difficult, our job being to see that enemy bandits did not break through.

It was one big air circus, with tons and tons of 'flak to walk on' – all of it directed to the hundreds of Dakotas and C.47's, many of which were dropping sticks of airborne parachutists, and many of which were bringing in Horsa gliders filled with the boys who wear the red beret in calmer times. I suppose it was well coordinated, but to us it looked like mass confusion. The air below us was filled – literally filled – with parachutes with bodies, armed, hanging beneath them. In the confusion, I asw one ghastly mistake, where a very big coloured supply 'chute was dropped from above the paratroopers' planes. I could not believe the bad luck that the supply 'chute draped itself over the tail unit of a Dakota. It smothered the tail unit, and down went the Dakota, with troops trying to abandon the diving 'plane.

We started back there on a late afternoon show, but my own aeroplane developed both undercarriage and fuel trouble (it wouldn't feed the droptank) so I had to abort. By late afternoon all the troops to be dropped had been dropped, so the patrol was more of an armed reconnaissance. Reports are that the ground fighting is fierce. Our troops are trying to secure the Rhine, and all bridges.

I realized, quite suddenly today, that this may be the beginning of the end. Now that we are over the Rhine, there seems little to stop us. Of course, our troops are taking town after town only after much street fighting and house-to-house fighting, but all the stories coming back from captured Germans are stories of horror, from the air – and this means *us*. The Huns can hardly get a truck or a staff car on the road without the fear that any one of our fifty-plus squadrons will swoop in from the sky, raking it with cannon and point fives – or blasting it with 60 lb rockets.

We don't see any tanks, to speak of – but German flak is still very deadly.

March 25th, 1945, B.85, Schindel, Holland

It was still dark this morning when Corporal Turner shook my shoulder and said, very quietly, 'There's a show on, Mr Smith. Briefing, right away.'

Then he moved to the next bed and woke up Sandy Powell. Then to Peter Coxell, Larry Hyland, Dave Fyfe, and some of the newer bods. We moved quietly through the hut and outside to our jeep, parked in two inches or more of slack sand. (The only hard standings on this aerodrome seem to be at dispersal, and the runway). Dave Fyfe jumped into the driver's seat, and we all piled on. He took us over to briefing. Spy Johnson, who is now the Wing IO did the briefing. 'Dawn Patrol, chaps. Get airborne as soon as you can – certainly by first light. Patrol the Rhine, between Arnhem and Emmerich. We fully expect the Hun to come up in force, purpose – to bomb the bridges. If they can knock out even one bridge, they will arrest our ground assault, so that our troops cannot cross. It is vital that we protect those bridges, Patrol, until relieved. Take a good look at the map, here, and memorize the bridges. Get in the air, *soonest*. . . . Okay? Questions?' No questions. 'Good hunting, chaps.' Even as Flying Officer Johnson was speaking, I sensed that this would be the day for an air show. In the cockpit, waiting for 'Contact' – I felt like a hunter, I felt it would happen this morning. Fyfe led Red Section, Sandy Powell, Yellow, and I led Blue Section. The air was smooth as silk as we took off – the first streak of daylight in the east. As the sun came up, a beautiful day was revealed. Take-off 0550. We patrolled back and forth, ten minutes or more on each leg, and watched the day establish by the rising sun. So much time passed, the turns became routine, and I was about to put the show away as another 'no incident patrol'. We were patrolling west,

Personal Combat Report
P/O E.A.W. Smith

Date:	25th March, 1945.
Squadron:	127.
Type and Mark of A/C:	Spitfire XVI.
Time Up and Down	0550
Time of Attack:	0725
Place of Attack:	S.W. of Bocholt.
Height of Enemy on First Sighting:	8,000 feet.
Own Height on First Sighting:	7,000 feet.
Own casualties:	Nil.
Enemy Casualties:	1/2 ME109 destroyed.
Gyro:	Used.
C.C.G.	Exposed.

Personal Narrative:
I was flying Blue leader on a Fighter Patrol when we were vectored on to a dog fight by Control. As I came into the melee, I could see a Spitfire on the tail of an Me 109 at about 400 yards. I did a steep climbing turn to starboard and closed in to the tail of the E/A. I carried on firing through his evasive action and saw strikes on his tail. When he eventually stopped his evasive action I closed in to very close range. At one point I had to throttle back to avoid overshooting as I was then only 25 yards from the Messerschmidt. Large pieces fell off the tail-plane and then glycol streamed out from port and starboard. Here I narrowly missed Blue 2 who was closing in with me and I pulled up and broke off the engagement. The Me 109 dived steeply and crashed into the ground.

I claim 1/2 Me 109 destroyed, shared with F/Lt. A. Willis.

....
E.A.W. Smith, P/O.

....
Intelligence Officer.

at angels seven, when my number two, Alan Willis, broke r/t silence . . . *excitedly*: 'Monty Red Leader, this is Monty Red Two. There's a dogfight, six o'clock *above*. Into sun. Can we attack?'

Dave Fyfe broke in. 'Longbow – this is Monty Red leader. Dogfight behind us, angels eight. Permission to tangle? Over.'

Even as Dave was speaking, I whipped into a steep turn to starboard, and saw what Willis's very keen eyes had spotted. Tiny little aeroplanes circling across the sun. In my rearview mirror, I saw that Willis, Coxell, and Van Helden were following me.

'This is Longbow, Monty Squadron.' This quietly, almost languid. 'We rather think it's under control, but you have permission. Over.'

Suddenly, there they all were, Tempests, Spits, 109's – and two FW190's.

I picked out a 109 and pre-empted a Spitfire trying to 'tail' it. One steep climbing turn to starboard. Gunsight on – graticule to Me109 – gunswitch to 'Fire'. I started firing at one hundred yards – exulting as my cannons and point fives began clattering in unison. Two second burst. No strikes. Another burst as he steep turned violently, port, then starboard. His evasive action was violent, but rudimentary. At one stage he throttled back, and suddenly he was less than twenty five yards ahead. Out of nowhere, four Spitfires were coming at us, at a closing speed of nearly 600 miles an hour. In one split second I could see all four of them sparking as they fired at the bandit – and me. I saw big pieces fall from the bandit's rudder and tail unit, from my guns. Next, his canopy, ejected or shot off, zipped past me. His glycol came streaming from port and starboard – and then – fright of my life – a Spitfire starboard wing came boring in from my port side. Instinctively I wheeled to starboard. As I did so, I saw the arcs of two airscrews, missing each other by a foot, no more. Why Willis and I did not collide, is a miracle. The bandit went in on a vertical dive. At a thousand feet or less, he ejected, and his parachute popped. I believe I was still shouting with glee, as we re-formed. Back at base, I decided to split the kill with Willis. I did so in dictating the combat report to Spy Johnson.

We had breakfast with some of the boys from 66, and a few from 331. They were curious to know why Willis and I both did 'Victory' rolls as we came over the field. So, we told them. We did a good combination lineshoot.

I did another show after breakfast, with Freddie leading, to the same area patrol, relieving 66. A curious thing happened, when we had patrolled for about forty minutes. Way above us, coming from east to west, were two hundred or more bombers, nearly all B.17 Fortresses, with a few B.24 Liberators. They were strung out over five miles, between 20,000 and 30,000 feet. I was screwballing my neck, up, down, round and round. Some instinct made me look directly above. There, as large as life, was a black Me163 rocket plane. My mind said, 'Two in one day!' I pushed the throttle to the gate, flipped the r/t switch, shouted, 'Bandit twelve o'clock – high!' and pulled the control column back to my stomach. I went to stall point, and to my dismay saw the rocket fire, and saw the plane disappear in a second. As I nosed over to prevent a stall, the r/t came alive with 'Call sign! Give your bloody *call sign.*'

I apologized to Red Leader – and r/t went quiet again.

All the way home I wondered whether the Me163 was a self-induced figment of my wishful imagination. When we got to de-briefing, Sandy and Robbie Robinson confirmed that, yes, it *was* there, and yes, it was a 163.

Today was an exciting day. We had a small celebration for the Me109, and Freddie told some of his great stories. He told us how he landed on Malta at the height of the bombardment of the island, from air and sea. How he found his way into a tent, within an hour of landing, with the purpose of locating his brother, Derek, an army captain decorated with the Military Cross. With so many communications disruptions, it was a miracle that he actually got his brother on the field telephone. The conversation was unbelievable but true.

'Come off your high horse, captain. This is your little brother, come to plague you.'

'Freddie! Where the hell are you?'

'I'm right on the airfield!'

'Where? Where, on the airfield.'

'North. I'm on the *Northside*!.

'Where – on the Northside?'

'At dispersal!'

'*Where* – at dispersal?' and so on. Finally, Freddie gave some irrevocable identification then – 'Oh! For God's sake, Freddie! Get up off your arse and come out of that tent!'

So Freddie stood up, pushed the tent flap aside, walked into the Malta sun, and confronted brother Derek, coming out of a tent not twelve feet away! There is no teller of stories like Frederick Wooldridge Lister.

March 26th, B.85, Schindel

Today, Flight Sergeant Simpson and I were detailed to go up to the forward check points to visit with a control car operation. We arrived at a big Dutch house, which has at least twelve bedrooms, and is surprisingly unscathed. Almost every house we saw, in the vicinity, has roof damage, at the very least. The family that owns the house is confined to two rooms at the back, and a large basement. There is a wooden fence all the way around the grounds, about three acres. The house is commanded by RAF Intelligence, and a very large living room on the ground floor has been converted into a control centre. The Intelligence officers have monitoring speakers, and they monitor all r/t channels. There is a sandy courtyard of sorts, and parked there were half a dozen scout vehicles. Incongruously, there were peacocks walking around. One cock, and three peahens. The hens, on our arrival, flew into the trees, while the cock hissed at us and spread his magnificent plumage.

We were ushered into the control room right away, and were given a one hour briefing on how they conduct 'cab rank' and other forward operations. The briefing was interesting, but not nearly as exciting as listening to the radio/telephone dialogue of marauding Typhoon and Spitfire sections. We did not arrive until afternoon, and were not offered anything to eat. The briefing was done by a senior Intelligence officer, by the name of Wing Commander Framingham, a flying type, with DFC and bar. I recognized his voice immediately, a distinctive, gravelly voice. We were taken over the bomb line by scout car, but disappointing, to me, was the fact that there was no action that we could see, parked as we were in a small copse. We saw two section of r.p. Typhoons, which passed over at about angels four.

We were on our way back to the house, talking, while Wingco Framingham's radio operator changed from one channel to another.

Suddenly: '*Listen*, these are your chaps.'

My hair at the back of my neck tingled, as I heard the familiar voices: Eckert, Hyland, Feltham, James, and Freddie Lister.

Then Feltham: 'Rail transport – three o'clock below, Monty Red Leader. One engine and petrol tankers. . .'

'This is Monty Red Leader. In five seconds, in we go!'

There was a silence for a full minute. Then the air was rent with 'Jesus, Skipper, can you believe this! My God!' One exultant yell followed another – then –

'Monty Squadron! this is Monty Red Leader. No more passes! Get away! Get away! Monty Squadron – re-form – angels seven!'

The r/t went silent again. Then Freddie's voice, calm, now. 'Monty Squadron. Over to B. Baker, *over*. . .'

Back at the control centre, we got the full story. Freddie and the boys had destroyed an entire train of petrol tankers. Well over one hundred thousand gallons of petrol, that the Hun would never use. Flames to two hundred feet – and smoke, to angels *ten* – or twelve!

Simpson and I were both silent, all the way back to Schindel. He was thinking what I was thinking. How come that I missed the biggest party of all – a trainload of fuel?

When we got back here, there was, as I might have expected, a small piss-up in progress. All the old jokes were regaled again, and Freddie added some new ones. One was about his speed skating, and how his brother, Derek, acting as his manager, contracted for Freddie to jump forty-one barrels on an ice rink – a feat which had never been accomplished. This was one more barrel than Freddie *last* jumped, when he broke a bone in his ankle. . . .

Until the gin ran out, the conversation kept coming back to the train in flames. I could have written a book about it.

March 29th, 1945, B.85, Schindel, Holland

I drove my first car today, though it was not a car – it was the squadron jeep, which of course, only Freddie the skipper drives, except when he directs whoever is leading a show that Freddie isn't flying.

The entire incident was a humiliation. I was wakened at first light by Warrant Officer Jones, one of our new pilots who joined us from Thruxton just in time for our *rest*, at Fairwood Common. Jones and I were detailed for Pink Section, which I have not drawn since Eckert stole it from me because he didn't like the sound of the mission. This was the show where Joe Birbeck was shot down.

Jones picked up the telephone on the first ring. Then he came down the hut to wake me up. I got up and dressed in the semi-darkness, and walked outside the hut, expecting to find the three tonner to transport us. It wasn't there. My first words to Jones were – where is our transport? My next words were – please go back in the hut and call flight. Jones came back out after three minutes. He told me that the three tonner had broken down. Suggestion, that we go to flight in the jeep.

With this, I woke Freddie, who was not a bit pleased at me ruining his pleasant dreams. I said I was sorry for waking him, and explained the circumstances. He reached under his pillow, produced the keys for the jeep, and put them in my hand. 'Don't slam the door,' was all he said.

I tried to hand the keys to Warrant Officer Jones, who recoiled, visibly, with, 'Oh, no, Mister Smith, I couldn't take *that*. You see, sir, I 'ave never driven a car in my life, you see.' Jones has an accent that is a delight to the ear, but brings no solution to practical problems.

Slightly annoyed, I climbed into the driver's seat as Jones jumped onto the passenger side. I put the shift lever into 'neutral', and started the motor. I put the shift lever in second gear, and engaged the clutch. The jeep moved easily but slowly through the slack sand that comprises this entire airfield, and we were on our way. Twice in the mile and quarter drive, Jones suggested, tentatively, that perhaps I should shift into fourth gear, or at least third. My retort was first, not yet, and secondly, *not bloody likely*. . . .

When we got to dispersal, I could see that good and faithful Corporal Fowler was already standing on my port wing, readying my cockpit by laying out my parachute and harness straps. I drove up as close to the port trailing edge as I dared, braked, and switched the jeep motor off.

Corporal Fowler said, 'Well, Mr Smith, I didn't think you were going to make it. Hardly *dawn*, you must admit, sir!' (He pointed to the rising sun).

'Aw, *can* it, Fowler,' I replied. 'We're here, aren't we? By the way, would you do me a favour in the next two hours?'

Fowler leaned towards me. 'And what might that be, Mr Smith?'

'Would you be good enough to start that jeep, put it in reverse, and turn it around, facing the way I *came* from?'

Corporal Fowler scratched his chin, contemplating the request. 'I'll tell you what I'll do. I'll do it, if you can give me a good reason, *why*.'

'Fowler,' I said, 'with the humility it deserves, I confess that until this morning I have never sat behind the wheel of a motorized vehicle in my life. I would not dare to try to reverse that jeep for fear of pranging that bloody tailplane.'

Corporal Fowler turned away, shaking his head. Then he turned again, to face me. ''Ow many flyin' hours in your log book, Mr Smith?'

'Over thirteen hundred, as of now. . . .'

'I don't bloody well believe it. What a turn-up!'

Today, Zhilbare shocked us with a visit, picked up his money belt – his 'flak jacket' from Larry Hyland, and his gear, and departed. He won't be coming back. The bullet wound in his right calf has left him with a 'warrior's limp'. He was drinking a bottle of Dutch beer with Hyland, Sandy and some others, in what serves as a mess bar. After a while of bantering, he sidled over to me and flashed a leave pass under my nose. He chuckled that peculiar Zhilbare chuckle that is so hissingly distinctive; the rolled tongue clenched between strong teeth. 'Hey! Smitt! Dees is a *leave* pass. *Ten days* to Paree! Den I go to Free French Head-quar-tah in London! Hey! Smitt! You want a bullet?'

Then, he *guffawed*. Good luck – Zhilbare.

March 31st, 1945, B.85, Schindel, Holland

We only flew one op today, and I was not on the show. I was just as happy. The wind has been constant, and swirling, and changing direction without warning. Sandy or someone said that you can take off into wind, do one circuit of the airfield, and come in to land, finding a ninety degree crosswind. The sand gets into everything, including our Merlin engines. They cough and choke even running them up, and they sometimes stall when you need them *most*, on take-off. You look down the runway watching a section take off, and one of them chokes, emits blue smoke, and then you see it careen off the end of the runway, and you see a cloud of dust like a sandstorm. This means two hours, at least, for the ground crew to get into the engine and clear the blockage. Our airmen are in pitiful shape, being half-blinded with sand, with sand blocking their nostrils, and sand blocking their ears. Sand gets into their mouths, and grates on their teeth, and still they get us into the air.

Virtually all of our ops for the last seven days have been supporting Field Marshal Montgomery's massive operations into Germany. It has been one armed recce after another. Instead of doing twelve men recces, we have been doing them in fours. In this way, we have found more targets to shoot at.

I led a section at dusk, a few days ago, and we had quite a party.

Four METs badly damaged, and many Hun soldiers, running for their lives. We strafed the woods three times. Then it got too dark to see much on the ground, so we had to return home.

We did an escort (Mitchells) to bomb Olpe – east of Cologne. It was nine-tenths cloud, and they had to bomb blind, so we did not see the results. Surprising, that the flak was not heavy. After all, the Jerry radar is very good – so they don't need sightings to throw up a lot of 88m shells.

Yesterday, I led Blue Section, Peter Coxell, Sandy Powell, and Sergeant Van Helden to an armed recce, Mengelo-Osnabrück area. Nothing concrete. We shot up some METs in the woods, but we didn't see live bods, so they could have been abandoned.

We got a commendation late today from Montgomery. As usual, I have got a copy for my log book. The Adj said, 'Gentlemen, we have just received a signal from none other than Field Marshal Montgomery. He salutes us all, for the fine work – well, read it for yourselves.'

Somebody – Alan Willis, I think, said, 'How fuckin' considerate of Monty!'

This is the commendation:

> The following signal received by the C. in C. from Field Marshal Montgomery begins:- I would like to express to you my great appreciation of the good work done for Second Army by 83 and 84 Groups RAF during the Battle of the Rhine. Over a long period of very high class performance the standard reached before, during and since the crossing of this great river obstacle has been remarkable: the splendid support given by the whole of 2nd TAF has been the admiration of the soldiers. I would be grateful if you would convey to all concerned my grateful thanks and my high appreciation of what they have done for the Army.

Extracts from the Operations Record Book 127 Squadron, R.A.F. 132 (Norwegian) Wing

Fairwood Common, 1st March 1945: Between 1st and 16th March 301 non-operational sorties were flown consisting of Dive Bombing Air to Air and Air to Ground (practice). Hours Non-Ops. 189.45 Bombs dropped. 657 .20 millimetres Ammo expended, 18,493 – .5 Ammo expended 6,720.

B.85, 17th March: Twenty aircraft were airborne under S/Ldr Lister at 1355 hours to attack the railway bridge at Dieren (E.8885) twelve 500 lb and twenty three 250 lb MC eleven seconds delay bombs were dropped by sections in a dive from 6,000 to 0 feet. One bomb was seen to hit the bridge (which however is still intact) but the majority fell on the south–west approaches cutting the tracks whilst another cut was achieved on the north–east approaches. One 250 lb bomb hung up and was brought back. Two aircraft painted light blue were seen parked in a clearing at the edge of a Wood E.8788. Medium accurate light flak was experienced from E.8975 and E.8888. The squadron landed back at base at 1450 hours.

Twelve aircraft were airborne again at 1705 hours on the same mission. Twelve 500 lb and twenty-three 250 lb MC eleven seconds delay bombs were dropped. There were no hits on the bridge and the majority of the bombs fell within thirty yards. One 250 lb bomb hung up and was brought back. The squadron landed at 1815 hours.

B.85, 21st March: 66 and 127 Squadrons were detailed as escort to Mitchells bombing Borken. Eleven aircraft of 1276 Squadron were airborne at 1030 hours and made rendezvous with the bombers according to plan. The escort was uneventful and the bombing appeared good, a big fire being seen in the target area. There was intense inaccurate heavy flak from the target area, and the north-east of Bocholt. The squadron landed at 1145 hours.

66 and 127 Squadrons again operated as escort to Mitchells. Eleven aircraft of 127 Squadron were airborne at 1610 hours. Rendezvous as planned and escort uneventful. The bombing appeared good. There was moderate, accurate, heavy flak from the target area and Borken. The squadron landed at 1735 hours.

B.85, 22nd March: Eight aircraft led by F/O James were airborne at 1000 hours on rail interdiction in the Amersfoort-Zwolle area. Two cuts were observed on the line at Z.5108 and Z.5209. One hit was scored on the railway embankment at Z.9924. All aircraft landed at 1120 hours.

The squadron was released from 1200 hours until 1200 hours on 23rd March 1945.

B.85, 23rd March: Twelve aircraft under W/Cdr Ryg (132 Wing) were airborne at 1420 hours and attacked an airfield at Steenwick which seemed deserted. No aircraft were seen on the ground but barrack buildings were strafed, numerous strikes being observed. Six MET and some horse-drawn vehicles were seen moving west at Z.9538 and attacked. Two MET and two horse-drawn vehicles were damaged. One aircraft returned early due to technical trouble. The squadron landed back at base at 1525 hours.

B.85, 24th March: The squadron was detailed to patrol Arnhem, Emmerich

No 127 Squadron on rest and repatriation, Fairwood Common, February 1945. *Front row:* second from left is Paddy Crozier. Harry Lea and Freddie Lister are front centre. F/O 'Jimmy James' is far right. *Second row:* F/Sgt Simpson, Eckert, Pollock, W/O Jones (shot down and killed 1st April 1945), Sgt Baecke, holding propeller (shot down and killed, 1st April 1945), Larry Hyland, Jock Wallace, Robbie Robinson, A. T. Willis (shot down on 127's last mission and, incredibly, survived from a crash into trees at 200 mph).

(Left) The author (left) on leave, with Len Silk, Bob Bode and Mickey Cross. (Cross was just repatriated from POW camp in Germany.)

(Below) On leave with Bob Bode, 1945, at the Fox and Goose (centre). A proud publican, Arthur Nice, in light suit. Author's father, second from right, stands with Mickey Cross.

and Rees. Eleven aircraft under S/Ldr Lister were airborne at 0915 hours and commenced patrolling at 0930 hours at 12,000 feet. No enemy aircraft were sighted but one section went down and destroyed a motorcycle moving north at E.9473. One aircraft landed at B.89 due to tank trouble. Moderate inaccurate heavy flak was experienced east of Arnhem and intense, accurate, light flak from Woods (E.9475). The squadron landed at 1050 hours.

The squadron was detailed to carry out an armed recce in the areas Arnhem, Zwolle, Oldenburg and Emmerich. They operated in two sections of four, the first section being airborne at 1225 hours. One MET moving south-west at V.1102 and one MET at A.1398 were destroyed.

Whilst two MET moving south as A.1084 and one MET moving east at V.0035 were damaged. There was intense inaccurate light flak from Doetinghem A.0175. The last section landed by 1420 hours.

Twelve aircraft led by S/Ldr Lister were detailed to carry out a Fighter Patrol in the areas Arnhem, Emmerich and Rees. They took off at 1620 hours and patrolled uneventfully at 5,000 feet. Moderate inaccurate heavy flak came up from Arnhem. The squadron landed at 1745 hours.

Twelve aircraft led by S/Ldr Lister were detailed to carry out a Fighter Patrol in the areas Arnhem, Emmerich and Rees. They took off at 1620 hours and patrolled uneventfully at 5,000 feet. Moderate inaccurate heavy flak came up from Arnhem. The squadron landed at 1745 hours.

B.85, 25th March: Fighter Patrol–Arnhem–Emmerich and Rees. Twelve aircraft led by F/Lt Fyfe got away at 0550 hours and whilst on the patrol line were vectored on to a dog fight south-west of Bocholt. F/Lt Willis and P/O Smith got on the tail of an Me109, knocking off portions of the tail and causing glycol to stream from the engine. The enemy aircraft then went down in a spiral dive and was seen to crash to the ground. The pilot baled out. The destruction of the Me109 is shared between two pilots, although nearly everyone claimed to have got in a squirt at it. The squadron landed at 0725 hours.

The squadron continued their patrol of Arnhem, Emmerich and Rees. Twelve aircraft under S/Ldr Lister were airborne at 0945 hours and patrolled the line at 5,000 feet. At 1045 hours an Me163 was observed north-east of Wesel but it disappeared northwards into cloud. Five stationary barges were seen on the canal between Doesburg E.9081 and Keppel East 9878. The patrol was otherwise uneventful and the squadron landed at 1120 hours.

Operation Armed Recce Arnhem, Zwolle, Enschede, and Emmerich. The squadron operated in three sections, eleven aircraft in all. The first section took off at 1255 hours. South of Borken six tanks were seen in two groups of 3, all camouflaged with branches of trees. One group of tanks was attacked and one was left burning at A.3858. Approximately twenty plus field guns towed by carriers were seen under trees by the roadside near Montferland E.9867 also many troops. These were strafed and two carriers are believed destroyed, two guns shot up and six troops killed. Two MET stationary facing west at E.9886 were attacked and damaged (smokers). Thirty troops marching south along the road at A.0228 were strafed and the majority are claimed killed. The area Zwolle-Deventer-Amelo was reported deserted. There was intense accurate light flak from A.3858 and E.9886. One aircraft returned early due to technical trouble and the last section landed at 1410 hours.

The squadron continued the search for movement in the Arnhem-Zwolle-Enschede and Emmerich areas. Three sections of four aircraft each operated, the first one was airborne at 1515 hours. Two camouflaged MET stationary facing west were damaged at V.0008, whilst one MET moving south at E.9683 was destroyed. Two covered stationary barges were strafed at E.8878 and many strikes were seen. One aircraft landed at B.91 with engine trouble and the last section was down at base at 1645 hours.

Two sections of four aircraft each operated in the above area, the first taking off at 1830 hours. Thirty to forty MET facing south were seen parked along the roadsides north of Ede E.5886 in concentrations of four to five, and also 200 to 300 troops. One section went down to strafe and four were claimed damaged. The troops disappeared into the woods and both sides of the road were well strafed. Failing light rendered it impossible to remain in the area longer and both sections landed by 1915 hours.

B.85, 26th March: The squadron was detailed as area cover to aircraft of two group bombing Dorsten. The squadron operated in two flights one of six and one of five aircraft, the first flight taking off at 1015 hours. Owing to thick cloud in the area nothing was seen and the squadron was recalled. One aircraft returned early owing to technical trouble and one acted as escort. The remainder of the squadron landed at 1135 hours.

Armed Recce Zwolle-Enschede-Emmerich areas. Twelve aircraft operating in three sections of four aircraft each, the first section being airborne at 1315 hours. One MET stationary at E.6882 was attacked and damaged, whilst two covered barges at E.9876 were strafed and many strikes seen. Twenty rail trucks were seen at A.0889 several of which were burning also the woods on the north side of the line. Two MET were sighted at A.1490 but disappeared under trees. The wood was strafed but no results could be seen. Moderate, accurate, light flak was experienced from A.0889 and E.9816. The squadron landed at 1510 hours.

Fighter Sweep Nordhorn, Plantlunne, and Furstenau.

66 and 127 Squadrons took part in the above operation. Nine aircraft led by S/Ldr Lister took off at 1635 hours. One Ju88 and three single-engined enemy aircraft were seen in a dispersal at Rheine airfield, but no attack

could be made due to intense flak. MET activity was seen at Twente airfield and three barges on the canal between Rheine and Lingen. Twenty petrol tankers drawn by a small shunting engine were found south of Enschede at A.4396 and were strafed. A huge fire was caused with flames 200 feet high and all tankers which are presumed to have been full, are claimed destroyed. The squadron landed by 1800 hours.

B.85, 31st March: Armed Recce Zutphen, Zwolle, Enschede, and Osnabrück.

Ten aircraft operated in pairs in the above area, the first section taking off at 1350 hours. One MET facing south-east was damaged at A.1094, whilst another MET facing north at A.0911 was also damaged. One MET with trailer attached moving north-west at V.3410 and another MET with trailer moving north-east at A.1397 were attacked and damaged. One motorcycle moving north–east at V.2001 and one MET moving east at V.1519 were destroyed. A large MET towing two caravans at V.3152 was strafed as a result of which the MET exploded and strikes were seen on the caravans.

Fifteen horse-drawn vehicles interpaced with three ambulances and three or four MET were seen moving north-east at V.1802 but were not attacked, but three camouflaged lorries also moving North East at V.1600 were strafed and strikes seen. Thirty plus MET were seen on roads in the Amelo-Borne-Delden area. The pilots also report that Rheine airfield was on fire. There was intense accurate light flak from A.0397 and north of Enschede. The last section landed by 1600 hours.

(signed)
for Squadron Leader, Commanding
No. 127 Squadron, R.A.F.

X

April

April 2nd, 1945, B.85, Schindel, Holland

Yesterday was April Fool's day, and some person or persons at GHQ decided that we would be the fools. The weather was most foul, with winds and driving rain. We went to briefing at noon, and we were given direct orders from Group that every serviceable aircraft would be in the sky for Rhubarb (low level) ops as soon as possible. Not only was this a 132 Wing briefing, but an additional five squadron wing briefing from the other side of the airfield. (French, Dutch, Belgian – and two British.)

When it was our turn for take-off, we had but eight aeroplanes serviceable. (The sand has taken quite a toll of engines). We sectioned off in two's, with me, leading Flight Lieutenant Bushen, a new pilot coming to us from Mosquitos. (On his last Mossie flight, his plane blew up. His navigator went *in*). Sandy Powell paired with Flight Lieutenant Foulston, Larry Hyland led little Sergeant Baecke, and Jock Wallace led our Welshman, 'Taffy' Jones. The briefing was about as curt as you can get.

'You *all* know what a rhubarb is. Low level, in and out of cloud. No bombs. Droptanks. Plenty of Huns out there, and your chance to get into mischief. Ten minute intervals for take-offs. I don't have to give you any specific areas to find your mischief – must find it clear of the bomb line. Look *here*. Almelo – Deventer – Zwolle – Meppen – Lingon – Hengelo. Don't come back until your guns are empty.'

We took off in pissing rain, and soon found that visibility was poor, at about 1,000 yards. The highest cloud base that Bushen and I could find was 700 feet, and at times it was down to three hundred feet. It was perfect for 'rhubarb' all right – so much disturbance that poor Bushen had a dreadful time trying to formate on me. The r/t was one mess of cacaphonic distortion. God knows how many voices were on our frequency. We found two METs – three ton trucks, and a scout car. Was it a flak trap? I led in at about 350 mph and sucked in my guts as tracers thicker than the rain came pissing past my cockpit. There was flak everywhere, and we bounced back into turbulent cloud time and again for protection.

There was so much clatter on the r/t that it was pointless for me to talk to Bushen. For his part, bouncing wildly in and out of lightning-charged clouds, he couldn't spare a hand to flip the r/t switch. The last words I said, after 'Over to "D" Dog,' was 'Jettison tank'. That, we did. It would have been suicide to press a low level attack with droptank connected. There must have been over 100 marauding Spitfires in the area, as well as rocket firing Typhoons. Because it was impossible to take advantage of cloud cover due to the turbulence, the marauders became the target – to the ground gunners. I was certain that I saw a Spitfire go in from a direct hit, as his starboard wing folded back. I heard at least two confirmations on the r/t. One was, 'Jesus Christ! What was that?' and a laconic reply: 'That was Red Two. Flamer.' The other was 'Bay Boy Yellow Four. On fire – baling out.' As I waggled my wings to Bushen, I noticed the sweat trickling down my back. After fifty minutes of madness, Longbow recalled us.

When we landed, I could see that all dispersals were virtually empty, except for unserviceable aircraft. After a while, perhaps after one cigarette, they started coming back in ones and two's. Two names were asterisked on the squadron 'team' board. Baecke and Jones. Bushen asked what the asterisks meant. Baecke and Jones would not return. Baecke blown up, Jones, a flamer. Either he couldn't, or didn't, jettison his drop tank.

After de-briefing, we strolled over to the adj's office. He was not there. On his desk, Sandy found this communiqué:

> SECRET, 84 GP, H.Q. A/O 127 SQUADRON, 1ST APL. 45.
> Air effort in Armed Recce now 'All out.' Every risk of bad weather, flak, cross winds, must be accepted.
> OC's Wings are to ensure that every effort is increased to 'All Out' regardless of all considerations.

Corporal Turner came in, and furnished a copy for Sandy and me. Then he told us more shocking news. In the one hour rhubarb, our wing lost eight aircraft, and the airfield fourteen. So much for April Fool's day.

Sergeant Baecke was twenty years of age. Taffy Jones was 22, as are Sandy, Larry Hyland and me. Eckert is still 21. We got drunk. It pissed rain all night.

Year 1945 Month	Date	AIRCRAFT Type	No.	Pilot, or 1st Pilot	2nd Pilot, Pupil or Passenger	DUTY (Including Results and Remarks)
—	—	—	—	—	—	— Totals Brought Forward
APR	1	SPITFIRE XVI	9N-Z	SELF	~	RHUBARB NORTH OF ALMELO B.L.
PR	2	SPITFIRE XVI	9N-Y	SELF	~	AIR TEST
PR	2	SPITFIRE XVI	9N-Z	SELF	~	ARMED RECCE NORDHOR LINGON AREA. DUSK B
PR	3	SPITFIRE XVI	9N-O	SELF	~	SCRAMBLE.
PR	7	SPITFIRE XVI	9N-O	SELF	~	ARMED RECCE GRONINGE EMDEN AREA R.L.
PR	8	SPITFIRE XVI	9N-O	SELF	~	ARMED RECCE, ABORTIVE
PR	9	SPITFIRE XVI	9N-O	SELF	~	DEFENCE PATROL BREMEN BRIDGES.
PR	10	SPITFIRE XVI	9N-O	SELF	~	ARMED RECCE NORT OF GRONINGEN B.L.
PR	11	SPITFIRE XVI	9N-O	SELF	~	LOW LEVEL BOMB & STRAFE NEUVREES,

GRAND TOTAL [Cols. (1) to (10)] 1375 Hrs. 50 Mins.

Totals Carried Forward

SINGLE-ENGINE AIRCRAFT				MULTI-ENGINE AIRCRAFT						PASS-ENGER	INSTR/CLOUD FLYING [incl. in cols. (1) to (10)]	
DAY		NIGHT		DAY			NIGHT					
Dual	Pilot	Dual	Pilot	Dual	1st Pilot	2nd Pilot	Dual	1st Pilot	2nd Pilot		Dual	Pilot
(1)	(2)	(3)	(4)	(5)	(6)	(7)	(8)	(9)	(10)	(11)	(12)	(13)
80·55	1107·00	11·10	6·55	72·20	64·30		14·20	7·35		22·45	49·20	17·00

N UP W/O JON [redacted]

SECRET 84 G.R.H.Q.
A/O 127 Squadron
1st. Apl.45.

Air Effort in Armed Recce now "All out". Every risk of bad weather, flak, cross winds, must be accepted. The wings are to ensure that every effort is increased to "All out" regardless of all considerations.

ORN BURNING.

Pilot (2)	Remarks
1·10	HUNS WERE MUSTANGS. HOOK-HOOK! APRIL 6TH SGT PALMER KILLED TESTING MY "Z". HIS FIRST TRIP.
1·30	SAW SIX M.E.T.'S COULD NOT JETTISON TANKS. BROUGHT SECTION HO
·05	PANIC CIRCUIT BIG SWEAT. ENGINE TROUBLE.
2·30	NO HUNS — THOSE BIG BLACK MUSHROOMS AGAIN!
1·35	TWO HORSE DRAWNS DAMAGED 3 M.E.T. FLAMERS.
1·45	W/Co BERGS GRAVE FOUND. WONDERFULL JOB. EVERY BOMB FOUND A TARGET IN MAIN STREET. ALSO STRAFED LINDERN. CONTACT CAR 'OP'

(1)	(2)	(3)	(4)	(5)	(6)	(7)	(8)	(9)	(10)	(11)	(12)	(13)
80·55	1118·05	11·10	6·55	72·20	64·30		14·20	7·35		22·45	49·20	17·00

April 3rd, 1945, B.85, Schindel, Holland

The spirit of 127 was never better, I feel, even with the unexpected losses of Baecke and Jones. People like Robinson and Alan Willis are absolute builders of confidence. They are loud, and they are irrepressible. They don't seem to recognize danger in any form. I was personally so sad when Baecke and Jones went down, because you couldn't find two more non-aggressive people. Both of them were very quiet, and neither asserted himself in our get-togethers beyond buying a beer, and quietly observing the loud mouths (most of the rest of us).

We have so many new bods, and most of them are intimidated by us old hands. Larry Hyland is *quite* intimidating. He reminds me of a pit bull terrier. Larry *is* Larry. He was born and grew up in the shadows of the Northern steel mills. When he was no more than eight, his daily task at twelve noon was to rush home from school, pick up a bucket, run to the local pub to get it filled with beer, and rush it to the steel mill to quench the thirsts of his father, and his uncles. He says that their trade was 'puddlers' but doesn't explain it, so we don't know what it means. Obviously, 'puddling' is thirsty work. Larry, like me and Peter Coxell, is a grammar school type, from a 'free' scholarship from elementary school.

If the spirit were not as strong as it is, I don't think I could survive, mentally. Truth is, that I am feeling tremendous pressure, as I am increasingly called on to fly Blue Leader. In spite of being scared to death on nearly every show. I know I have to go in lower, and lower, so that my two, three and four will not guess the fear that is in me. I know no sweeter words than those spoken at sunset. 'Squadron Released!'

Yesterday I was Blue Leader on an armed recce at dusk – Nordhorn – Lingon area. I hate dusk operations, because by the time we find a target, it is almost too dark to prang it, properly. We saw nothing but some ambulances, and raging fires at Nordhorn.

When I brought the section home I couldn't lower my undercarriage. I told the others to pancake, and I flew three more circuits trying to get wheels down. Finally Control told me to turn upside down, and move the control lever while the undercart weight would not be on the pins. I did this, and it worked, but in rolling over I lost my horizon and directional gyro. By now it was dark, and I had to make it down to a shitty apology for a flare path without two instruments.

Today we got a commendation of sorts for the bad days at the end of March. This is it:

> The following signal received by Col Mehre from AOC begins:- Please convey to all pilots my congratulations on the excellent results achieved by your Squadrons on the 30th & 31st March. The high rate of effort maintained on the 30th under the difficult conditions at B.85 was a fine achievement on the part of all ground staff. Please convey my appreciation.

Today we had a scramble. Control thought we were running into a gaggle of 109's. Of course, it turned out that they were P.51 Mustangs.

April 6th, 1945, B.85, Schindel, Holland

We saw Sergeant Palmer killed today, and there was not a thing we could do about it. I was about to take my 'Z' on air test. (Most of the time I get my own aeroplane these days, as is the perquisite of section Leader. Eckert, Paddy, Sandy and Hyland have the same privilege).

Harry Lea came along as Corporal Fowler was preparing my cockpit, i.e. parachute straps, restraining harness. He asked me if I wouldn't mind Sergeant Palmer doing the test, so that he could finally qualify – experience on type (detailed as 'sector reconnaissance'). Five or six of us, then, were standing around, 'shooting the shit' as it were, when we moved fast to get out of the way of blasting sand, as Palmer gunned the motor to taxi out.

We were still talking as he opened the throttle and went down the runway. We watched as he got airborne, flaps up, undercarriage up. Suddenly the engine started choking – and oily black smoke came pouring out of the exhaust stacks. He hit the ground with an appalling – B-O-O-M. The meat wagon went tearing down the runway, but there was nothing to do but take Sergeant Palmer's body from the cockpit and transport it to the mortuary. He died of a broken neck, which was caused by the rejerk as his face smashed into the gyro gunsight. Incredibly, while his tank blew up, it did not flame.

The cause – unbelievable. Nobody thought to give Palmer a

cockpit re-check. So many days have gone by since his cockpit orientation that apparently Palmer forgot one fact. These Mark XVI's have no auto-prop control, as do the Mark IX's. Palmer pulled the pitch, control lever back into full coarse – and not 'automatic', as he thought. Naturally, he stalled, and pranged. This was his first and last take-off, as a 127 pilot. A rotten shame.

April 10th, 1945, B.85, Schindel, Holland
It has developed into an armed recce war, almost exclusively, it seems. We don't seem to get many escorts, though the Mitchells and Marauders and Bostons, must still be bombing. (Is there much left to bomb, by bombing yardsticks?) They say that the Germans say that *we* are the *worst* – the Spitfires, and the r/p (rocket-projectile) Typhoons. They say Jerry calls us the *Terrorfliegers*. I suppose, to them, we are terrorists without principle *or* conscience. They are right, but as Churchill has said, they are the ones who sow'd the wind – and they are reaping the whirlwind.

We are going to *have* to move, soon. We are getting so far out of range that we are having to use ninety gallon drop tanks, and these present three problems. The first is, on take off. They are real bastards on take off, because they cannot be totally filled, so they slop from side to side, and the Spitfire is very difficult to control. The Spitfire has always had tremendous torque on take off, to starboard, and this has to be corrected with full left rudder, and full left rudder trim. With the drop tank slopping left, then right, it is very easy to overcorrect. Secondly, we all fear crashing on take-off, because these tanks are made of plywood, and they are built like a boat carried under the belly, with very poor aerodynamics. A prang on take-off almost certainly means a total fire, and petrol explosion.

The third problem is, that there is no certainty that the tank will jettison, and in this case it means an abortive operation. Learning the lesson of Wingco Berg, not one of us is game enough, or intrepid enough, to attack with a partially empty drop tank on board. This is an open invitation to the dreaded and much feared, 'Good night, Nurse.'

As usual, we will probably get the order to pack up and move without warning.

66 Squadron has been getting their share of 'Big Twitches' lately. Yesterday, Woody Woodhouse got a direct hit in the engine, 20 mm.

He baled out, but it was very close. They got him as he got into a strafing dive, at about 1,000 feet. Woody pulled up, ejected the canopy, disconnected oxygen and r/t, and rammed the control column forward. Then, to his horror, his parachute got stuck, and he was half-in/half-out of the cockpit. He kicked the stick with his left foot, and was sprung – but he hit the tail unit with his left knee. He parachuted down all right but injured the knee again, on landing, when his leg collapsed. He won't be walking for about a week.

Today, Mike Larson, the 'scabrous one,' had to bale out right over the airfield. He was trying to get back to land, having been hit in the engine, losing his glycol, and with temperature gauges 'off the clock.' The engine seized solid, so Mike hit the silk, as we say. Uncannily, he was actually in the circuit when it happened, and he parachuted to 66's dispersal, standing upright, watching the last sub-section land! He actually was there when the last two aircraft taxied in. With all of Larson's brass and bullshit, he has finally put in for 'Tour-ex'. He has been bragging for weeks and weeks: 'Not to worry, lads, Mike Larson is the one fooker who *will beat the game.*' Today, at squadron release, he has decided that perhaps he can *not* beat the game.

Yesterday, we flew a defence patrol of Bremen Bridges. Apparently our GHQ were very concerned that Jerry might send in some suicide dive bombers. All that *we* saw was a lot of big black mushrooms from 88s. Nobody was hit, fortunately.

Today, I flew one show as Blue Leader. An armed recce north of Groningen. First, we found three MET's (trucks). Stupidly, they tried to outrun us, streaking desperately towards the security of woods. We got all three in flames. Then, with our guns almost empty, we went down on some horse-drawn vehicles. We left them damaged. Thank God, the horses bolted. I feel very guilty about attacking horse-drawns, but our orders are – *all out* warfare.

We have no beer or booze, since we drank it all up on April Fool's day, when Baecke and Jones bought it. Yesterday, Harry Lea heard that the French squadron bought and slaughtered a few pigs, and made every bit of pork into sausage. Coincidentally, they sent a gharry to Rheims, and it arrived, loaded with cases of champagne. Harry told a few of us, and we went over with the jeep and crashed the party. The sausage was bloody marvellous, the best I ever tasted. We felt like kings, washing the sausage and new french bread down with champagne. We all ate and drank too much. My head was heavy this morning. I cured it by jumping into the cockpit this morning, putting on my oxygen mask, and turning the oxygen on at full blast, 30,000 feet on the gauge.

April 11th, 1945, B.85, Schindel, Holland

The first disturbing news today was at least the finality of knowing that Wingco Rolf Berg is dead. I, for one, have allowed myself the occasional daydream that perhaps it *wasn't* the Spitfire R.A.B. that went in with a flaming droptank. Now we know. The most professional pilot I, or any of us will know, will *not* be in a victory parade in Oslo when this war is over. The man who led us on so many successful operations. The man who knew no fear for himself, but had so much compassion for us, individually, or collectively. The man, who, without a second thought, spent his leaves partly by flying as crew member on bombing operations. The man who told us, times over, never – *never* go in on a bombing assault if we cannot jettison our drop tanks. Surely none of the ancient Vikings was more a warrior than Rolf A. Berg.

I was asked, and I agreed to fly Yellow Leader today. In the shuffle between being available (readiness) and the need for experience, I got the nod. Once airborne, it made no difference. There were only eight aircraft detailed, and I led a new pilot, Sergeant Williams, and two nearly new flight lieutenants, Adcock and Parish. The target was a village, Neuurees. It was a contact car operation, and we had tanks and two 250-pounders. The contact car officer, under code name Red Fox, handled his part so well that there was no reason or room for doubt about which buildings to bomb. It was preceded by red smoke shells fired by the troops forward, and every shell found a proper target. We saw no flak, and virtually every 250 lb bomb hit a target in the main street. At deck level it was hard to miss. We started fires, and then Longbow ordered us over to the town of Linden. We strafed Linden until our guns were empty. We got down around 1700 hours, just in time for tea. Good tea, because for some reason they have stopped putting saltpetre in it. Same old rock cakes. They probably put one egg in for every pound of flour. A hungry airman could probably crack his molars on them.

April 12th, 1945, B.85, Schindel, Holland

We are wondering when we will be given orders to move. We are getting very cross about the situations that call for drop tanks. We still haven't licked the problem of the occasional air lock. We are told *not* to switch drop tank *on*, before closing main tank, after take off on 'mains.' Some of the boys say that this is bullshit. Better to have the drop tank feeding fuel, rather than gasping for air. An air lock usually only lasts a few seconds, but it certainly leaves one close to panic when the engine is about to cut.

Most of all, we don't like drop tanks which won't jettison, and nobody but a b.f. goes down with a fume-filled drop tank.

We had a very serious note injected into our briefing today. There is a very real fear, according to reports from the Dutch underground, that Jerry might try to do the *unforgiveable*. That he might try to blow up the main dyke that holds back the Zuider Zee. Nobody has the slightest idea how he could do this, since he would have to bring hundreds of tons of explosives, and all the lorries needed would stretch from one end of the Zuider Causeway to the other. And, of course, there are only so many hours of cover of darkness. Still, the fear is very much there. They told us that if the Zuider dyke is breached, Holland will be under salt water for a hundred years. Our orders are that we are to shoot at anything that moves, on the Zuider Causeway.

I flew one more droptank armed recce today, which ended in another 'arse-like-a-ball-bearing.' Two hours, ten minutes. Covered a hell of a big area, east of Bremen. We found one big truck, and we flamed and destroyed that in one pass. Then we found six railroad trucks. Apparently there was nothing inflammable in them, so we put them down as 'smokers.' Very often, the wood construction trucks do go on fire, later. They *were* smoking well, when we left.

We got a good word about yesterday's bombing of Nuurees. The defenders gave up within an hour of our bombing and strafing. I suppose they didn't look forward to another dose.

April 13th, 1945, B.85, Schindel, Holland

I looked around at the faces today, and I realized we (the squadron, that is) has changed in character. When we were going through the terrible times, after Frank Bradley left us 'tour-ex' until Freddie Lister came back to lead us, we were heavily non-com. Some days, on some shows, we had as many as eight common rankers. Eight out of twelve! Today, since Paddy Crozier, Sandy Powell, and I, all received commissions, there are only a few non-coms left. Larry Hyland has been warrant officer for quite a while. Peter Coxell and Jock Wallace are both warrant officers. Reg Eckert's commission hasn't come through, so Eckert is still warrant officer. That leaves Norm Simpson as flight sergeant, Jimmy Harris, ditto, and the new bod, Sergeant Williams. The rest of the pilots are all officers.

I led an armed recce today in the Leeuwarden-Gronigen area. We were airborne one hour when we first sighted game. Right on the western end of the Zuider Causeway. One big truck. I went right down to the deck, Robbie Robinson, Alan Parish and Norm Simpson behind me. We destroyed it, two running soldiers were blasted away. The truck was left in pieces, packing case sized. Then wc went back west fifty miles, found two trucks on a highway, and left them smoking. Armed recce, as the communiqué said on April Fool's day, is certainly '*All out*.'

In the Gronigen area today, I went north about twenty miles to give a cursory look at the strange collection of sand dunes. I was hoping to find the Spitfire flown, (and shot down) by my namesake on 66 Squadron, Flight Lieutenant Foster-Smith.

This was two days ago. Foster-Smith has been with 66 only since B.79, and since I am the only 'other' Smith, there has been a mild confusion, from time to time. This was caused because hyphenated Foster-Smith allowed his name simply, Smith.

I was standing in the lunch line, two days ago, when up came Johnny Turk, the open, frank, candid Australian with the ball of flaming red hair. He was carrying his mess tin. 'Smitty old Sport,' he said. 'For *now* you can forget the confusion between *you* and Tommy Foster-Smith. He got shot down.'

I was startled. 'Oh, God! Where did he get it?'

'Over Gronigen. He made it up to that Dutch desert – you know – where all the sand dunes are?'

'Oh, yes!'

'He said, "I'm pancaking. Too low to bale out."

'I said, "I'll cover for you. I'll see you get down safe, sport."

'*He* said, "For Christ's sake don't use your guns. If they capture me, they'll *kill* me!"

'I said, "Okay sport. Let me watch you ditch it."

'That was all. He made a beaut crash landing. Lots of sand. I flew right down to the deck. Saw him jump out, and start runnin' like a fuckin' *gazelle* . . .'

'My God, Johnny,' I said. 'Do you think he has a chance to get to *our* side?'

Johnny Turk winked a big wink. 'Smitty', he said, 'if the long legged bastard keeps goin' the way he started out, he'll be back tonight!'

Only Johnny Turk.

April 16th, 1945, B.85, Schindel, Holland

There are two groups in 2nd TAF, 83 and 84 Groups. In 84 Group, there are 24 attack squadrons, comprised of Spitfires and Typhoons. It is reasonable to assume that this force is doubled, with 83 Group. To the Hun, this total assault must be beyond comprehension, now that his air force is kaput.

Whatever they call us, (*Terrorfliegers*) is well justified. The only time the German army can move, is dusk to dawn. They can hardly get a motor bike moving in daylight, without Spitfires zooming down from the sky. The Hun still has his flak – but he lost a barge unit, today, courtesy of Flight Lieutenant Alan Willis.

Talk about 'Armed Recce Now *all out*!' We operated in twos, all day long, and I drew Alan Willis, or, more properly, he drew *me*.

We took off as last section of the day, right after tea time. We found no mischief until it was almost dusk, and since we were not carrying drop tanks, we did not have all that much fuel. We had flown twice along the Zuider Causeway, twice coming up empty. We made one last pass, and we found one truck. Just as I was pressing the centre of the rocker-arm gun button, Willis shouted on r/t 'Watch out for flak!' I was attacking east to west, and twenty mill, and small arms tracers came ripping across my nose from starboard side. I got down to the truck's level and gave a two second burst of cannon and point fives. As I steep turned away, to port, the truck was on fire, split in half from stem to stern, and the flak was going harmlessly, overhead. I looked for Willis in my rearview mirror. He was not following me on the strafe.

Then, suddenly, he broke r/t silence. 'Monty Blue Leader, this is Blue Two. Flak Barge! I'm going down!'

Before I could even answer – there was Willis in a dive, with tracers whipping over his wings and fuselage. I saw his cannons open up on the waterline of the barge, then hold for three seconds where the barge gunners were standing. He was pulling out, not more than three hundred yards past, at sea level when there was a bright yellow/red explosion. The barge blew up. Willis must have hit the ammunition hold. Of course, it was potentially suicidal. Besides this, it was not an ordered attack. It was a moment of bloody, wonderful –

madness. I was surprised, on landing, to find not one single bullet hole or flak hole in Willis's aircraft. This ex-heavyweight boxer, champion of Southern Rhodesia, is a truly fearless bastard! I am thankful that I will never have to box him. He is the essence of a new spirit that has been building since the day that Freddie Lister came back. If Freddie or Harry Lea ever feel a flak twinge, none of us will ever know it. We are building a tremendous record of bomb and strafe carnage. Jerry is reaping his whirlwind. As Paddy or Sandy Powell would spontaneously elucidate – fuck his Irish luck.

April 18th, 1945, B.106, Twente, Holland
Armed recces continue. A new problem has arisen, and it causes dangerous, frightening problems. Some of the Dutch population, being bombed and strafed out of their homes, have taken to the roads. We have to be very, very careful when we go down to strafe. What, from five thousand feet looks like horse-drawn transport and soldiers marching turns suddenly into civilians as one of us is about to blast them to kingdom come. The r/t comes alive with 'Monty! Monty! Don't shoot! They're civvies! They're civvies! Over!'

This is almost a repeat cry of last August, when Patton's convoys invariably overran the bomb line. We would come screaming down and the US Army lorry people would stop, jump out, and rip the canvas bonnet covers away, revealing white stars, at the split second we would have our collective Hun on gun panel.

As our armed recces have stepped up so rapidly, our toll of troops and material have almost turned into a hunting 'bag'.

People like Robbie Robinson and his oppo.

Alan Willis, and of course people like Larry Hyland have been keeping score on a blackboard which they liberated from operations. They are trying to make a contest of it between Red, Blue, and Yellow Sections. Since they are now sending us out in twos, they can't get a proper fix on which 'bag' belongs to which section.

I do have to repeat that morale was never as high as now, and likewise to camaraderie. Today I was told that the booze rations and cigarette rations are in, so that probably means an impromptu party soon.

I am very wary of this low level work, every day, and I always try to get on the first section, to get mine in, for the day. I have become very superstitious, which I suppose is an old hands' disease. I have this feeling that morning shows are my 'lucky' times, and that if I'm

No 74 Squadron, RAF Colerne, March 1946. The author is front centre, leaning on nacelle of Gloster Meteor Mk III jet.

74 Squadron Gloster Meteor in flight

(Left) Reg Eckert after his return to Adelaide from the war. It was on disembarkation that he learned he had been commissioned while he flew with 127. *(Right)* The author in his first civilian clothes, May 1945.

going to get the chop, it will be late in the day. The best of my dreams is dangling on my parachute in total darkness. All of Europe is blacked out, after nightfall.

It was Mike Larson of 66 who finally decided that in the long run, he couldn't 'beat the game,' and I am not sure that anyone can beat the game. The problem with some of our mob is that they still believe this *is* a game. Wherever my old pal Bill Williams is, I'm sure that he has no illusions that this armed recce stuff is anything but get Jerry before Jerry gets you.

Yesterday I was Blue Leader on armed recce Western Holland. I had Willis as number two, Jock Wallace number three, and Jake Conroy, a fairly new bod as number four. I made a wrong turn, coming out of cloud right over Utrecht. Don't tell me Jerry is running short at intermediate (37 mill or 40 mill, whatever) flak.

It was very intense, and they more than caught our attention. Then we found our bag. I suppose the four of us spotted these METs at the same time, but it was Willis's excited voice that broke the r/t silence. 'Monty Blue Leader, METs at two o'clock below!'

My reply – 'In we go.' It was a bag of nine. We destroyed four, three in flames, and we put the other five out of commission. I wonder what the total bag is, on days like this, with fifty squadrons looking for mischief?

My show today was (what else?) Western Holland. I led Willis, Peter Coxell, and the new fellow Hal Bushen. I don't think Bushen has got over his Mosquito blowing up with his navigator in it – and I wouldn't blame him.

There wasn't much to bag today, because we didn't take off until after tea. (1545 hrs). We finally found a big transport and trailer on the outskirts of Amsterdam, and we left that in flames.

I've got to stop. Damn it, they've done it again. We just got word that we are moving up to B.106 Twente. That's pronounced 'Twent-er' *not* 'Twenty.') Fifteen aircraft, take off in thirty minutes. For me, same team.

April 20th, 1945, B.106, Twente, Holland

As usual, we stuffed our blankets and small kits into the gun ports, before we took off. At least we can sleep warm, and be clean. As usual, our kit bags and steel chests have gone astray, somewhere. Of course, they will turn up in a day or two.

We did not miss a beat in the transition. Twenty-six individual armed recce sorties, East and north of Oldenburg. I drew Bushen, Willis, and the new kid, Sergeant Talbot. If anyone can look younger than Talbot, I haven't met him. Anyway, we were just about to attack, when my gun panel blew off. I ordered Willis to take over, and I came back alone. Airborne, thirty minutes.

B.106 is the best damn airfield/base in all of Europe, I am sure. The sleeping quarters and the rooms and offices are *all* immaculate. The mess hall has tables and chairs that are as new as you can imagine. The kitchen equipment is superb. Electric appliances abound, and these include meat grinders and spud mashers, enough to excite the dullest of cooks. We have blast walls around the huts, just the same as those at Woensdrecht. Also, the windows have steel shutters like Woensdrecht, but they are gaily painted with white designs on base blue, which reminds one of country cottages. Now, rumour or not, we have heard that this entire base was one of the famous 'Strength Through Joy' camps.

These I remember reading about in *Picture Post*, before the war began. Working on Hitler's theory of 'The Pure Aryan', it was decided that Aryan women of the purest Saxon blood, who gave themselves to the Third Reich, would be used to breed a whole new pure race. The women who signed themselves *over* to the programme were sent to 'Strength Through Joy' camps to have a three week holiday, or more. They would be put in an exercise program that included all sports, tennis, swimming, running, climbing, gymnastics, etcetera. For every Aryan woman, there was a young Aryan man. It was expected that the woman would become impregnated as a matter of nature. The child would be brought up at the expense of the State.

Looking at the amenities of this camp, with its boating and swimming lake, and its tennis courts, I would not doubt that it would qualify as 'Strength Through Joy.' Until recently, this base was for night fighters. It is a perfect location for knocking down bombers in the main stream. Since the Yanks came into the bomber war, I am certain that the base has been operating around the clock.

Two trips today, both as Blue Leader. The first show was dive bombing gun positions at Aschendorf. It was a squadron show, and it was a contact car operation. We asked for red smoke and got it. Freddie led it, and directed us to pick out our own special target. Nearly every bomb was *bang on* – and our contact car leader praised us highly. Then we went down to the deck and strafed until our guns were empty. I am sure that our troops had no more problem storming those gun positions.

My second trip was railway interdiction north of Oldenburg. (Robinson, Willis, Talbot). We had quite a party. We got two cuts and two near misses on the railway lines. With bombs gone, we went looking for mischief. Soon, Robbie and Talbot found a motorcycle dispatch rider. They blasted him to bits, at high speed. Then we found ten railway cars, and we left them smoking. Here, the flak was like rain going the wrong way. We all got out of it without a flak hit. We came back guns empty.

I have just heard that Frank Bradley, DSO is posted here. He is now a Wingco. Is he going to take over 132 Wing? Nobody knows. I'll bet a lot of Hun soldiers would wish he wasn't back – if only *they* knew. . . .

April 23rd, 1945, B.106, Twente, Holland

Our sergeant photographer, Jenkins, came in with some hot 'gen,' today. He was down in the village, photographing the church which somehow was blitzed, probably by one of our bombers, returning with hangups, 'accidentally-on-purpose' dumping its load. The rest of the village is intact. Some of the villagers came up to Jenkins, brandishing their fists, indignantly, as if *he* were the cause. After a very short while they quieted down, and then one of the men revealed the fact that he can speak English.

He told Jenkins that there were two flyers, RAF buried in the churchyard. Only a week ago, with the Germans gone, did the villagers feel safe enough to place wooden crosses on the graves. Jenkins asked to be shown the graves, so that he could photograph them for the War Graves Commission. When Jenkins got to the graves, he realized that he was a small part of history. The first grave cross reads 'Squadron Leader Warwick, DFC,' and his regimental number. The other cross reads 'Guy Gibson, R.A.F.'

This, of course, marks the last Mosquito flight by Gibson, the Dambuster. He was posted missing only a few months ago. Next to Geoffrey Cheshire, Guy Gibson is probably the biggest bomber hero of the war. He was awarded the Victoria Cross, for his gallantry in the breaching of the Möhne and Eder dams. Prior to *that* he was DSO and bar, DFC and bar. These are *all* very big gongs. The story is that having done two tours as bomber pilot, one tour as night fighter pilot, and the special duty raid on the Dams, Gibson refused to rest.

He came back as 'MC' (Master of Ceremonies) orchestrating the big night raids from the Mosquito cockpit.

So, it was here that he crashed. The villager says that Gibson's navigator was wearing his identitags, but Gibson had only a silver bracelet on his wrist. Hence, 'Guy Gibson – R.A.F.'

Jenkins is very proud. It's what journalists call 'a scoop'.

Two shows today. Blue Leader on railway interdiction north-east of Oldenburg. Coxell and Bushen both got line cuts. My bombs missed, but all three went directly through three houses which were standing isolated from the level crossing. Foulston, one of the new bods, missed everything. We drew a rain of flak for our efforts.

My second show, Blue Leader, dive bombing factory strongpoints west of Oldenburg. This was a squadron show. We left the factory on fire, then strafed until all guns were empty. If I say so, without deliberate attempt at punning. This was a *Bloody Good Show*.

I think we are having a piss up, tonight. The booze rations finally got here.

April 27th, 1945, B.106, Twente, Holland

Today, Alan Willis got shot down. I hope to God that he didn't get the 'chop,' but it seems likely that he did, because the last thing the boys heard on r/t, and what they saw, he had half his elevators shot off; and he had little control over his aircraft, and he was diving into woods beyond a 'steam up' train, too low to bale out. It was, indeed, a flak trap.

It could have been *me*, or any of us, except that I had another drop tank hangup, just as I had yesterday.

Yesterday I was up with Willis, and again, those eagle eyes of his picked out three trucks. I had a tank jettison failure, so I stayed aloft. We were doing armed recce north-east of Bremen. Willis went down alone, and destroyed all three in two passes.

Today's operation was bombing (interdiction) NE of Bremen, then armed recce. It was led by Freddie, and I was Blue Leader with Ross, Conroy, and Larry Hyland behind me. I couldn't *believe* it. Not one of the four of us could jettison the drop tank! Freddie ordered me to return, with bombs. Just as I was saying, 'Roger, Longbow – Monty Blue section going over to Able Control' – Willis must have seen the train. In that split second between changing channel from 'D' Dog to 'A' Able, I heard an excited Willis: 'Look below – Monty Red Leader!' – and I pressed button A. . . .

I ask myself – why didn't Alan Willis have the hangup? Willis is the only father of two, or even father of one, I believe. Perhaps the saving grace might be that at least he wasn't on fire. Then again, you can easily get killed, without a funeral pyre to accompany the prang.

Harry Lea brought out a bottle of Gilbey's after release, this evening. Nobody had the taste for it.

April 30th, 1945, B.106, Twente, Holland

We have been wondering why we were not called to operate either yesterday, or the day before. The weather was good, yet the entire airfield was quiet. When I asked, yesterday, I was told, by Spy Johnson, no less, that I should enjoy it, not question it. Or, words to that effect.

This morning after breakfast, we were brought out, on parade. There *we* were, facing 66, and, on our left, 331 facing 332.

Group Captain Morris addressed us: 'Gentlemen,' he said. 'It is out, and took places in between the four squadrons.

Group Captain Morris addressed us: 'Gentlemen,' he said, 'It is my pleasure to bring you greetings from the AOC. He notes that every one of you in 132 Wing have served the cause well, and ably, and on occasion, magnificently. The Hun is on the run, and will not recover. It is time for us, now, to consider the reduction of petrol, ammunition, aircraft – and – lives. As soon as transport becomes available, all four squadrons will be flown to 84 GSU Lasham. In a reasonable period, the Norwegian squadrons will be flown home to Norway.

'What you have done, in these many months since D-Day, is *history*. Today, April 30th, 1945 marks the day of disbandment. For me, it is a Great Day, and a sad day. I will miss you all, very much. I am happy that I flew with all of you, on one occasion. Those of you who were there will long remember the day this Wing destroyed the Panzer Barracks at Bussum.

'For all of you, the long fight is over. May God go with you.'

That was all. We were dismissed – but we stood still for a while, in *shock*. Hours later, we still are.

I have just totalled my log book.

Total Flying Hours:	1392.40
Ops time for Month:	27.05
Total Ops Time:	115.30

Total Missions:	90
Total Bombing Sorties:	33

We are having a piss up tonight. We leave for Blighty tomorrow. *May Day*. How ironic.

Extracts from the
Operations Record Book 127 Squadron, R.A.F. 132 (Norwegian) Wing
c/o B.L.A.

B.85, 1st April 1945: The squadron was called upon to carry out armed recces in the Deventer–Zwolle–Meppen–Lingen and Hengelo areas. They operated in pairs at ten minute intervals and eight aircraft took part. The first section was airborne at 1320 hours. Fifty plus troops and four horse-drawn vehicles were found moving north-west at V.1208 and strafed. All four vehicles were damaged and it is claimed that there were many casualties amongst the troops. There was also much dispersed horse-drawn vehicles movement northwards towards Doesburg. Two sections experienced intense, accurate, light flak from V.6012 and V.1010 and Sgt Baecke (Belgian) and WO Jones were hit. Contact was lost with the former and he is not yet returned but WO Jones' aircraft was seen to be hit in the drop tank, burst into flames and crash to the ground. The cloud base was low in fact as low as 200 feet in places and the operations were then stopped. The last section landed at 1425 hours.

B.85, 2nd April: Armed Recces in the Nordhorn–Zwolle–Meppel areas was the programme for the day. Ten aircraft operated in pairs, the first section was airborne at 1540 hours. Four MET stationary at W.0946 were strafed and strikes were seen on two. At V.8635 nine plus horse-drawn vehicles moving north east were attacked and strikes seen. One stationary camouflaged MET at V.1134 and one MET moving South at V.0021 were destroyed. Sightings which were not attacked include – one unidentified single engined aircraft in a wood near Nordhorn airfield – thirty MET at Z.8402 moving towards Apeldoorn – finally our own tanks were seen moving north-east from Nordhorn at 1700 hours. One aircraft landed at B.100 short of fuel. The last section landed at 1735 hours.

Eleven aircraft again operated in the above area from 1820 hours to 2040 hours, but the patrols proved uneventful and no movement was seen.

B.85, 3rd April: At 1900 hours nine aircraft of 127 Squadron were scrambled for thirty plus Huns reported in the Enschede area flying south-west. The squadron patrolled base at 20,000 feet uneventfully and bogies eventually proved to be Mustangs. All aircraft were down by 2015 hours.

B.85, 6th April: Sgt Palmer killed while carrying out a Sector Recce.

B.85, 10th April: Armed recce – Oldenburg area. Operating in section of four aircraft each, twelve aircraft of 127 Squadron flew armed recces during the morning but again Hun activity on the roads was exceedingly scarce. One train with twenty plus TRGS was found, strafed and stopped and the locomotive claimed damaged. The remainder of the score consisted of three MET destroyed and also one horse-drawn transport with three trailers destroyed. The first section was airborne at 0910 hours and the last section was down by 1335 hours.

Fighter patrol Verden–Heustadt area. The other operation undertaken by the squadron consisted of fighter patrols in the Bremen area in support of our ground forces. Twelve individual sorties were flown, all of which proved completely uneventful as the Hun made no attempt to challenge our air supremacy. The first section was airborne at 1420 hours and the last aircraft was down at 1700 hours.

B.85, 11th April: Escort to Mitchells bombing Soltau. Three squadrons were briefed for this operation and twelve aircraft from the squadron took part. The rendezvous was made according to plan over Osnabrück and the bombers escorted to and from the target without incident. The bombing did not appear too accurate according to reports from the pilots. The squadron took off at 1130 hours and landed back at base at 1410 hours.

Bombing Village of Neuvrees – eight aircraft were detailed for this mission and with forty-five gallon long range tanks and two 250 lb bombs were briefed to low level bomb this target. A mechanical fault prevented the CO from taking part but seven aircraft under F/O James were airborne at 1605 hours. One bomb hung up and was brought back while the other thirteen all fell in the target area, hits were seen among building and a fire started. After the bombing attack the target was strafed before the squadron was diverted to strafe the village of Linden, which was attacked twice and strikes seen on some buildings. The squadron landed back at a base at 1750 hours.

Bombing of Friesoythe. A mixed squadron of eleven aircraft from 66, 127 and 322 Squadrons under F/Lt Lea were briefed for this operation. With forty-five gallon long range tanks and two 250 lb bombs four aircraft of 127 Squadron were airborne at 1735 hours and reached the target at the appointed time of 1815 hours. Due to some unknown hitch in the signals communications it was impossible to contact the control car and the squadron was forced to remain in the target area 25 minutes before they could obtain permission to attack. All bombs are believed to have fallen in the village but there was only time to make one attack and no time to strafe the target afterwards. Moderate, inaccurate, light flak was experienced from south of the target and the squadron returned to base at 1925 hours.

Armed Recce – Area West. Five sections of four aircraft each flew Armed Recce in the Meppel–Groningen–Emden–Bremerhaven–Bremen–Oldenberg area during the day, the first section being airborne at 1055 hours. By using ninety gallon long range tanks it was possible to get further afield but even so, little Hun transport was found. Two sections of four aircraft each were specially briefed for a recce over Rotenburg airfield but thick haze reduced visibility to some two miles and caused the mission to be abortive. From this operation one aircraft returned early with mechanical trouble and the last section was back by 1945 hours. The day's claims amounted to: one MET and Trailer destroyed, three TRGS damaged, and one Staff car strafed NRO (No result observed).

During the day a message of appreciation was received from our forward troops regarding the bombing of Neuvrees. It read: 'Very good results. Many houses destroyed. Cannon strafing shows up well. No difficulty today capturing target area.'

B.85, 13th April: Armed Recce – Northern Holland. Three sections, eleven aircraft in all flew armed recces in the foregoing area but poor weather with cloud as low as 300 feet in places greatly interfered with the operation. A few scattered transport were found and the total results of the mission amounted to: two MET (one with Trailer) damaged. One MET strafed N.R.O. – One horse-drawn transport damaged. The first section was airborne at 1635 hours and the last section landed at 1846 hours.

B.85, 16th April: Armed Recce – Northern Holland. Operating in sections of two aircraft, twenty six individual sorties were flown during the day in the above area. After so many days of little or no movement, the pilots eagerly took advantage of Hun activity in the area around Utrecht and Amsterdam and a very satisfactory score was obtained. In addition to a flak barge which exploded and an ammo truck which also exploded, five other MET and one horse-drawn vehicle were destroyed, and eleven MET, two Articulators, three trailers, ten horse-drawn transport, and one Motorcycle were damaged. The first section took off at 1240 hours and the last section landed at 2015 hours.

B.85, 18th April: Armed Recce – Western Holland. In weather excellent for armed recces, three sections of four aircraft each searched for transport in the Amsterdam–Utrecht area and even further north but there was practically no Hun movement on the roads. The first section was airborne at 1520 hours and the last aircraft landed by 1710 hours, and the total claims for the above mission amounted to: one Staff car destroyed. One MET with trailer destroyed. One Staff car damaged. Six Huns killed and one MET damaged.

B.85, 20th April: Bomb and strafe gun positions south of Papenburg. Eight aircraft under S/Ldr Lister were airborne at 0845 hours and proceeded to target area where eight 500 lb and sixteen 250 lbs bombs MC .025 seconds were dropped in a dive from 8,000 to 3,000 feet. No gun positions were seen but of four houses in the target area, two were destroyed, and two damaged. Altogether twenty-one bombs fell in the target area, and only three were wide. The squadron went down to strafe twice and the slit trenches north of the houses were also attacked. There was meagre, inaccurate, light flak from east of Papenburg. The squadron landed back to base at 0950 hours.

Bomb and strafe defended locality south of Papenburg. Eight aircraft operated (four aircraft each) and led by P/O Powell were airborne at 0910 hours. One aircraft returned early due to mechanical trouble. The other three however dropped three 500 and six 250 lb bombs in the target area. The north side of a road in the area was also strafed. The aircraft landed back at base at 1005 hours.

Bomb and strafe rail lines Leer–Emden–Oldenburg and Wilhelmshaven. The squadron operated in three sections of four aircraft, the first of which took off at 1505 hours. Four 500 and eight 250 lb bombs were dropped with the result that one cut was made on the railway at R.0812, two cuts at R.2208 and a further cut at R.3112, whilst hits were obtained on the embankment at Q.9116 and Q.9813, and no misses at Q.8817 and 3113. Two houses at Q.8817 were set on fire. One heavy duty vehicle at Q.9813 was destroyed as also was a motorcycle at R.2708. Forty plus TRGS at R.2208 were strafed and several detailed. Of fifteen TRGS at R.1809 which were strafed, ten were damaged. There was intense, accurate, light flak from the woods at R.1809. The squadron landed at 1805 hours.

B.85, 23rd April: Rail Interdiction–Oldenburg–Brake–Wilhelmshaven. Twelve aircraft operated in sections of four, the first being airborne at 0610 hours. Eleven 500 and twenty-two 250 lb MC eleven seconds delay bombs were dropped from 6,000 to 1,500 feet. One direct hit obtained at R.4324 and the line was cut in two places. One direct hit on two houses at R.4425. Six bombs fell fifteen to twenty yards from ten plus TRGS at R.3819, and one direct hit was made on eight TRGS at R.3716 as a result of which three TRGS were destroyed. One 500 lb and two 250 lb bombs were brought back as the pilot lost formation. There was intense, inaccurate, light flak from R.4017 and intense, accurate, light from R.4327. The last section landed at 0935 hours.

In the same area eleven aircraft operated in sections, the first taken off at 1035 hours. Eight 500 lb and sixteen 250 lb bombs were dropped as a result of which one cut and one 1/2 cut were made on the rail line at R.3012, whilst at R.3113 six bombs fell wide and the other six bombs were not observed. One section of three aircraft brought their bombs back abortive due to weather. At Zwischenshon airfield (R.1711) brilliant yellow fires were seen burning. There was intense, accurate, light flak from R.3113 and meagre, inaccurate from R.2414. The last section landed at 1240 hours.

Bomb and strafe factory west of Oldenburg held by enemy troops. Led by S/Ldr Lister twelve aircraft took off at 1740 hours to attack a factory held by enemy troops in front of our forward troops. Twelve 500 lb and twenty-four 250 lb bombs were dropped in a dive from 8,000 to 2,000 feet. All bombs fell in the target area and the northern group of buildings received direct hits and were set on fire. The remaining buildings and chimney were strafed three times and strikes were seen on all of them. There was no flak. The squadron returned to base at 1900 hours.

B.85, 26th April: Armed Recce – Bremen. Eight aircraft operated in three sections, the first of which was airborne at Q,835 hours. One staff car moving north at R.1414 was destroyed and two heavy-duty transport (one carrying troops) damaged at R.1316. There were several Hun casualties. Otherwise little movement was seen. The last section landed at 1130 hours.

Armed Recce – Bremen. Eight aircraft operated in sections of four aircraft each, the first taking off at 1410 hours. One MET was damaged at R.5267, a tractor towing a trailer was attacked and the tractor was destroyed while the trailer was damaged. Six dummy JU87s were strafed at R.1032. One section was fired at by our own Ack-Ack in the Bussum area (W.6773) whilst returning to base. One motorcycle was destroyed at R.0547. At R.1316 a staff car was destroyed (Flamer) and the occupants casualties, whilst a building nearby (believed to be an ammunition dump) was set on fire. White smoke was seen rising to 5,000 feet. The last section landed at 1620 hours.

Armed Recce – Bremen. Eight aircraft operated in three sections, the first of which was airborne at 1900 hours. One MET was damaged at R.1416. One MET destroyed at R.9165, one MET destroyed (Flamer) at R.7837, one MET damaged at R.4929 and one Staff Car damaged at R.2209. There was intense, accurate, light flak from R.9582. The last section landed at 2055 hours.

B.85, 27th April: Armed Recce – Area Y. Eight aircraft led by S/Ldr Lister were airborne at 0705 hours. Eight 250 lb bombs were dropped in a dive from 5,000 to 2,000 feet on the line north of Bremen (R.7029). Fifteen to eighteen TRGS stationary attacked at Leas of which three were damaged.

Two direct hits and two near misses were obtained on the line at R.7352 – Two cuts being claimed. One MET and three heavy duty transport moving West at R.7359 were destroyed. One MET stationary at R.7061 was destroyed (Flamer). F/Lt Willis' aircraft was hit by flak and is believed to have crash landed in enemy territory. (Aircraft category E). The remainder of the squadron landed back at 0855 hours. There was intense, accurate, light flak from E.3921.

B.85, 28th April: Nothing doing.

B.85, 29th April: Another quiet day.

B.85, 30th April: Squadron – Disbanded.

(signed) D.W. Riley, F/O for
Squadron Leader, Commanding
No. 127 Squadron, R.A.F.

XI

May

May 1st, 84 G.S.U. Lasham

The party was a Boy Scout Rouser! With tensions off, with no more shows to fly on, with no more dicing with death, we had a hell of a bash. The evening was filled with gross lies of bravado, hand clasps, promises of friendships forever, and teary-eyed decantations of liquids and lachrymose.

Everyone seemed to be loving the next man, as a brother. Rivalries and attendant uglinesses were buried, between *us*, and 66, and the Norwegians.

Robbie Robinson got into a minor row with Sandy and Larry Hyland. They were trying to console him, over the loss of Alan Willis. Robbie wasn't having any. I heard him say, 'Why won't I drink? Why *won't* I drink to me old mate Willis? Because A.T. Willis is *not – fuckin' – dead*, sport! One day *soon*, he'll prove it to you!'

Today, everyone has a well-deserved hangover. I caught a lift to flight, this morning, the object being to cure *mine*. When I got in the cockpit of 9N-Z – I realized I had already packed my helmet and oxygen mask – so no oxygen. I sat in the bucket seat without parachute, until it became too uncomfortable. I thought my thoughts, and said a prayer of thanks.

I thought of something Alan Willis said the other night, when he asked us all to *admit* that fear, when flak is flying, makes everyone duck down behind the instrument panel. He said 'Ever think that when you duck, you remove your bloody head from the protection of bullet-proof glass, and give it all the protection of three-sixteenths of *aluminium*!' I smiled at the recollection.

I shook the hands of Fowler, Martin, and 'Chiefie' Wills, and all the ground crew. We were due to be airborne at 1300 hours. We had the use of two Dakotas, one, mostly for gear.

I saw the boys piling into one Dakota, which was parked less than fifty yards from our hut. I walked into the hut. Only Sandy Powell and Paddy Crozier were there. 'Fellows,' I said, 'we have to get on the plane. You about ready?'

Paddy turned around to face me. 'Eddie,' he said, 'Eddie.' He pulled Sandy over, by the shoulder epaulette. With his other hand, he pulled me in. He grabbed Sandy's hand, and then he grabbed mine. 'God bless you *both*,' he said. 'God bless you both.' His eyes welled with tears, and ran down his cheeks. 'Thank God, for keepin' us safe.'

We dragged our kitbags out in the sun, and then we got on board the Dakota. The pilot banked, and banked again, and flew twice around Twente airfield. I thought of Twente, and Schindel – and Woensdrecht.

Then, I thought of Pete Attwooll.

And then, I thought of the rest of them.

I thought of Macey, Malone, Housden, Bell, Whittington, Davies, Fosse, Lloyd, Shillitoe, Smik, Taymans, Birbeck, Richardson, Bundara, Baecke, Jones, Palmer, Willis. Willis, still a question mark. Somewhere, in those thoughts, was Wing Commander Rolf Berg.

I looked down again as we crossed the coast, vectored for Blighty. I thought of 9N-Z, and our total of Spitfires. Who would fly *them* back to Blighty? Would the pilots think about our Spitfires, and would they wonder what the Spitfires might be thinking? Would *any* of us, in this Dakota, ever see one of our Spitfires again? Would it matter?

What mattered, was: we would not be coming back.

Aftermath of War

Reg Eckert, who was posted 'Tour-Ex,' a week before the disbandment, was staying at my home when I got there. Bob was at a unit close to North London, and could get away without formal leave passes.

The squadron convened at the Fox and Goose for a hell of a party, in which we presented Arthur Nice, the publican, with a large framed Nazi Manifesto. This was, literally, the basic rules of *Die Arbeiterpartie*. We performed 'The Guardians' and brought the house down. May 8th dawned, and the war was over.

A few days after the Victory celebration, and the RAF flypast, I met Sandy Powell, and Paddy Crozier in Piccadilly. Reg Eckert was with me. We walked down the Strand, towards the Law Courts. In our meanderings, we were confronted, suddenly, by the sign 'Rhodesia House.' I suggested that we go in. Sandy challenged me. 'Why? You know it's almost a *certainty* that Willis was killed. . . .' So I replied, 'I'm going *in*!'

The young lady at the desk answered my query directly. 'Flight Lieutenant Alan T. Willis? He was in here about an hour ago. Since it is already pub time – why don't you try to find him in the pub across the street? I'm sure you'll find him in the Standard.'

The four of us went into the saloon bar. It was seemingly full of Rhodesians. There was no sign of Willis. I saw Billy Hallam, a Rhodesian I trained with, at Bulawayo, Salisbury, and Heany. I had not seen Billy since 1942 at 15 AFU Leconfield. I introduced Billy to Sandy, Paddy, and Reg. Billy had just been repatriated after more than two years as a P.O.W. He was shot down over Cologne in a Halifax. The lives of him and his crew were saved from a lynch mob at 3:00 am by officers of the SS of all people. It was an incredible story of luck – as the SS officers just happened to be cruising the streets. Billy's crew parachuted down to a Cologne park.

The door marked 'Gentlemen' opened. Into the bar walked Alan

Willis. With a loud 'Hello, you bastards!' he bounded over, lifting me off my feet. We four were speechless. We ordered pints from the barmaid, and Willis told us about his almost unbelievable *luck*.

'It *was* a flak trap – no doubt about it. They shot away most of my elevators, man. I was too low to bale out. I was diving straight down to the woods, balls out. I grabbed the elevator trimwheel, and pulled it back, in desperation. It *worked*, man! I pulled out of the dive! I got her to straight and level – and I was sure that I would clear the forest I was flyin' over. And then, she nosed in. I cut the throttle just as I hit the fir trees. I don't know why I survived. The wings were ripped off – and somehow the fuselage held together. By a bloody miracle, I didn't hit a tree trunk. Poor old Betsy died in a skid that seemed to last forever. When it finally stopped, I jumped out – ran about a hundred yards, expecting Betsy to blow up. Then I hid behind a tree, and got a cigarette out of my tin. Before I'd even finished it man, half the bloody German army was in the woods, carrying rifles and machine pistols! I surrendered. The truck they put me in, to take me to interrogation had half of Betsy's tail unit in it! They transferred me to a staff car, and I was blindfolded by an SS officer. I was interrogated by another SS bloke while we were driving at about sixty miles an hour. I gave my name, rank, and number, again and again. I was shit-scared, man, that some Spitfire would see us, and come down and end my lot. Maybe, one of you bastards! I was blindfolded for days, sleeping in barns, being transferred from staff cars to trucks and back. Eight days later, we ran into the American Army. Man, was I *relieved* . . .'

When the Standard closed at 2:30 pm, we went over to Wardour Street, to the White Monkey, an after hours' club. Two weeks later, Alan was on his way back to Rhodesia. Reg Eckert and Robbie Robinson went back to Australia.

I was posted to three aircraft ferry units over the next few months, ferrying variously Typhoons, Hurricanes and a Mustang Mark IV. In December, I was posted to RAF Pocklington, Yorkshire – an ex-heavy bomber airfield. I was posted there, with hundreds of other Pilot Officers. The object was, to convert us all to redundancy – i.e. ground staff – adjutants.

I decided on a gambit, so that I could keep flying. I telephoned Wing Commander Frank Bradley, DSO, and explained my plight. Frank was at Staff College, Uxbridge. He asked me, if he could pull it off – would I like to fly jet fighters. Would I? Ha!

An hour after I made the call, I walked into the officers' mess, and the first person I saw was Paddy Crozier. I was *ecstatic*. I told him of my call to Bradley, and said that I would pick up the 'phone right away, and have Brad add his name to mine for a jet posting.

His reply: 'You'll do no such bloody thing, Eddie. I got out of that bloody squadron alive, and I have no intention of ever climbing into a cockpit again. Enjoy yourself. I'm serving the rest of my time on the ground. Then, old sport, I'm goin' back to the Mountains o' Mourne.'

Early 1946, I joined 74 Squadron, made famous by the Battle of Britain, and 'Sailor' Malan. By dint of good fortune, I was probably one of the first 300 pilots who ever flew a jet. 74 Squadron was a peace-time treat, at RAF Colerne – near Bath. I flew about fifty hours in Meteor – Mark III's.

I was demobilized in May 1946. Freddie Lister came out of the RAF pursuing a career of sales, for an American company, Gilbert and Barker (Gilbarco, petrol pumps). We had a great time for some months, while he lived with me and my family. Freddie was awarded the DSO, along with his DFC. I went with him to Buckingham Palace, for his investiture. It was an event to remember.

I read the *London Gazette, avidly*, looking for the announcement of my DFC, which Freddie had recommended. Sandy Powell was cited, as was Paddy Crozier. Harry Lea was cited.

One day, a manila envelope came through my letter box. I opened it:

By the KING'S Order the name of
Flying Officer E.A.W. Smith,
Royal Air Force Volunteer Reserve,
was published in the London Gazette on
1 January 1946
as mentioned in a Despatch for distinguished service.
I am charged to record
His Majesty's high appreciation.

(signed) Stanesgate
Secretary of State for Air

On another day, I received a letter from Bill Williams. Here it is:

Monday 13th

567 E/O Williams, S.L.
198 SQDRN.
123 WING
R.A.F.
BLA

Dear SIR,

I 'ardly know 'ow to fank yer fer yer kind le''er. It touched me bleedin' 'art, that it did. Like I says to me mate 'ere, arter all these monf's I goes and git's a le''er from im.

Cor!! Aint it arf good to know yer OK, and congratcherlashons (Phew!) on yer com-mish-son.

You seem to shoot the shit about bein' touer hexpired and on rest free monfs. Well, Cock I also was tour Ex. for two bleeding months and I found myself back out here with B.L.A. There is two things that are diff. now. There's no war and we are now BAFO instead of BLA.

Flash: I've just got me gongs – 3 –. Bags of drift now. I shall be coming on leave 28th of this month with the object of getting married on 1st Sept.

Yes, your eyes aren't playing tricks with you, it does say 'to get married' at long last I've wilted.

I only decided a week ago and wrote and told mum. So far I haven't had a reply from her.

I hope the shock wasn't too great, for her. Anyway how about popping down that weekend and I can mix pleasure with pleasure (it will be legal as well) less of that, – 'for a change' business, from you.

Ken Brown (POW) got back to England OK and I am hoping to see him on the 1st as well.

Unlimited supplies of wallop, women, food and my company. Who could ask for more? *You* just try, that's all.

Just because you have got yer commish – yer don't ave to git bleedin lairy and put a bleedin 2-1/2 bleedin stamp on me bleeding letter eiver!

Bleeding trying to be flash aincha? Well don't it don't become yer.

My ole man found that art last week.

Tought if ad a la-di-da talk we wouldn't get knocked orf any more so he goes to the library and gits all the griff.

He gits a book called 'The art of Swift Rep R.T.' by some geeser called Smiff.

When he got knocked orf he put on 'is accent and the copper, and the judge fought he was takin the piss. So he got 9 monfs instead er 6.

I got ter go to the Scrubbs to see if he can git a day orf for me weddin.

You can get 48's darn there naw.

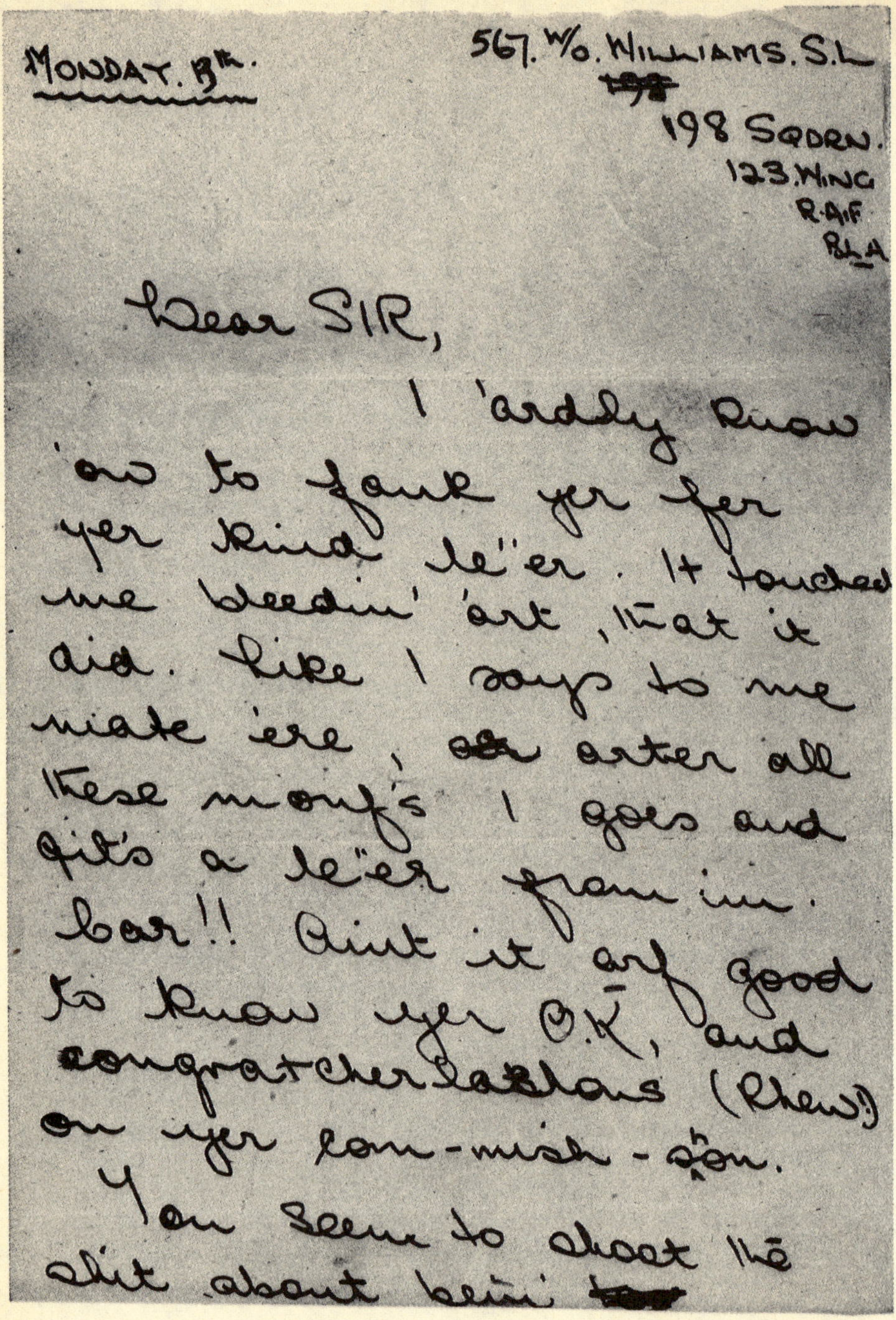

Monday. 13th.

567. W/O. Williams. S.L
~~198~~
198 Sqdrn.
123 Wing
R.A.F.
B.L.A

Dear Sir,

I 'ardly know 'ow to fank yer fer yer kind le'er. It touched me bleedin' 'art, that it did. Like I says to me mate 'ere, ~~oh~~ arter all these monf's I goes and git's a le'er from im. bar!! Aint it arf good to know yer O.K., and congratcherlatlons (Phew!) on yer com-mish-son.

You seem to shoot the shit about bein' [illegible]

Well china, I'm going along OK and so are the folks (I think – er. I hope!) and I hope all is well at home for you.

I'll close and hope to hear from you soon, to tell me I shall see you on the first.

I am,
Sir,
Your Obedient Servant,
Williams

Cheerio old Pal,
Always your Oppo
Bill – P.S. I *was* at Lasham for 5 days and I *did* see Dicky Peters. Please excuse me if I got one of your numbers wrong.

I never saw Bill Williams again.

Jock Wallace went back to his beloved Scotland, and became a professional plumber. He retired in Edinburgh.

Paddy Crozier went back to the Mountains o' Mourne. No further contact.

Likewise, Larry Hyland, who went back, presumably, to the North Country.

Sandy Powell married an English girl, from the Midlands. I was his best man. Sandy stayed in Europe for some years, working for the European Graves Commission. I lost contact.

Reg Eckert left the RAAF to start a new career in Adelaide, with Australia's Telecom Telephone System. He retired in 1983. He died in Adelaide, January 12th, 1986.

Alan Willis went back to Southern Rhodesia. No further contact.

Robbie Robinson return to Wagga Wagga, New South Wales. No further contact.

Peter Coxell joined the Thames Police Force, and served his time for a full retirement pension.

Harry Lea entered civilian life, by going back to his pre-war job – at Spillers, a dog food company, in sales. He joined the Auxiliary Air Force. When the Korean conflict began, he volunteered to serve, full time. He never got to Korea, but he did take advantage of earning his commercial licence. He got a job flying for European Airlines, and flew as Captain for many years, until the airline merged with British Airways. He retired, and went to live in Portugal.

Freddie Lister left the petrol pump business after one year, and returned to the Royal Air Force. During his peace time career, he commanded No. 1 Squadron, perhaps the most historic, prestigious, of all fighter squadrons, flying Hawker Hunter jets. He retired to Bourne, Lincolnshire.

Wing Commander C.F. Bradley pursued a full career in the Royal Air Force. He retired as group captain, to live in South Africa.

Flight Lieutenant Feltham was posted to India, and ferried spitfires from Karachi through Burma, Korea, and Indo-China. He became a squadron leader, was demobilized in 1946, and received his DFC in the mail – with a note of congratulations, signed 'George R.' His career was spent in public relations; notably, he was PRO for many years for the Brooke Bond Tea Company. Today, he lives in Putney, and runs his own PR Company – Polygon Promotions.

Flying Officer 'Jimmy' James left the service in 1946, and went into publishing as the best choice in a civilian job, next to flying. For years he was with the Canadian Publishing Company, Maclean Hunter. He retired in August 1987. He lives in Brighton, Sussex.

I applied for a Government grant to pursue a career in advertising. I worked in Piccadilly for two years with an advertising firm called G.S. Royds. On July 23rd, 1948, while the London Olympic Games, Wembley, were in full swing, I went to Southampton, Freddie Lister's home town, to sail to the United States. The *Marine Jumper* berthed in New York – August 3rd 1948.

Appendix A: Pilots of 127 Squadron

These are the pilots who comprised The Boys of One-Two-Seven, between the dates of August 1st 1944 and April 30th 1945

Attwooll
Asboe
Adcock

Bradley
Butcher
Bell
Boudreau
Bundara
Birbeck
Bushen
Berg
Baecke

Crozier
Campbell
Covington
Coxell
Conroy

Doyle
Davis
DeKerdrel

Eckert

Fyfe
Feltham
Fosse
Foulston

Gollins
Griffin
Gotze

Hillwood
Hyland
Harris
Harrison

Jenkins
Jack
James
Jones

Lloyd
Lister
Lea
Langston

Marriott
McNally
Macey
Malone
Morisson
McCallum
Mallandaine

Nowlan

Powell
Pollock
Parish
Palmer

Richardson
Reeves
Roth
Round
Robinson
Ross

Savage
Schofield
Smith
Shillitoe
Smik
Sampson
Simpson

Truscott
Talbot
Taymans

VanHelden
Vanlerberghe

Whittington
Wallace
Wade
Willis
Williams

Appendix B: No 127 Squadron

No 127 Squadron was formed at Catterick as a day bomber squadron in February 1918 and was disbanded in the following July.

In June 1941, after the Gladiators of No 4 Flying Training School had played their part in the defeat of Bashid Ali at Habbaniya, four of these Gladiators, with four Hurricanes, were flown to Haditha, in Iraq, as the equipment for the newly formed No 127 Squadron.

On 12th July No 261 Squadron reformed at Habbaniya and took over the personnel and Hurricanes of No 127 Squadron. On 2nd August some officers and ground staff disembarked at Port Tewfik, and were organised into a squadron which was given the number 249 Since however there was a No 249 Squadron already operating at Malta this new squadron at Kasfareet was renumbered No 127 Squadron on 2nd August 1941.

After various moves the squadron eventually arrived in the Western Desert in June 1942, at the time when Rommel had driven the 8th Army back to the frontiers of Egypt. The squadron Hurricanes went at once into action and during the following months flew continuous sorties over the El Alamein line and in patrolling forward areas. Towards the end of the year, with the retreat of the Afrika Korps towards Tripoli, the squadron were engaged in patrolling Malta bound convoys and in anti-submarine duties.

In January 1943 the Squadron left the Western Desert and returned to Palestine where it was in No 209 Group, forming part of the Air Defences, Eastern Mediterranean. It was stationed at St Jean, with detachments at Nicosia, Cyprus and Beirut, Syria. The main operations at this period were standing patrols and convoy patrols. In November 1943, a detachment operated from Teheran, Persia.

On 1st April 1944 the squadron left the Levant and arrived at North Weald on 1st May where it re-equipped with Spitfire IX. It speedily became operational and on the 19th May was escorting

Mosquitos over Lille and Courtrai. Wireless transmitters and trains were attacked and various targets were bombed.

On D Day and subsequently, the squadron protected convoys, swept the landing beaches, and escorted bombers in attacks on enemy armour and on port and railways. Rocket and flying bomb sites, storage and manufacturing centres also received attention.

On 21st August, operating in No 84 Group, No 127 Squadron flew across to France and operated from various airfields in France, Belgium and Holland. During a deck level bombing attack on the goods yard at Zwolle on 28th November 1944 the Commanding Officer, Squadron Leader O. Smik, a Czech, was shot down in the intense and accurate heavy and light flak barrage which was met. Until its disbandment on 30th April 1945 the squadron was continually engaged in armed reconnaissance, in bombing and in fighter sweeps.

Bases

Catterick	1 Jan 1918
	to 4 Jul 1918
Hadiths (K.3)	29 Jun 1941
T.1	30 Jun 1941
Tahoune Guemac	6 Jul 1941
	to 12 Jul 1941
Kasfareet	2 Aug 1941
Hurghada	17 Sep 1941
St. Jean	16 Fen 1941
Shandur	2 Jun 1942
LG.92 Amriya	25 Jun 1942
LG.172	14 Jul 1942
LG.88	20 Aug 1942
Kilo 8	9 Sep 1942
LG.89	10 Oct 1942
LG.37	23 Oct 1942
LG.20	9 Nov 1942
LG.08	18 Nov 1942
St. Jean	6 Jan 1943
Ramal David	26 Jan 1943
Paphos (D)	13 Nov 1943
	to 20 Nov 1943
Left for UK	4 Apr 1944
North Weald	23 Apr 1944
Lympne	17 May 1944
Tangmere	4 Jul 1944
Southend	12 Jul 1944
Tangmere	23 Jul 1944
Funtingdon	6 Aug 1944
Ford	12 Aug 1944
B.16 Villons les Buissons	20th Aug 1944
B.33 Camp Neuseville	6 Sep 1944
B.57 Lille/Wambrechies	11 Sep 1944
B.60 Grimbergen	6 Oct 1944
B.79 Woensdrecht	23 Dec 1944
Fairwood Common	21 Feb 1945
B.85 Schijndel	17 Mar 1945
B.106 Twente	21 Apr 1945
	to 30 Apr 1945

Equipment	*Service*	*Serials and codes*
D.H.9	Jan 1918 – Jul 1918	
Gladiator II	Jun 1941–Jul 1941	K8048
Hurricane I	Jun 1941 – Jul 1941 Mar 1942 – Jun 1942	Z4115
Hurricane IIB	Jun 1942 – Oct 1943	BN160
Hurricane IIC	Aug 1943 – Mar 1944	KZ113
Spitfire VC	Jan 1943 – Oct 1943	AB321
Spitfire IX	Mar 1944	
	Apr 1944 – Nov 1944	ML235
Spitfire XVI	Nov 1944 – Apr 1945	RR257 (9N-Y)

Index